HISTORY & TRUTH
IN
HEGEL'S
PHENOMENOLOGY

HISTORY & TRUTH
IN
HEGEL'S
PHENOMENOLOGY

THIRD EDITION

MEROLD WESTPHAL

INDIANA UNIVERSITY PRESS

Bloomington and Indianapolis

This book is a publication of

Indiana University Press
601 North Morton Street
Bloomington, Indiana 47404-3797 USA

www.indiana.edu/~iupress

Telephone orders 800-842-6796
Fax orders 812-855-7931
Orders by e-mail iuporder@indiana.edu

The paper used in this publication meets the minimum requirements of
American National Standard for Information Sciences—Permanence of
Paper for Printed Library Materials, ANSI Z39.48-1984.

Manufactured in the United States of America

Library of Congress Cataloging-in-Publication Data

Westphal, Merold.
   History and truth in Hegel's Phenomenology / Merold Westphal. —
3rd ed.
     p. cm.
   Originally published: Atlantic Highlands, N.J. : Humanities Press,
1979, c1978.
   Includes bibliographical references and index.
   ISBN 0-253-33422-5 (cloth : alk. paper). —
   ISBN 0-253-21221-9 (pbk. : alk. paper)
   1. Hegel, Georg Wilhelm Friedrich, 1770–1831. Phänomenologie des
Geistes. 2. Spirit. 3. Consciousness. 4. Truth. 5. Knowledge,
Theory of. 6. History—Philosophy. I. Title.
B2929.W47 1998
193—dc21   98-14995

     2 3 4 5 03 02 01 00

With appreciation to
Arthur F. Holmes
and
John E. Smith
mentors, scholars, friends

CONTENTS

PREFACE TO THE THIRD EDITION

"By substance I understand what is in itself and is conceived through itself. . . ."
                                                                    –Spinoza[1]

"Yet all that Hegel thought within this horizon [of absolute knowledge], all, that
is, except eschatology, may be reread as a meditation on writing. Hegel is *also*
the thinker of irreducible difference."   – Jacques Derrida[2]

During my first semester in graduate school I was introduced to Hegel's
Phenomenology in a seminar taught by Paul Weiss. As we began the opening chapter
on Sense Certainty, he warned us most solemnly to be careful. If Hegel got us here
he had us and there was no escaping. It was as if, to invert Platonic images of ascent,
the text was a slippery slope on which, once footing was lost, there was no stopping
until one landed in a heap at the bottom, claiming to be the embodiment of Absolute
Knowing.

Of course, Weiss was wrong. But not entirely. It is true that the argument
against Sense Certainty represents a point of no return. For it is not so much a
critique of a single philosophical position as a recipe for undermining "the myth of
the given" in all its forms.[3] Whether the appeal to immediacy occurs in the context
of classical foundationalism, common sense realism, or any other appeal to intuition
as ultimate, Hegel seeks to show how such appeals undermine themselves.[4] It is no
accident that the *Phenomenology* and both versions of the Logic begin with a
critique of immediacy. If Hegel gets us with his critique of Sense Certainty there is
indeed no turning back. We are decisively cut off from a whole family of strategies
for achieving the goal of philosophy, the knowledge that can rightly be called
Wissenschaft, which Hegel calls both knowledge of the Absolute as it truly is and
Absolute Knowing.[5]

But it does not follow that Hegel has got us in any stronger sense. For in place
of the strategies that appeal to intuition in some form, Hegel offers a strategy
grounded not in immediacy but in total mediation. And, as Derrida and all those who
can be called "Hegelians without the Absolute" remind us, this claim that there is
another path to the same goal remains open to debate among those who have
abandoned "the myth of the given."

Hegel's argument follows the tripartite analysis of human thought in the

Encyclopedia Logic, according to which its three moments are Understanding, Dialectic, and Speculation.[6] The critique of Sense Certainty signifies our departure from Understanding, which Hegel describes as thinking in its abstract mode. But abstraction for Hegel means, not extracting the universal from the particular, but isolating the part from the whole. Correspondingly, Understanding is the atomism that claims for particular meanings and facts the stand-alone structure of Spinoza's substance. They are in themselves at least in the sense that they are to be conceived through themselves. This is not the denial of otherness but the claim that otherness is external, that the only truly internal relation is identity. All forms of the appeal to immediacy presuppose this semantico-ontological pointillism.

The critique of Sense Certainty is our introduction to Dialectic, which can be summarized as the Spinozistic claim that no particular meaning and no finite fact can be conceived through itself alone. Every meaning and every fact refers us beyond itself to other meanings and facts without which they would not be themselves and to which, accordingly, they are internally related. Dialectic, we might say, is the general form of field theory; it is a holism or contextualism at both the semantic and the ontological levels (which, for dialectical thinking, are themselves internally related).

Dialectical holism[7] tolls the knell of parting metaphysics and epistemology, the end of philosophy *as practiced by the Understanding*. It is, Hegel tells us, a skeptical *via dolorosa* in which doubt (*Zweifel*) takes on the character of despair (*Verzweiflung*).[8] This skepticism is "complete despair about everything that the understanding holds to be firm" and it is "completely certain about its central point, i.e., the nullity of everything finite."[9]

But dialectic is not despair simpliciter; just as a certain skepticism about the sensible/temporal served as the introduction to a metaphysics of the intelligible/eternal in Plato, so Hegelian holism turns us away from Understanding toward Speculation. But if we are cut off from all ascents up the divided line that appeal to some foundational immediacy for *Episteme* or *Wissenschaft*, if everything is mediation, can the subject and object of knowledge be anything but flotsam and jetsam on the Heraclitean flux?

Like Spinoza, Hegel refuses to give in to this question. Mediation (essential otherness, referential deferral) is a barrier to Absolute Knowing only if it cannot be completed. There can be only one Substance for Spinoza because only the Totality is in itself and can be conceived through itself. Speculative thought achieves its goal not by fleeing mediation but by gathering all the parts, which point beyond themselves, into a Whole, which points, not beyond itself, but back to the parts which constitute it. Hegel's only quarrel with this strategy is the choice of Substance rather than Spirit as the name for the Totality. It is not *Deus sive Natura* but *Gott oder Geist* that summarizes his speculative philosophy.

Total mediation rather than immediacy—that is the Hegelian strategy. Philosophy is essentially a totalizing gesture. In defiance of the assumptions of his contemporaries and ours, he takes this to be its pride and glory, not its tragic flaw or Achilles' heel. Needless to say, this is not to claim some kind of empirical omniscience for philosophy, which should know how many insects there are in Swabia or be able to deduce Herr Krug's pen.[10] But what then does totality mean? What would it be to bring mediation to a close?

In introducing the *Phenomenology*, Hegel seeks to answer this question several times by telling us what the speculative goal of the dialectical journey is. For example, "the goal is fixed just as necessarily as the sequence of the progression. It is that point where knowledge no longer has need to transcend itself, where it finds itself, and where the concept corresponds to the object and the object to the concept. The progression toward this goal is consequently without halt and at no earlier stage is satisfaction to be found."[11]

If we are skeptical, we can take this talk about necessary progression and progress without halt with a grain of salt; but surely Hegel is right in claiming that the philosophical urge to knowledge will know no rest short of the point that realists express as the correspondence of the concept to the object and idealists as the correspondence of the object to the concept. Dialectical holism reminds us that both concepts and objects refer us beyond themselves to other concepts and objects, so it is clear that we should not look for this correspondence short of semantico-ontological totality. But the only clue we get here as to what that might mean, short of the bad infinity of numerical completeness, is the idea of knowledge no longer needing to transcend itself. And what might that mean?

We get a strong hint when Hegel tells us that consciousness will have become Absolute Knowing when it reaches "a point where it casts off the semblance of being burdened by something alien to it, something which is only for it and which exists as an other."[12] We know that Hegel is not out to abolish difference and otherness altogether, so what we need to know is how consciousness or knowledge can have an other which is not alien. The Introduction, from which these passages have been cited, does not tell us. We can learn the answer to this question only on the journey itself; or, if we want to cheat, we can look to the Preface, written from the standpoint of the completed journey.

There we read that the goal is to get to the place where we can "lay aside the name of love of knowledge [philosophy] and be actual knowledge . . . [the place where] the separation of knowledge and truth is overcome. . . ." Where this goal of the *Phenomenology* is reached, the moments of Spirit "spread themselves out in the form of simplicity which knows its object as itself. They no longer fall apart into the opposition of being and knowledge but abide in the simplicity of knowledge."[13] For

Hegel knowledge and truth or knowledge and being are no longer alien to each other only in that knowing that "knows its object as itself." Absolute Knowing is self-consciousness. Of course, this is not the immediate self-consciousness of the Cartesian cogito (or its empiricist cousins, who incorrigibly know themselves to be in pain); nor is it the reflective self-consciousness of the transcendental ego of Kantian/Fichtean idealism. It is the self-consciousness of Spirit, which occurs only in a certain philosophical reinterpretation of Christian religious knowledge.

But that belongs to the substance of Hegel's argument, and we are here concerned with his strategy. Once again the *Phenomenology* is a kind of recipe, for the strategy of achieving closure or totality through the completion of mediation is the strategy Hegel regularly adopts for both his structural and his historical analyses. It is the ever-recurring historical analyses and their adumbration in the structural analyses that gives an eschatological character to Hegelian thought.[14] The structural version of the Logic is complemented by the historical version of the *Lectures on History of Philosophy*; the structural version of the *Philosophy of Right* is complemented by the historical version of the *Lectures on the Philosophy of World History*; and the structural version of the *Encyclopedia*'s account of Absolute Spirit is complemented by the historical versions of the *Lectures on Aesthetics*, the *Lectures on the Philosophy of Religion*, and, in a repeat appearance, the *Lectures on the History of Philosophy*.

It is a stunning performance! Not even Aristotle can claim to be so comprehensive. But philosophers are not easily intimidated, and even the System's stun gun could not keep them stunned for long. We are familiar with story of how as early as 1843 Kierkegaard and Marx declared the Hegelian closure premature. Finding Hegel to be insufficiently dialectical, Kierkegaard claimed that the identity of thought and being that Hegel sought in Speculation could be found only in Eternity and that the thoroughly temporal Hegel made himself ridiculous by claiming to embody that identity. Finding Hegel to be insufficiently historical, Marx claimed that Hegel was right to claim that *Wissenschaft* could occur only as the "ideology" of the Kingdom, but worse than ridiculous in claiming that modern, capitalist society was that Kingdom.

Both thinkers were eschatological. Denying that Hegelian closure was even possible under present circumstances, they looked for it in a future still to come. For while Plato's eternity lies behind the soul, to be recollected, Kierkegaard's eternity lies ahead of the existing individual as the future of all futures; and Marx's revolution is obviously a future event.

Enter Derrida. Like Kierkegaard and Marx (and ever so many others) he is an Hegelian without the Absolute, without closure, without eschatology. Or, to be more precise, like Kierkegaard and Marx he is an eschatological thinker who challenges the realized eschatology which for Hegel is not an accidental conclusion but the utterly essential condition for the possibility of philosophy as *Wissenschaft.*

Derrida tells us that *"différance* instigates the subversion of every kingdom."[15] In the epigraph above, he tells us that he, too, is an Hegelian, but without the Kingdom, thus without Absolute Knowing. This is of interest because it gives us a way to read not only Derrida but the complex variety of texts sometimes lumped together under the rubric 'postmodern.' For if Derridean deconstruction, Foucauldian genealogy, and the other strands of French poststructuralism have a common theme uniting them, it is that of mediation without closure. And it is hard to see how this can be dismissed as an inevitably irresponsible relativism short of the claim to reside in the safety of some quasi-Cartesian immediacy or some quasi-Hegelian totality.

The suggestion is that the strategy Hegel introduces in the *Phenomenology* provides a point of reference from which to see some unity in the diversity of texts about difference, but also to see this tradition (and I don't think that is too strong a term) not as an outer fringe of philosophical esotericism (as much as that image may be cultivated at times by the epigones) but as part of the philosophical mainstream. For isn't just about everybody these days posing the question in more or less the same way: given the failure of Cartesian-style appeals to immediacy and the hubris of Hegelian claims to total mediation, how shall we construe the mediation without closure that seems to define the human condition? The spectrum of answers stretches from cynical skepticism to dialogical hope, but there is important common ground on which these are articulated.

Is Hegel then just a whipping boy, a Nixon for the philosophical press to kick around when we grow tired of bashing Descartes? Not at all. What really interests me about the epigraph from Derrida is the suggestion it makes for a different way to read Hegel himself. When he says that Hegel is *also* the philosopher of absolute difference, his *also* does not mean 'in addition to me (Derrida)', but, 'in addition to being the philosopher of closure and totality.' Like Kierkegaard, he reminds us that Hegel is the philosopher of dialectic as well as of speculation, and he invites us to deconstructive readings of Hegel in which speculation is *aufgehoben* in dialectic rather than the other way around.[16]

This does not mean that the text becomes but a laboratory for doing Derridean exercises. For, as already indicated, deconstruction is not the only mode of postmodern philosophy, nor is postmodernism the only philosophical tradition that finds itself in the misty flats between Cartesian archeology and Hegelian teleology. To read Hegel as *also* a philosopher of *absolute* difference is to read him as someone who, in spite of his own predilections for closure, can help us better to understand the wide open seas on which we sail, whether with Nietzsche at the dawning of the death of God or with Kierkegaard in hope of eternity.

It has now been almost two decades since *History and Truth* was first published. What has changed for me is not so much my understanding of what goes on in Hegel's text as the context in which I read it. When I wrote the book it was hermeneutical phenomenology that for me primarily defined the space between immediacy and totality. Now it is postmodern reflections on the interminability of mediation. I do not see these as mutually exclusive perspectives from which to read Hegel. But they are different. In suggesting another angle of vision on the *Phenomenology*, I am following Nietzsche's admonition to seek objectivity, not by fleeing perspectives but by multiplying them.

January 1998

NOTES

1. *Ethics*, First Part, Definition 3.

2. *Of Grammatology*, trans. Gayatri Chakravorty Spivak (Baltimore: Johns Hopkins University Press, 1976), p. 26.

3. For "the myth of the given" see Wilfrid Sellars, "Empiricism and the Philosophy of Mind," *The Foundations of Science and the Concepts of Psychology and Psychoanalysis*, Minnesota Studies in the Philosophy of Science, Vol. I, ed. Herbert Feigl and Michael Scriven (Minneapolis: University of Minnesota Press, 1956). Richard Rorty draws heavily on this essay in his critique of "privileged representations" in chapter 4 of *Philosophy and the Mirror of Nature* (Princeton: Princeton University Press, 1979) and has written an introduction to its republication as *Empiricism and the Philosophy of Mind* (Cambridge: Harvard University Press, 1997).

4. See chapters 7 and 11 of my *Hegel, Freedom, and Modernity* (Albany: SUNY Press, 1992). Following Al Plantinga, I use the term 'classical foundationalism' to signify the strong claim that only propositions that are self-evident, or evident to the senses, or incorrigible are properly basic in one's epistemic structure. Each of these ways of building on certain foundations is an appeal to immediacy. See "Reason and Belief in God," *Faith and Rationality: Reason and Belief in God*, ed. Alvin Plantinga and Nicholas Wolterstorff (Notre Dame: University of Notre Dame Press, 1983), pp. 48–59.

5. See pp. 2–3 below.

6. ¶¶ 79–82.

7. See chapters 5, 7, and 10 of *Hegel, Freedom, and Modernity*.

8. See section 1B below.

9. *Encyclopedia Logic*, ¶ 81, *Zusatz* 2.

10. On Herr Krug's pen, see Hegel's 1802 essay "How the Ordinary Human Understanding Takes Philosophy (as displayed in the works of Mr. Krug)," *Between Kant and Hegel: Texts in the Development of Post-Kantian Idealism*, trans. George di Giovanni and H. S. Harris (Albany: SUNY Press, 1985), pp. 293–309.

11. See p. 11 below.

12. See p. 19 below.

13. See p. 26 below.

14. For the eschatological character of the *Phenomenology*, see sections 2A and 2B below, and note 46 on p. 54. For a similar theme in the Logic, see *Hegel, Freedom, and Modernity*, pp. 95 and 103.

15. "Différance," *Margins of Philosophy*, trans. Alan Bass (Chicago: University of Chicago Press, 1982), p. 22.

16. See Derrida's essay, "From Restricted to General Economy: A Hegelianism without Reserve," *Writing and Difference*, trans. Alan Bass (Chicago: University of Chicago Press, 1978).

INTRODUCTION

This essay represents my attempt to write the book I looked for in vain during my own first encounter with the *Phenomenology of Spirit*. I felt the need for something more detailed and comprehensive than the chapter or two which so many good books on Hegel devote to this aspect of his work, and less overwhelming both in size and complexity than the two great French commentaries of Hyppolite and Kojève. More specifically I desired help in discovering what Hegel's overall strategy was and how the widely varied parts of the text contributed to carrying out his plan.

My goal, consequently, has been an ambitious one—to show that a single argument runs through the text from start to finish. For those coming to the *Phenomenology* as newcomers, whatever success I have had will make it easier not to lose sight of the forest while wandering through the 750 pages of trees and heavy underbrush. For Hegel scholars, I hope to have put to rest discussions about the unity of the text, not by further analysis of its *Entstehungsgeschichte*, but by showing that unity in the text. My thesis is that the key to that unity is Hegel's radical discovery that transcendental subjectivity has a social history and that absolute knowledge is both an historically conditioned and essentially collective or social event.

The following summary of the argument correlates the chapters of this essay with the chapters of the *Phenomenology* discussed in each. While I have treated every part of Hegel's text, no attempt has been made to comment on all of them in equal detail. The degree of attention given to any particular section has been dictated by its importance for tracing Hegel's unifying argument. This accounts for the relatively brief treatment of Hegel's Chapter Five, for in my view it reiterates and anticipates but does little to advance the argument. An abbreviated table of contents for the *Phenomenology* would look like this:

Chapter Six   *Spirit*
Chapter Seven *Religion*
Chapter Eight *Absolute Knowledge*

Chapters One and Two (dealing with Hegel's Introduction and aspects of his Preface). The Introduction presents the task of the *Phenomenology* in exclusively noetic terms. Its target is the prevailing scepticism, Kantian and otherwise, which denies to philosophical reason the capacity to know the Absolute, which other traditions refer to as the Unconditioned, God, Truth, or Being Itself. By contrast the Preface directs our attention to the present standpoint of Spirit, the historical-cultural crisis of a European civilization which in 1807 had lost the substantial life and immediate unity with the divine it once possessed.

It is easy to relate the early, abstractly epistemological chapters of the *Phenomenology* to the former account of Hegel's project, the later socio-historical analyses to the latter. Such learned students of Hegel as Haering, Hoffmeister, and Pöggeler have concluded that the text is schizophrenic, with Hegel's philosophy of Spirit rather arbitrarily appended to an introduction to his *Science of Logic,* an introduction essentially completed midway through the text we now possess. The issue was raised first and most dramatically by Rudolf Haym when he rhetorically asked what possible relation could exist between the madness of Diderot's musician or the fanaticism of Marat and Robespierre as portrayed in Chapter Six and the earlier analyses of sense perception.

But this was not Hegel's view. Not only in the *Science of Logic* did he affirm the entire published *Phenomenology* to be the systematic presupposition of a truly philosophical logic; in the Preface of 1807, written after the rest of the text was completed, he affirmed the fundamental unity of the anti-Kantian and history-of-Spirit dimensions of his work. In doing so he provided important preliminary guidance for finding one's way through his labyrinthine text.

Chapters Three and Four (dealing with Hegel's first three chapters, collectively entitled Consciousness). Hegel begins like a true epistemologist, with the analysis of sense perception and natural scientific knowledge. This is not because he is primarily interested in the career of the sciences. His concern is always with philosophical knowledge, knowledge of the Absolute. He must begin where he does because of the tendency of the natural sciences to preempt the claim of philosophy to be scientific knowledge, a tendency to which various forms of philosophy, so-called, have increasingly contributed. These critical philosophies, which had set out to determine "the nature and limits of human understanding," had all too regularly concluded that human knowledge was by nature suited only to grasp the finite objects of sense perception and scientific theory, and could never transcend the limits of what Kant called the conditioned. To show that and how knowledge of the Absolute is possible, Hegel must undercut these various scepticisms. So as not to assert this possibility dogmatically over against equally dogmatic sceptical denials, Hegel must develop what he considers to be truly philosophical knowledge out of the very sort of reflection on sense perception and natural science which, when cut short too quickly, generates a scepticism which might be called critical finitism. The first step along this path is Hegel's reiteration of Kant's discovery that knowledge does not so much conform to its object as the object conforms to our knowledge of it. One can therefore speak of a subjectivity or selfhood which contributes essentially to the object as present in our knowledge of it, thereby shaping or constituting the world in which we live. Kant uses the term transcendental to designate that subjectivity, and his usage will be adopted in the chapters which follow.

Chapter Five (dealing with Hegel's fourth chapter and the latter two sections of his fifth). The crucial move beyond Kant does not come in a critique of the thing in itself, though the ending of his third chapter can be read as such a critique. It comes rather in Hegel's fourth chapter with the discovery that transcendental subjectivity as Kant presented it, within the limits of the purely theoretical, is a highly rarefied abstraction. Where Kant finds the conditions for the possibility of experience in transcendental subjectivity, Hegel asks what the conditions for the possibility of transcendental subjectivity may be. It is in answer to this question that he introduces the central notion of Spirit. As the practical-social condition for the possibility of transcendental subjectivity, Spirit forms the bridge from the epistemological framework to the historical-cultural framework. Haym's question shows that he has not understood the central concept in Hegel's book.

Chapter Six (dealing with Hegel's sixth chapter). It is by this deepening of critical reflection that the question of knowledge becomes the question of the historical career of Spirit. There follows a socio-political interpretation of European history from classical Greece to the post-revolutionary world of Hegel's present. This culminates in the bold claim that Spirit, man's historical self-development, has become absolute, and that in the process the wisdom which previous philosophy merely loved or longed for has become actual as Absolute Knowledge.

Chapter Seven (dealing with Hegel's seventh chapter). Since Hegel finds it necessary to describe this result in theological language, its full clarification requires a retelling of the same story as the history of religion. While his sixth chapter interprets history as the apotheosis of the social, his seventh narrates the historical socializing of the divine. In this way the two accounts reinforce one another and render transparent the jointly theological and political nature of Hegel's conclusion, thereby incorporating into his systematic thought the central concerns of his so-called "early theological writings."

Chapter Eight (dealing with Hegel's eighth and final chapter). Hegel recapitulates this result in order 1) to refute (clairvoyantly) Marx's misinterpretation of the *Phenomenology* as a Stoic-idealist withdrawal from the actual, 2) to mediate his historicist account of Absolute Knowledge with the ideal of philosophy as eternal truth, and 3) to indicate briefly the tasks remaining to philosophical science once the historical conditions of its possibility have been presented.

In the chapters which follow I have *tried* to present this long and complex argument without speaking Hegelese myself. At the same time I have quoted him extensively. In other words, I have *tried* to present the argument in two different languages, Hegel's and ours. There are two reasons for this. There is first of all the usual matter of documentation, providing the reader with the texts upon which my interpretation primarily rests. More important, however, is my view of Hegelese. It is a dead language and should remain so. No one should learn to speak or write it. But it is obviously necessary to learn to read it if one is to study Hegel for oneself. I *hope* the alternation between our language and Hegelese will provide something of an entrance into that language for those to whom it is somewhat new, as well as some clues on graceful exiting for those who fear or have already fallen prey to its seductive charms. The italicized words in this paragraph are my confession that my goal has exceeded my grasp. I can only take comfort from the poet's assurance that that's the way it ought to be, or what's a heaven for?

Finally I would like to express my appreciation to John Smith for his guidance and encouragement in my first serious encounters with Hegel, and to David Carr and Ed Casey for their helpful comments on early drafts of my manuscript. I am also grateful to Yale University for the Morse Fellowship which permitted me to do some of my research in Heidelberg among some of Germany's most distinguished Hegel scholars.

GUIDE TO FOOTNOTES

A typical reference to the *Phenomenology* will be: PhG, x/y/z.

x   = pagination of the first edition, also available in the Ullstein edition and to be included in the new critical edition in GW (see below).

y   = pagination in Hoffmeister's 1952 edition, the handiest German text.

z   = pagination in the Baillie translation.

Where other references are divided with a '/' the German is given first, then the corresponding English translation, as given below.

HTJ   = *Hegels Theologische Jugendschriften,* ed. Nohl. English translation, where given from *On Christianity: Early Theological Writings,* tr. and ed. Knox and Kroner.

Volksreligion = *Volksreligion und Christentum*

PCR I = *The Positivity of the Christian Religion* (1795-96)

PCR II = *The Positivity of the Christian Religion* (1800)

SC = *The Spirit of Christianity and its Fate*

Fragment = one of the fragmentary drafts appended to HTJ.

GW   = *Gesammelte Werke* (Deutsche Forschungsgemeinschaft Ausgabe)

Differenz = *Differenz des Fichte'chen und Schelling'schen Systems der Philosophie*

Skepticismus = *Verhältniss des Skepticismus zur Philosophie*

Glauben = *Glauben und Wissen*

Naturrecht = *Über die wissenschaftlichen Behandlungsarten des Naturrechts*

Werke   = Werke in zwanzig Bänden (Theorie Werkausgabe, Suhrkamp)

The German Constitution is cited from this German text and in English translation from Pelczynski *Hegel's Political Writings.*

Sittlichkeit   = *System der Sittlichkeit,* ed. Lasson.

Realphilosophie = *Jenaer Realphilosophie* (see Ch. 3, n. 37).

SL = *Wissenschaft der Logik,* ed. Lasson. English translation, *Science of Logic* by A. V. Miller.

SW = *Sämtliche Werke,* ed. Glockner

HP = *Vorlesungen über die Geschichte der Philosophie.* English translation, *Hegel's Lectures on the History of Philosophy* by Haldane and Simson.

LL = *Encyklopädie der philosophischen Wissenchaften im Grundrisse.* Part I, the Logic is known as the Lesser Logic. English translation, *The Logic of Hegel* by Wallace.

CHAPTER ONE: The Task of the *Phenomenology:*
A) The Introduction

In his first critique of Kant Hegel defines the task of true philosophy as the absolute overcoming of all oppositions. This is accomplished only in knowing the Absolute. The Kantian philosophy, however, takes as its task not the knowing of the Absolute, but the critique of our knowing capacity. Thus it remains in the realm of opposition and in the strictest sense cannot be called philosophy. In fact it mistakes the death of philosophy for its highest fulfillment.[1] We can therefore expect Hegel's philosophy to take the form of a continuous debate with the critical philosophy; and we should not be too surprised when he defines philosophy as the refutation of Kant.[2]

It is in these terms that the *Phenomenology* presents itself in its Introduction. This is our starting point, if we read the book as it was written, for the longer and more famous Preface was written several months after the rest of the book was completed. The advantage of hindsight was greater than usual in this case, for the project grew considerably in the course of writing. Originally the plan was that the *Phenomenology* would not be an entity in itself, but only an introduction to the Logic, which would appear with it in the first volume of Hegel's System of Science. In light of this fact and the marked differences between the Preface and Introduction, it is natural to ask whether the latter remains an accurate statement of the *Phenomenology's* task, and even whether there is any single project which unifies the enormous whole of the text.

It is the thesis of this essay that we can meaningfully speak of *the* task of the *Phenomenology;* that there is a single coherent argument running through its entirety; and that when properly understood, the Preface can be seen not only as complementary to the Introduction but as growing directly out of it. This chapter and the next are concerned with a comprehensive view of the task of the *Phenomenology* as set forth in the Introduction and Preface. It will then fall to the remaining chapters to trace the argument from Sense Certainty to Absolute Knowledge.[3]

1A. Critical Philosophy as the Fear of Error and the Fear of Truth.

The Introduction defines phenomenology in terms of its opposition to all critical philosophy *as previously practiced.* Criticism is portrayed as a fear of error leading to the belief that knowledge must be examined before philosophy can get on with its job of knowing the Absolute, here defined as "what truly is" and "what is in itself." It argues that "since knowing is a faculty of a determinate kind and scope, without the more precise determination of its nature and limits we might take hold on clouds of error instead of the heaven of truth."[4]

It is clear from this description as well as from other writings of the Jena period[5] that Hegel's target is not just the transcendental critical philosophy of Kant and Fichte, but also the work of Locke and Hume and even of such lesser contemporaries as Jacobi, Schulze, and Krug. In fact Hegel is declaring his independence from the whole epistemological project as modern philosophy inherited it from Descartes.[6] "Now no more useful inquiry can be proposed than that which seeks to determine the nature and the scope of human knowledge . . . This investigation should be undertaken once at least in his life by anyone who has the slightest regard for truth, since in pursuing it the true instruments of knowledge and the whole method of inquiry come to light. But nothing seems more futile than the conduct of those who boldly dispute about the secrets of nature . . . without yet having ever asked whether human reason is adequate to the solution of these problems."[7]

It is Locke's formulation of this project which Hegel quotes in the Kant critique mentioned above as being definitive of the prevailing philosophical enterprise, with the comment that one can read the same thing in Kant. "For I thought that the first step towards satisfying several inquiries the mind of man was very apt to run into, was, to take a survey of our understandings, examine our own powers, and see to what things they were adapted . . . Thus men, extending their inquiries beyond their capacities, and letting their thoughts wander into those depths where they can find no sure footing, it is no wonder that they raise questions and multiply disputes, which, never coming to any clear resolution, are proper only to continue and increase their doubts, and to confirm them at last in perfect scepticism. Whereas, were the capacities of our understandings well considered, the extent of our knowledge once discovered, and the horizon found which sets the bounds between the enlightened and dark parts of things; between what is and what is not comprehensible by us, men would perhaps with less scruple acquiesce in the avowed ignorance of the one, and employ their thoughts and discourse with more advantage and satisfaction in the other."[8]

This is the background for Hegel's opening sentence: "It is natural to suppose that, before philosophy enters upon its subject proper—namely the actual knowledge of what truly is—it is necessary to come first to an understanding concerning knowledge . . ." It sounds as if he is introducing his favorite joke about the poor fellow who wouldn't enter the water before he had learned to swim. But the passage continues, "which is looked upon as the instrument by which to take possession of the Absolute, or as the means through which to get sight of it."[9] It is to this metaphorical account of knowledge as an instrument or means to which our attention is directed, not the difficulties of a philosophy which assumes we can know knowledge but questions whether we can know anything else.

Hegel is particularly hostile to the first of these metaphors. In his essay of 1802 on "The Relation of Scepticism to Philosophy," he reproaches Schulze for treating concepts and principles as instruments which philosophy uses to ferret out hidden objects, as if it were seeking a rock under snow. "It is impossible to conceive of what is rational and of speculation in a cruder manner . . . What happens here is not what the Devil demanded of Christ, to change stone to bread; rather the living bread of reason is eternally changed into stone."[10]

A similar scorn is directed against Kant in the *Lectures on the History of Philosophy.* "Knowledge is thereby represented as an instrument, as a method and means whereby we endeavour to possess ourselves of the truth. Thus before men can make their way to the truth itself they must know the nature and function of their instrument . . . This would appear as though men could set forth upon the search for truth with spears and staves."[11]

Hegel's lack of charity towards the instrument metaphor is not arbitrary. It represents his disenchantment with the assumption that knowledge is power and that method is the means to this end. It is well known that Kant called the *Critique of Pure Reason* a treatise on method.[12] But it is less frequently noticed that he prefaced the second edition, in which this statement appears, with a quotation from Bacon. Fichte in turn included part of the same quotation in his *First Introduction to the Science of Knowledge,* including the sentence, " . . . I am laboring to lay the foundation, not of any sect or doctrine, but of human utility and power." To which Hegel replied, when lecturing on Bacon, "Even now our countrymen like to adorn their works with sententious sayings culled from him."[13] Descartes' conception of method, like Bacon's, is linked to this idea of knowledge as an instrument of power, as not only the *Discourse on Method* indicates, but even the brief quotation given above from the rules; and his influence on subsequent developments was not limited to providing the adornment of sententious sayings. The same could be said of Locke. Hegel can rightly claim that the instrument metaphor pervades the epistemological tradition he is seeking to transcend.

His deepest objections to the view of knowledge as method and power, as "controlling knowledge" (Scheler, Tillich) or "the logic of domination" (Marcuse), are moral. He agrees with Schiller that "utility is the great idol of the times,"[14] and he gives his own critique of this Enlightenment idol in Chapter Six of the *Phenomenology.* But in the Introduction he limits himself to epistemic matters. Knowledge conceived as an instrument is a means to the end of power. The goal of philosophy, however, is not to gain power over the Absolute but to know it as it truly is. This is the source of the difficulty of importing into philosophy two metaphors for knowledge which derive from the knowledge-as-power tradition. "In both cases [assuming we are doing philosophy and not engineering] we employ a means which immediately brings about the opposite of its own end; or, rather, the absurdity lies in our making use of any means at all." This is best seen by taking each case separately. "For if knowledge is the instrument to take hold of the Absolute, one is immediately reminded that the application of an instrument to a thing does not leave the thing *as it is for itself,* but brings about a shaping and alteration of it. Or, if knowledge is not an instrument for our activity, but a more or less passive medium through which the light of truth reaches us, then again we do not receive this truth *as it is in itself*, but as it is in and through this medium."[15]

The thoughtless use of the instrument and medium metaphors is not an isolated inadvertence within the critical tradition. That tradition is pictured, not as a miscellaneous conclusion here and an isolated pronouncement there, but rather as a network of interrelated elements. The "fear of error" which is its hallmark has both its "presuppositions" and its "consequences", i.e., it is a system of logically related elements. At least four of these are distinguished: 1) the idea of knowledge as an instrument or medium, 2) the idea of the Absolute as something separated from us and our knowledge, 3) the idea that in addition to the absolute truth and knowledge there are lower kinds of knowledge which can be said to possess "truth of another kind," and 4) for employment in stating these three principles, a whole set of basic categories whose meaning is assumed to be familiar to everyone, such as absolute, knowledge, objective, subjective, etc.[16] Just as Kant finds "a whole nest of dialectical assumptions" underlying and undermining the cosmological argument, so Hegel finds a whole system of presuppositions at the basis of critical finitism.[17]

Hegel's differences with that tradition are thus revealed to be systemic. If we distinguish an external question as "a question which concerns the collective justification of all the true propositions contained in any particular realm of discourse," from an internal question, which is "the question of the justification of a judgment within the particular realm of discourse [at hand]," then the issue between Hegel and critical philosophy begins to look more like an external than an internal question.[18] That is, Hegel's own stress on the systematic nature of criticism's stance suggests that this debate with it is more like discussing the relative merits of Euclidian and Riemannian geometries than correcting a pupil for doing a Euclidian proof incorrectly. The difficulties of carrying on a debate under these circumstances are enormous. Hegel does not underestimate them, but rather gives primary attention to them in the second and third parts of the Introduction. In the Preface he says one must teach the opponent to "walk on his head," so fundamental is the change of attitude that is necessary, but at the same time one must remember that all genuine criticism is internal.[19]

A more immediate result emerges, however, from this

analysis of criticism. It is the discovery that the entire enter-prise, *as traditionally practiced*, is as dogmatic in its procedure as it is sceptical in its conclusions, for it rests on unexamined pre-suppositions. It sets out to examine the categories and princi-ples of knowledge, but it employs categories whose meaning has not been clarified and principles whose truth has not been established. It thereby opens itself to a variety of epithets which suggest mindlessness and even bad faith: random talk, opaque distinction, useless ideas, accidental and arbitrary ideas, pre-tense, fraud.[20] Hegel's language is strong here because he wants to do philosophy and because he has long been convinced that this kind of absolute and unanalyzed assumption means that "all philosophy is routed from the field of battle."[21]

This being the case, "one should not overlook the possibil-ity of reversing this procedure [of distrusting Science] by plac-ing distrust in this very distrust and becoming concerned about another question: Is not this fear of erring already the error it-self?" Since conclusions based on arbitrary presuppositions can have no normative force, we are entitled immediately to dismiss the whole business as the fraudulent effort "to avoid the toil of Science and to give at the same time the impression of earnest and zealous effort." The fear of error turns out to be the fear of truth.[22]

This is far from being Hegel's last word on the subject of critical philosophy. He neither abandons critical questions completely, as he seems about to do, nor does he leave his critique of critical finitism in the form it takes here. But he never abandons this charge that carelessly adopted assumptions underlie its negative conclusions. This raises the question whether he has, in Collingwood's terms, discovered the "abso-lute" or most basic of these presuppositions. Of the elements he has singled out, the most basic seems to be the idea that the Ab-solute is an object which stands over against us, escaping our gaze by escaping our grasp. This leads to the idea that knowl-edge is an instrument for seizing the Absolute (the verbs used with this metaphor are *bemächtigen, habhaft werden, fassen,* and *erfassen*) and a medium through which to see it; then, since this is bound to distort the object, the face-saving appeal to that elu-sive "truth of another kind."

A rigorous questioning must ask on what presupposition, if

any, rests the idea that the Absolute is separated from us and hidden from our view like a bird which we would catch with a lime-twig or a stone under the snow, rather than being "in and for itself already close to us of its own accord."[23] Hegel has not overlooked this question. Underlying this basic theoretical presupposition he finds a more basic pre-theoretical presupposition, the fear (*Furcht*) of error and an anxiety (*Besorgnis*) which is its constant companion. So he introduces the presuppositions mentioned above with the following formula: "In fact, this fear of erring presupposes something, indeed a great deal, as truth." Similarly, it is "the anxiety about falling into error" which "posits a mistrust in Science," just as it is "this anxiety [about grasping clouds of error instead of the heaven of truth]" which "will surely transform itself into the conviction . . . that between knowledge and the Absolute there lies a boundary which completely cuts off the one from the other."[24]

This makes it clear that a full understanding of critical philosophy, upon which any attempt to go beyond it must be based, can only rest on an understanding of its affective roots, its fundamental fearfulness. The critique of criticism will have to uncover both the nature and the origin of the anxiety expressed in all its behavior. A kind of psychoanalysis seems to be called for, but Hegel offers nothing of the kind in his Introduction. Instead, he breaks off his line of thought very abruptly (in the middle of a paragraph in the German text, at *Aber die Wissenschaft* . . .) and begins to reflect on how the branch of philosophical Science he calls phenomenology can mediate between the pseudo-philosophy of the critical tradition and genuine, i.e., speculative philosophy.

Hegel is here seeking to avoid the genetic fallacy. He knows that the theoretical presuppositions of critical philosophy cannot be discredited simply by reference to more basic pre-theoretical presuppositions. Even when his philosophical psychoanalysis is completed and a fuller comprehension of critical philosophy is available the task of generating philosophical Science by deepening critical reflection will only be begun, by no means completed. If we are to be prepared for what is to come Hegel must give us some indication of how he thinks this is possible.

1B. Phenomenology as the Way of Doubt and Despair.

In other places Hegel seeks to dismiss critical finitism briefly and decisively.[25] While the initial paragraphs of the Introduction suggest the same procedure, the sudden shift we have just noted indicates that a different strategy is being adopted. It is based on the belief that a quick battle is not genuinely decisive, whatever its rhetorical success in embarrassing the opponent. At best one silences him temporarily, creating a vacuum as abhorrent to truth as to nature.

The new train of thought begins with the recognition that "Science, in the very fact that it comes on the scene is itself a phenomenon [*Erscheinung*]; it is not yet Science in its fully realized and propagated truth simply by virtue of coming on the scene . . . [Consequently] it cannot simply reject an untrue form of knowledge as a merely common view of things and give assurance that it is a completely different way of knowing . . . By giving this assurance it would declare that its force resides in its being; but the untrue knowledge also appeals to the fact that it is, and gives assurance that to it Science is nothing—one barren assurance carries as much weight as another."[26]

The issue is now posed as a quarrel between Science and "another kind" of knowledge or consciousness, variously characterized as phenomenal, untrue, unreal, incomplete, and natural.[27] Science can conquer its opponent only "by turning against it," i.e., by actually coming to grips with it and engaging it in battle. It cannot in good faith either simply ignore finite knowledge and the philosophy which absolutizes it, or help itself to assumptions which beg the question against them. Science must become the medium which contains natural consciousness and yet invalidates its pretensions to exhaust the scope of human knowledge, showing how natural consciousness transcends itself and leads to Science. "These, then, are the reasons for proposing to undertake a description of knowledge as it appears, a presentation of knowledge as a phenomenon."[28]

There is an elegant ambiguity in the phrase *das erscheinende Wissen*. It can be rendered either by "knowledge as a phenomenon, as it appears," or by "phenomenal knowledge." The former case indicates that knowledge is an object available for investigation, while the latter carries a pejorative connotation derived from Kant. Hegel intends both meanings. It is the first which belongs to the idea of a description or presentation [*Darstellung*] of knowledge in various of its modes, but the second is called for in the immediately following sentence—"In view of the fact that this presentation has for its object only phenomenal knowledge, the presentation itself seems to be unscientific, for unlike free Science, it does not seem to move in a shape peculiar to itself. But it can be regarded . . . as the way of the natural consciousness which is striving toward true knowledge."

The point is this: the whole of the *Phenomenology* is now given as the critique of criticism, not just the Introduction. For it alone is this presentation of phenomenal knowledge as a phenomenon, the "turning against" which is not simple, dogmatic negation. Not only in this Introduction but again and again in the earlier Jena writings Hegel has been telling us about the antithetical relationship between the natural consciousness (sometimes called, following Kant, healthy human understanding or common sense—*der gesunde Menschenverstand*) and genuine philosophy.[29] Now he is accepting the challenge to show us what he has been telling us, namely that human knowledge is not finally subject to the kinds of limitation and finitude attributed to it by Kant and the critical tradition. This he intends to do by placing before us the various finite forms of knowledge validated by this tradition that we may see for ourselves how they lead beyond themselves. Thus at least part of the meaning of the often discussed "we" and "for us" which occurs in the text is Socratic. Hegel seeks as pedagogue to evoke in each of his readers the insights he has already achieved for himself. This carries no implication, as is often charged, that one must already be in the realm of Absolute Knowledge to follow Hegel's argument. It only supposes that like the slaveboy in the Meno, the reader can see for himself what is there to be seen and does not need to take anything on Hegel's authority. How Hegel himself may have come to the insights he seeks to evoke is no more relevant here than the same question about Socrates' geometrical knowledge would be. What matters is the insight, not the occasion under which it arises. In his final chapter Hegel will himself describe the philosophical understanding to which we are led in terms of re-collection, deliberately invoking this Platonic model.

Anticipating the final outcome, Hegel emphasizes above all else the destructive nature of his presentation. "Natural consciousness will show itself to be merely the concept of knowledge, or unreal knowledge. But since it immediately takes itself to be real knowledge, this way has a negative significance for it, and what is actually the realization of the concept [of knowledge] is for it rather the loss and destruction of itself. For on this road it loses its truth. The road may thus be viewed as the way of doubt, or more properly, as the way of despair." In this way philosophy begins with a "thoroughgoing scepticism."[30]

It is not just any old scepticism, however, which marks the beginning of true philosophy. It is a triply distinctive scepticism whose determination is a trio of negations. In the first place, it is not a temporary doubt, "entertaining a disbelief in this or that presumed truth only to return to that same 'truth' once the 'doubt' has been appropriately dissipated, so that in the end matters stand pretty much as in the beginning. On the contrary, this way is the conscious insight into the untruth of phenomenal knowledge." Temporary doubt is merely the resolve to take nothing on authority but to test everything by reason. But since it reveals itself to be an empty intention by holding fast to "a system of opinion and prejudice, it matters little whether one bases himself on the authority of others or on personal conviction; the only difference is the vanity which is peculiar to the latter."[31]

We are likely to think of Descartes in this context, though Hegel more likely has Fichte in mind.[32] The point, however, is not so much to discredit Fichte or anyone else, but rather to give us the standard by which Hegel wishes to be judged, not the promises of his Introduction but the performance of the 750 pages which follow. It is only there that his scepticism can be thoroughgoing in its examination of the various modes of theoretical and practical knowledge which belong to natural consciousness.

Secondly, if phenomenological scepticism is not temporary, neither is it paralyzing. It seeks to discover as well as to negate, and thus to be able to move on. To do this it must avoid the fallacy of simple negation, the flaw of that ancient scepticism of Pyrrho and Sextus Empiricus which Hegel otherwise so greatly admires.³³ This scepticism "sees in every result only pure nothingness and abstracts from the fact that this nothingness is determinate, that it is the nothingness of that from which it results." Thus it "cannot proceed any further but must wait and see whether anything new presents itself to it, and what this is, in order to cast it into the same abysmal void."³⁴

Such a scepticism cannot, like Socratic scepticism in the hands of Plato, become the introduction to metaphysics. But this is just what phenomenological scepticism must be, the negative side of genuine philosophical Science. It must recognize that the negation of one form of consciousness is itself a new form of consciousness which has a positive content of its own. For example, from an abstract point of view critical philosophy is a simple negation of philosophy as knowledge of the Absolute. But as Hegel has already shown, that negation rests on a variety of positive assumptions such as the absoluteness of the finite and empirical and the "undeniable certainty of the common consciousness and its whole realm of finite facts."³⁵ Because Hegel recognizes that every negation rests on some such position he can describe his phenomenological scepticism as "the way of the soul which is making its way through the sequence of its own transformations as through waystations prescribed to it by its very nature." At each stage "the transition is made by which the progression through the complete sequence of shapes [of consciousness] takes place of its own accord."³⁶

This continual movement is guaranteed not only because every negation is itself a position, but also because each new position must measure itself against the philosophical ideal, opening itself to a new negation. "For knowledge, however, the goal is fixed just as necessarily as the sequence of the progression. It is that point where knowledge no longer has need to transcend itself, where it finds itself, and where the concept corresponds to the object and the object to the concept. The progression toward this goal is consequently without halt and at no earlier stage is satisfaction to be found."³⁷

This description of the goal is only an account of what Absolute Knowledge would be. We are not told whether this goal is a postulate to be grasped by some sort of philosophical faith, a regulative ideal to be approximated in an infinite process, or a possibility to be realized by actual knowledge. We are only told that short of achieving this goal in actual knowledge there will be the kind of cognitive dissonance required to keep the process moving. For all we know, each new form of consciousness may be cast into the same "abysmal void" already mentioned. Negating will be positing indeed, but nothing positive will be able to sustain itself. Dialectical thought will produce the terror of absolute freedom and the frenzy of self-conceit. Far from being the way to Science, phenomenology will be the way of endless despair. This is not, of course, the conclusion that Hegel reaches. The point is only that he has not precluded this possibility at the start. One need not already have attained the goal in order to set out on the path toward it. One needn't even be persuaded there is a goal to be reached at the end of the path. One only needs to see how movement along the path is possible.

Finally, and most importantly, the scepticism which Hegel calls phenomenology is not a positivistic scepticism.[38] In his critique of Schulze, applied in the Lesser Logic to Hume as well,[39] he distinguishes ancient from modern scepticism. The latter is positivistic in taking as fixed and unshakeable the finite objects of common sense and natural science and consequently doubting anything which cannot be reduced to these spheres. One has only to think of the glorious book burning scene in which Hume plays Grand Inquisitor at the conclusion of the *Inquiry Concerning Human Understanding.* The "grand" and "noble" scepticism of antiquity, by contrast, is directed against "this dogmatism of common sense . . . against the finite and the knowledge of the finite, i.e., the understanding." It knows that "the beginning of philosophy must be the elevation above the truth provided by the common consciousness, and the presentiment of a higher truth." The ancient sceptics listed by Diogenes had "the insight that a true philosophy necessarily has its own negative side, which is directed against all that is limited, including the heap of facts of consciousness and their undeniable certainty . . . against this whole ground of finitude on which this modern scepticism has its nature and its truth." Of these the most brilliant example is Plato's *Parmenides.* "This Platonic scepticism does not lead to doubting these truths of the understanding . . . but to the total negation of all truth of such knowledge . . . It is the negative side of the knowledge of the Absolute, and it immediately presupposes reason as the positive side."[40]

It is just this contrast which Hegel wants to establish between his phenomenological scepticism and the "modern" scepticism of critical philosophy. Hence the cryptic statement with which he expresses the third characteristic of his own "ancient" scepticism—"But through that scepticism which directs itself to the whole compass of phenomenal consciousness, Spirit becomes suited for the first time to examine what truth is. For this scepticism brings about a despair over the so-called natural ideas, thoughts, and opinions."[41]

Both at the beginning of our analysis of Hegel's triply radical scepticism and here at the end we find him describing it in terms of despair rather than doubt. It is indeed a traumatic journey for the natural consciousness, a fact which Hegel goes out of his way to underscore. "Although what is limited to a natural life is by itself powerless to transcend its immediate existence, it is driven out by another power—and thus to be uprooted is its death."[42] This is how natural consciousness will experience genuine philosophical scepticism, and why "healthy common sense not only cannot understand speculation, but must also hate it if it experiences it, and, if it is not wholly indifferent in its security, must also abhor and persecute it."[43]

This clinging by consciousness to its familiar existence shows that it still belongs to natural life and has not yet achieved the life of Spirit. Shortly before writing the *Phenomenology* Hegel told his students that "Spirit exists only as transcending [*aufhebend*] that which it immediately is."[44] Similarly, in the Introduction he continues by contrasting consciousness to natural life. "But since consciousness is for itself its own concept, it immediately transcends [*das Hinausgehen ist*] what is limited, and because this limitedness is its own, it transcends itself . . . Consciousness therefore suffers this violence at its own hands, a violence through which it destroys for itself any limited satisfaction." Anxiety [*Angst*] is sure to result from this process, and a variety of escapes from it will be tried. But it is of the nature of consciousness that short of its goal it can find no rest, and it will continue to suffer this "violence at the hands of reason." As Hegel later put it in the Preface, "not the life that shrinks from

death and keeps itself undefiled by devastation, but the life that
endures, and preserves itself through death is the life of
Spirit."[45] In other words, it is not so much suicide to which
Hegel is calling the natural consciousness as it is initiation, the
process by which one dies to an old life and is reborn to a new.
In the light of this whole analysis of the phenomenological
journey with its emphasis on the attachment to an infinite goal
which produces only restlessness and negativity in the face of
everything finite,[46] it is no wonder that the *Phenomenology* has
been so frequently compared on the one hand to Goethe's *Faust*
and on the other to St. Bonaventure's *Itinerarium Mentis in
Deum.* What we do not learn from the Introduction is how seriously we are to take these comparisons and Hegel's use of
such terms as fear, anxiety, despair, violence, and death. When
Jean Wahl tells us that Hegelian doubt is more like that of Pas-
cal and Nietzsche than that of Descartes, and when Jean Hyppolite suggests that we have to do here with *une angoisse exis-
tentielle,* is it Hegel or the intellectual atmosphere of France in
the forties which is speaking to us?[47] Is Hegel dealing here with
the conflict between philosophical systems or with something a
little closer to where we all, even as philosophers, live, and
move, and have our being? The answer to this question about
what might be called the existential import of the *Phenomenology*
is, along with the analysis of criticism's fearfulness, the unfinished business with which the Introduction leaves us as it
moves on to its third and final part.

1C.   Phenomenology as Criticism without
Presuppositions.

The discussion of method which concludes the Introduction grows directly out of the first two parts. Hegel has tried to
show that critical philosophy brings with it a lot of presupposi-
tional baggage, which is not surprising if every negation also involves a position. What then about his own sceptical project?
We may have carelessly read him to say that Science "takes up
its work and actually knows without any hesitations," dispens-
ing with the critical task entirely. But it has become clear that
this is not the case, and what he actually says is that Science
"takes up its work and actually knows without any *such* hesita-

tions,"[48] i.e., such hesitations as stem from the anxiety over falling into error. Since the *Phenomenology* invites itself to be read as a long series of hesitations which must be dealt with before Science in its full and proper sense can get under weigh, Hegel puts the issue to himself sharply. "For if this presentation is viewed as a description of the way Science is related to phenomenal knowledge, and as an investigation and critical examination into the reality of knowledge, it does not seem possible for it even to take place without some presupposition which will serve as the fundamental criterion . . . Here, where Science first comes on the scene, neither it nor anything else has justified itself as the essence or as the in itself; and without some such basic principle it seems that an examination cannot take place."[49]

The dilemma is sharp. Criticism calls for criteria, but any choice of criteria involves either dogmatism or faith, in either case the abrogation of criticism. How can there be criticism without presuppositions?

The answer is found by attending carefully to the object of our investigations—consciousness. As it turns out, "consciousness provides itself with its own criterion, and the investigation will be a comparison of consciousness with its own self."[50] This happy discovery is really simpler than Hegel makes it sound. Every mode of knowledge distinguishes itself from its object or truth. It has at least a general idea of its object, of what would fulfill its intention or verify its assertion, and this serves as the criterion by which all putative knowledge is measured. Thus the question about each form of consciousness is not whether it conforms to our expectations, or Hegel's, but whether it satisfies its own demands. The self-understanding of natural science, for example, is significantly altered when reflection on the problem of induction or the paradoxes of confirmation reveals that it cannot live up to its own previously professed promises.

Hegel goes a step further. It is not just that consciousness provides its own criterion. It also compares itself with that criterion and thus examines itself. In this respect as well no contribution [*Zutat*] is needed from the phenomenological investigator, whose task becomes simply "the pure act of observation [*reine Zusehen*]."[51]

This is criticism without presuppositions. Though we are

given no concrete examples by Hegel, they are not hard to supply. The critical scepticism of Hume and Kant—what is it but
the metaphysics of continental rationalism comparing itself
with its own demands and coming up with a negative verdict?
And what is romanticism, at least in one important aspect, if not
the philosophies of faith and intuition which were offered in
place of that metaphysics, confessing that they cannot keep
their promises of satisfying the human spirit concerning the E-
ternal? A different sort of example was tucked away somewhere
in Hegel's files when he wrote the *Phenomenology*. We now know
it as *The German Constitution*. Like Voltaire's *bon mot* about the
Holy Roman Empire being neither holy, nor Roman, nor an
empire, Hegel's political criticism is wholly internal. Germany
qua Holy Roman Empire claims to be a state. But then it puts itself to the test by going to war and proves to anyone who cares
to watch that it is no longer a state but a living lie. "If Germany
were to profess to be a state and a constitution, although its con-
stitutional forms were without life, and the theory of them
without actuality, it would be speaking an untruth."[52]

Instead of such examples, however, Hegel summarizes his
discussion of method with the following most peculiar definition of experience: "This dialectical movement, which consciousness exercises on itself—on its knowledge as well as its
object—is, insofar as the new, true object emerges for consciousness as a result of it, precisely that which is called experience."[53] Concern over the unusual use of the term 'experience'
which Hegel employs (though he is after all talking about the
way in which objects are given to consciousness) must not dis-
tract from the really substantive dimensions of this definition.

In the first place there is the emergence of the new object
for consciousness. Consciousness compares itself with its own
criterion and in the process alters itself. But since each different form of consciousness is a new kind of knowing and each
new kind of knowing is new just because it is the knowledge of a
new kind of object, the process is one in which neither our concept of knowledge nor our concept of its object remains constant.[54] If Absolute Knowledge does not turn out in Chapter
Eight to be what we expected it to be, and the Absolute which is
the object (and the subject) of that knowledge is also a bit surprising, we should not be surprised. If we understand Hegel's

method we will expect to be surprised, for it is a method of watching the familiar repeatedly self-destruct and replace itself with a new mode of consciousness to which new objects correspond.

Secondly, the process by which a new form of knowledge and its new objects arise occurs repeatedly. This is "the dialectical movement which consciousness exercises on itself."[55] In other words, it is consciousness and not Hegel's method which is dialectical. Both here and in the Preface, where the discussion of dialectic is more directly related to the Logic than to the *Phenomenology*, this is the case.[56] The dialectical movement belongs to the subject matter of philosophy, whose task it is simply to describe this movement. Marxists sometimes speak of employing a dialectical method whose purpose is to change reality. But Hegel is suspicious of all methods, just because they are employed for someone's purpose, thereby introducing concerns extraneous to the subject matter into the process of knowing.[57] In his discussion of his own method he remains faithful to this distrust of method. His "method" is the *reine Zusehen* of human consciousness, the pure description of its dialectical restlessness and its striving to transcend its own finitude.

A further consequence of the fact that consciousness itself is dialectical is that the emergence of each new form of consciousness is no mere fact but has a rationality or intelligibility to it. This is because, as we already know from the discussion of scepticism, the new form is "the nothingness of that whose result it is, a result which contains what is true in the previous knowledge." It doesn't just come from nowhere. It comes from an "earlier" form of phenomenal knowledge by means of a feeling for its untruth. Since this feeling is not necessarily the conscious insight which Hegel seeks to evoke, the intelligibility of the transition may go entirely unnoticed. So he assigns to the phenomenological enterprise the task of pointing it out. Even if phenomenology is to be a descriptive science, this description is something other than the "gaping which always sees the opposite of what takes place before its eyes."[58]

The phenomenologist in this way has a role to play after all, even if he is deprived of the philosopher's favorite toy, a method. "This way of observing the subject matter is our contribution [*unsere Zutat*]; it does not exist for the consciousness we observe. But when viewed in this way the sequence of experiences constituted by consciousness is raised to the level of a scientific progression." Hence phenomenology can be called "The Science of the Experience of Consciousness."[59]

In making the distinction between observed and observing consciousness basic to his philosophical enterprise Hegel is placing himself within the tradition of transcendental reflection which stretches from Descartes to Fichte, who explicitly builds his *Science of Knowledge* around this distinction. This is one sense in which his own philosophy, which is the determinate negation of that tradition, "contains what is true in the previous philosophy." But in this respect Hegel is that tradition comparing itself with its criterion and thereby transcending itself. For the criterion which leads to transcendental reflection is the requirement that philosophy shall be without presuppositions. Descartes and Fichte, at opposite ends of the historical development are most explicit about this. But from the opening words of Descartes' Third Meditation, "I shall now close my eyes . . ." to the opening words of Fichte's *First Introduction to the Science of Knowledge,* "Attend to yourself: turn your attention from everything that surrounds you and towards your inner life," transcendental reflection had rested on this distinction of itself from knowledge of the external world and on the assumption which entitles the Second Meditation, that the mind is better known than the body, that inner sense is more reliable than outer sense.

This introspective orientation has a dogmatic character about it, for it rests on unexamined psychological assumptions about the directness and purity with which the self is available to its own inward look. Hegel counts it among the greatest sins of the critical tradition that it is so naive about its psychological assumptions,[60] not because this violates the canons which Hegel would impose on transcendental philosophy from without, but because it violates that tradition's own loudly proclaimed standards. The prejudice toward introspective inwardness is conspicuously missing from the way in which Hegel distinguishes observed and observing consciousness. To emphasize the point he explicitly tells us that "the phenomenology of Spirit is to replace psychological explanations as well as the more abstract discussions of the foundation of knowledge." In fact, this is the first thing Hegel wanted the public to know about his book beyond the fact that it presents "the becoming of knowledge."[61]

The Introduction concludes with a promissory note, that "consciousness will reach a point where it casts off the semblance of being burdened by something alien to it, something which is only for it and which exists as an other." In other words, the distinction between observed and observing consciousness will be overcome in a fully transparent self-consciousness. " . . . at that point where its appearance becomes equal to its essence, consciousness' presentation of itself [the *Phenomenology*] will converge with this very same point in the authentic Science of Spirit [the System]. And finally, when consciousness itself grasps this its essence, it will itself indicate the nature of Absolute Knowledge."[62]

This final part of the Introduction leaves no new unfinished business other than getting on to the text itself to see whether Hegel can produce what he has promised and in the way he has promised it, i.e., whether he can overcome critical philosophy by turning against the various forms of natural consciousness in a criticism which is without presuppositions. But there remain the earlier unanswered questions about the analysis of criticism's fearfulness and the existential import of phenomenological negation. Even a preliminary indication of what Hegel has to say about them would be a real asset in working through the text. Perhaps the Preface will supply what the Introduction has left undone.

NOTES

1. *Glauben,* GW, 4:325-26, 316. *das absolute Aufgehobensein des Gegensatzes.*

2. SL, I, 25/45.

3. Upper case will be used for these and other terms which Hegel uses as quasi-proper names for the modes or forms of consciousness he describes. Where Science appears in upper case it designates Hegel's conception of systematic philosophy in contrast to natural science. The justification for putting Spirit in upper case can only be the interpretation of that concept as given in Chapters Five through Seven below.

4. PhG, 3/63/131.

5. Hegel's first university appointment was at Jena, where he began in 1801 as *Privatdozent.* He was promoted in 1805 to *Ausserordentlicher Professor* but left in 1806 as Napoleon's armies approached for the fateful Battle of Jena, the official end of the Holy Roman Empire. It was not until ten years later that he had another university appointment, this time at Heidelberg.

6. Quite appropriately a recent collection of essays on Hegel's theory of knowledge, edited by Frederick G. Weiss, is entitled, *Beyond Epistemology.*

7. *Rules for the Direction of the Mind,* discussion of rule 8.

8. *An Essay Concerning Human Understanding,* Introduction, Section 7. Hegel quotes from a translation by Poleyen. I have given Locke's original. The ellipsis indicates an omitted sentence of which Hegel gives no indication.

9. PhG,3/63/131.

10. *Skepticismus,* GW, 4:201.

11. HP, SW, 19:555/III, 428.

12. B XXII.

13. HP, SW, 19:278/III, 170. Hegel gave his lectures on the history of philosophy for the first time while he was still in Jena. Whether the discussion of Bacon which is included in the editions we have was included at that time or comes from later versions of the lectures, long after the *Phenomenology* was written, it is impossible to tell at this time. So we cannot be sure that Hegel had Bacon in mind while writing his Introduction.

14. *On the Aesthetic Education of Man,* tr. Snell, New York, 1954, p. 26.

15. PhG, 3-4/63-64/131, my italics.

16. PhG, 5-7/64-65/132-34.

17. *Critique of Pure Reason,* A 609 = B637 f.

18. The distinction is Carnap's. These modified definitions are from Lewis White Beck's essay, "The Fact of Reason: An Essay on Justification in Ethics," in his *Studies in the Philosophy of Kant,* Indianapolis, 1956, pp. 200-01.

19. PhG, XXVIII-XXXI/23-25/85-87.

20. PhG, 5-7/65-66/133-134.

21. *Glauben,* GW, 4:350.

22. PhG, 5-7/64-65/132-34. In the interlude on misology in the *Phaedo* Socrates considers the possibility that someone might get so exasperated in the face of sophistical argumentation that he spent his life loathing and decrying argumentation "and so missed the chance of knowing the truth about reality—would it not be a deplorable thing?" 90d, Tredennick translation.

23. PhG, 4/64/132. cf. *Differenz,* GW, 4:15, "[The Absolute] is already at hand. How else could it be sought?"

24. PhG, 3-5/63-64/131-33.

25. See my essay, "In Defense of the Thing in Itself," *Kant-Studien,* 1968, Heft 1, 118-41.

26 PhG, 7-8/66/134.

27. PhG, 7-11/66-68/134-37. 'Natural consciousness' comes to be the most used designation. Included in its compass are not only our everyday awareness of the world and the knowledge of natural science but also the highly reflective activity of critical philosophy. There is a kind of gnostic or mystical perspective at work here which designates as merely natural all consciousness not engaged in actually knowing the Absolute. Thus everything short of Science is natural consciousness.

28. PhG, 8/66/135.

29. For example, *Differenz,* GW, 4:20-23, *Skepticismus,* GW, 4:206-16, *Glauben,* GW, 4:322-23, 355-57.

30. PhG, 9/67/135. Hegel has fun here with a word play on *Zweifel* and *Verzweiflung.*

31. PhG, 9-10/67-68/135-36.

32. The opening pages on doubt in *The Vocation of Man* are a classic expression of doubt as the public resolve to take nothing on authority.

As for the conceit which is supposed to go with this kind of doubt, one need only join the following statements from the *Science of Knowledge* and its *First Introduction*: "For my personal position I have no regard whatever. But I am hot for truth." "I thought and still think myself to have discovered the way in which philosophy must raise itself to the level of a manifest science." With reference to "these final results of idealism"—"Anyone who thinks otherwise simply does not know what he is talking about." *Science of Knowledge (Wissenschaftslehre)*, trans. Heath and Lachs, New York, 1970, pp. 90, 89, 26. *Sämmtliche Werke,* ed. I. H. Fichte, I, 87, 86, 447.

33. *Skepticismus,* GW, 4:213.
34. PhG, 11/68/137. cf. Preface, LXXIII-LXXIV/49/117-18.
35. *Skepticismus,* GW, 4:201-03. The first formula is typical of *Glauben.*
36. PhG, 9/67/135, 12/69/137.
37. PhG, 12/69/137-38. *über sich selbst hinausgehen.*
38. Though it is anachronistic to describe pre-Comptean positions as positivistic, I believe it is useful to do so to highlight their affinity with nineteenth and twentieth century views which repudiate metaphysics in favor of empirical science.
39. LL, #39-40 and *Zusätze* to #24 and #81. Perhaps Hegel is unfair to Hume here, though I think not. It is true that along with his twentieth century heirs, the logical empiricists, he has very sophisticated views of the ambiguous status of our scientific knowledge and does not share the naiveté of someone like Schulze. But he does share with all forms of positivism the view that empirical science and common sense (so far as it is assimilable to empirical science) are genuine knowledge, while metaphysics is spurious.
40. *Skepticismus,* GW, 4:215-16, 207.
41. PhG, 10/68/136.
42. PhG, 12-13/69/138.
43. *Differenz,* GW, 4:21.
44. *Realphilosophie,* 179.
45. PhG, XXXVIII/29/93.
46. See Fichte, *op. cit.,* pp. 231-33, 265-67. *Werke,* I, 261-65, 301-04.
47. Wahl, *Le Malheur de la Conscience dans la Philosophie de Hegel,* Paris, 1951, p. 7. Hyppolite, *Genèse et Structure de la Phénoménologie de l'Esprit de Hegel,* Paris, 1946, p. 10.
48. PhG, 5/64/132, my italics.

49. PhG, 13-14/70/139.

50. PhG, 15/71/140.

51. PhG, 16-17/72/141. cf. Fichte, *op. cit.*, 30, 120, *Werke*, I, 454, 123-24.

52. *The German Constitution, Werke*, I, 473/154. For context see 461-85/143-64.

53. PhG, 18/73/142.

54. PhG, 17/72/142.

55. PhG, 18/73/142. Dialectic might here be defined as self-transcendence through inner tension.

56. PhG, LXXX/53/123 f.

57. PhG, IV/11/69, LXVI/45/112. The entire second half of the Preface, from XLIV/33/97 on, is an extended treatment of this issue.

58. *Skepticismus,* GW, 4:199. The philosophical activity which Husserl calls phenomenology is also concerned with pure description and presuppositionless philosophy. The relationship between the two kinds of phenomenology is complex. Two important differences should be noted. What Husserl means by transcending the natural standpoint in order to philosophize is very different from what Hegel means by transcending natural consciousness for the sake of true philosophy. Second, where truth and certainty tend to coalesce for Husserl, Hegel constantly and deliberately holds them apart, claiming instead that truth is the whole, not the certain.

59. PhG, 19-21/74/143-44.

60. *Skepticismus,* GW, 4:200, *Glauben,* 4:322, 330-31.

61. From Hegel's own announcement of the PhG, which appeared in the October 28, 1807 issue of the *Jenaischen Allgemeinen Literatur-Zeitung.* The German text is found in the Ullstein edition of the PhG, p. 588. There is an English translation in Walter Kaufmann, *Hegel: Reinterpretation, Texts and Commentary,* Garden City, 1965, p. 366.

62. PhG, 21/75/145.

CHAPTER TWO: The Task of the *Phenomenology:*
B) The Preface

For the most part the Preface is best read as it was written—after the rest of the text. Unlike the Introduction, nearly every paragraph of which is crucially important for understanding what follows, most of the Preface does not provide the same sort of advance help for the reader. Indeed, parts of it are all but unintelligible apart from the substance of what follows; so one can say that the Preface requires the main text for its own understanding more than that text requires the Preface, a reversal of the usual relationship. For this reason, and because the Preface is four times the length of the Introduction, a close analysis of the whole Preface like that just given of the Introduction would not be appropriate.

At the same time there are a few central passages in the Preface which contribute significantly to the reader's preparation for the main argument. Furthermore, reflection on these helps us develop a fuller picture of the intellectual ferment which culminated for Hegel in the writing of the *Phenomenology*. So we cannot ignore the Preface entirely at this stage, even if we cannot treat it in the same way as the Introduction.

2A. The present standpoint of Spirit

On the basis of the Introduction alone it would be easy to suppose that Hegel was a philosopher's philosopher; that he took his problems from philosophers and addressed his answers to them, something in the style of G.E. Moore; that it was simply his attempt at Jena to come to grips with the dominant philosophical epistemology of his day that led him to write the *Phenomenology*. Since the task of phenomenology is given in such heavily epistemic language, it would not be arbitrary to suppose that the "existential" overtones detected by some readers are the result of taking too seriously the metaphors of a would-be literary stylist or of projecting their own interests and situation into the text. Such a view cannot be sustained past the first few chapters of the text, however, and it is the Preface which prepares us for this discovery.

To be sure, it still describes the goal in noetic terms. "To help bring philosophy nearer to the form of Science—that goal where it can lay aside the name of love of knowledge and be actual knowledge—that is what I have set before me."[1] Or again, "The goal is Spirit's insight into what constitutes knowledge."[2] Although the separation of knowledge and its object (truth, being) infects all the forms of consciousness through which phenomenology passes and is the defect which moves the process along, we are promised a vision of that state in which "the separation of knowledge and truth is overcome . . . With this the phenomenology of Spirit is concluded. What Spirit prepares for itself in this phenomenology is the element of knowledge. In this element the moments of Spirit spread themselves out in the form of simplicity which knows its object as itself. They no longer fall apart into the opposition of being and knowledge but abide in the simplicity of knowledge."[3] Statements of this sort stand in closest connection with the Introduction's idea that phenomenology is a re-doing of critical philosophy in such a way that the story has a happy rather than a sceptical ending.

Side by side with such statements in the Preface are others which formulate phenomenology's task in radically different language; language more likely to suggest Marx or Nietzsche than Hume and Kant; language which leads Kroner to say that the issue in the *Phenomenology* is no longer merely *Erkennen* but *Erlebnis* and Marcuse to say that the dualisms of subject and object, understanding and sense, thought and existence, are "not primarily an epistemological problem for Hegel."[4]

For example, it is essential to consider "what stage self-conscious Spirit occupies at present. It has passed beyond the substantial life that it formerly led in the element of thought, beyond this immediacy of its faith, beyond the satisfaction and security of the certainty which consciousness possessed about its reconciliation with the divine [*mit dem Wesen*] and its . . . presence . . . Not only has Spirit lost its essential life; it is also conscious of this loss and of the finitude which is now its content. Turning away from the husks, confessing that it lies in wickedness, and despising its situation, it now demands from philosophy not so much self-knowledge as that philosophy should help it to restore that substantiality and the solidity of being."[5] We have yet to learn more precisely what Hegel means by Spirit, but it is clear from this passage that he refers to the historical life of the human spirit. To say that the human spirit has lost its substantial and essential life is to say that "the times are out of joint" and that "things fall apart—the centre cannot hold." By evoking the image of the prodigal son Hegel suggests the experience of exile and estrangement, while at the same time underscoring the religious dimension of Spirit's loss. Having lost touch with the Divine Spirit the human spirit has lost its way.

This religious experience is juxtaposed to the scientific revolution of the preceding three centuries as Hegel continues: "Formerly men had a heaven, furnished with abundant riches of thoughts and images. The significance of all that is used to lie in the thread of light that tied it to heaven; and following this thread, the eye, instead of abiding in the present rose above to the Divine Being [*zum göttlichen Wesen*], to, if one may say so, a present beyond. The eye of the Spirit had to be directed forcibly to the things of this earth and kept there. Indeed, it took a long time to work that clarity which only the supernatural possessed into the must and confusion in which the sense of this world lay, and to make attention to the present as such, which was called experience, interesting and valid. Now the opposite need meets the eye . . . Spirit appears so poor that, like a wanderer in the desert who languishes for a simple drink of water, it seems to crave for its refreshment merely the bare feeling of the divine in general."[6]

Speaking for philosophy, Hegel accepts these demands. It is true that he vigorously repudiates those who think that philosophy can meet them with edification, ecstasy, and fermenting enthusiasm rather than with insight, the concept, and the coldly progressing necessity of the subject matter.[7] But this concerns only the form appropriate to Science, not whether it must address itself to the present predicament of Spirit. That predicament Hegel here interprets in terms of a scientific secularism which has tended to undermine "the significance of all that is," or at least radically alter it so that the human spirit has come to feel deeply impoverished. The *Phenomenology* is to concern itself with this historical-cultural crisis of the times and not merely with critical philosophy.

So perhaps Wahl and Hyppolite are not projecting their Paris into the Introduction when they give an existentialist reading to Hegel's focus on despair rather than doubt. Perhaps Hegel's references to death and to *Angst* do not concern the luxurious anxiety of the professional philosopher whose system has just been declared dead by the learned journals, but rather, as the texts just cited suggest, the experience (by no means unique to scholars) of living in the Wasteland.

It is not that Hegel has abandoned his confrontation with critical philosophy. It is rather that, like Husserl more than a century later, he is convinced that the intellectual crisis of his day is a "radical life-crisis of European humanity," which concerns "the total meaningfulness of its cultural life, its total *Existenz.*" Both see the development of modern philosophy with all its epistemological concerns as simply "humanity struggling to understand itself."[8]

Hegel's earliest Jena writings insist on this most clearly. For example, if critical philosophy separates its conceptual activity from the unconditioned and supernatural as something absolutely beyond it, this involves the separation of man from himself.[9] Philosophy is needed when this sort of estrangement [*Entzewiung*] prevails in the life of men from whom the power of unification [*Vereinigung*] has disappeared. The forms which estrangement takes are varied and they come to philosophy as contingently given. Such oppositions as those between spirit and matter, soul and body, faith and understanding, freedom and necessity, which involve "all important human interests" can be transposed into the form of such oppositions as that between subjectivity and objectivity. In the "northwest" the prevailing form is the opposition between thought and actuality, and the stronger this opposition grows "the more meaningless become the strivings of life to give itself a rebirth of harmony."[10] In other words, when critical philosophy talks about the relation of thought as subjectivity to actuality as objectivity it is only the abstract and technical form which makes this seem remote from all human interests. Just as Kant took note of "the interest of reason in these conflicts," when speaking about the antinomies, so Hegel tells us that the interest of reason is "the transformation of such congealed oppositions." Reason is not here conceived as an abstract psychological faculty which lives man like the Freudian id, but simply as human life in its totality seeking wholeness. The essential question, which sometimes takes epistemic form, concerns the meaningfulness of this search, whether man is a useless passion or not.

In order fully to appreciate the concreteness of the concern underlying Hegel's allusions to the loss of substantial life and a sense of the divine presence, however abstract the epistemological form in which these matters may be discussed, it is necessary to ask what sort of society is the archetype of health in relation to which the present cultural sickness is diagnosed. This question takes us back from the Jena period to the "early theological writings" of Tübingen, Bern, and Frankfurt. A detailed analysis of these papers and of Hegel's development during these years (1793-1800), on which there is a large and growing literature, will not be necessary in order to extract what is most helpful for reading the *Phenomenology*. But it will be helpful to mention briefly the two objections which have been raised to the publication of these materials, both in German and in English, as "theological" writings. There is first the claim that these papers are political rather than theological, and second the claim that they are more nearly anti-theological than theological. To the first contention it must be granted that political issues are prominent throughout the papers, but one only needs to read them to see that for Hegel this in no way lessens their theological significance. One might say that for Hegel they could only be theological if they were political as well, and this discovery is not unimportant for understanding the *Phenomenology*. It is also true that the fragments published by Nohl as "Folk Religion and Christianity," not included in the English translation, unfavorably contrast theology with religion in order to express Hegel's preference for a religion of the heart over religion of the cold, lifeless understanding. But the distinction is between two kinds of religion, which he calls subjective and objective, and the discussion is no less theological for its insistence that true religion is more than systematic theology. Hegel's intent is by no means secular, and this, too, is important for understanding the *Phenomenology*, where he once again will refuse to cast the conflict between orthodoxy and secularism in an either/or mold.

What pervades and unites these essays and fragments is the

contrast between Greek and Judeo-Christian culture. In the former Hegel finds unity, harmony, joy, and beauty; in the latter separation, estrangement, sorrow, and ugliness. In fact, he goes so far as to say that Christianity was able to conquer the ancient world because that world, in the time of the Empire, had lost the substantial life and sense of the divine presence which characterized city-state Greece and republican Rome. The success of Christianity was not due to its intrinsic spiritual superiority but to its congruity with the decadence of the period. The Empire meant that "the picture of the state as a product of his own activity disappeared from the citizen's soul." In that situation "without a fatherland, the citizen lived in a state with which no joy could be associated and all he felt was its pressure. He had a worship to whose celebration and festivals he could no longer bring a cheerful heart, because cheerfulness had flown away out of his life."[11] To such a miserable people, Christianity offered a "miserable sort of culture."[12]

The primary categories for drawing this cultural contrast are those of slavery and freedom, with the result that there is a striking resemblance to Nietzsche's contrast between slave morality and master morality. Like Nietzsche, Hegel looks behind Christianity to Judaism as the source of the slave mentality which permeates Christian culture. At the heart of Judaism lies not only a "mechanical slavery" but also a "pedantically slavish spirit of the people," an "obstinate pride in slavish obedience," a "maniacally servile disposition," and a "frenzied slavery of spirit." The Jews have a sense of their nothingness, but not of their selfhood.[13] All this is in reference to the Jewish ethic, based on the absolutely authoritative command of God and not on man's own reason, in Kantian language the heteronomy of practical reason.

By the time Hegel wrote this account (1800), which is also found in earlier papers, he had come to have severe reservations about Kant's theory of practical reason. But this Jewish heteronomy remained the very essence of depravity. "There is one God . . . What deeper truth is there for slaves than that they have a master? But Mendelssohn is right not to call this a truth . . . For truth is something free which we neither master nor are mastered by; hence the existence of God appears to the Jews not as a truth but as a command. On God the Jews are depen-

dent throughout." With a fervor that even Nietzsche never surpasses, Hegel describes Judaism as a tradegy which can arouse
neither fear nor pity, but only horror.[14]

Christianity represents no improvement. Jesus was largely
free from the spirit of Judaism, it is true, but it was his fate,
both because of the overwhelming force of the spirit of his time
and place and because he was not himself totally free from that
spirit, to become the founder of a religion which not only took
over in theory and practice the "perverted and immoral concepts of the Jews"[15] but increased their heteronomy. For to the
authority of the Lord was added the authority of the church,
and the church "has not stopped at prescribing a number of external actions whereby we are supposed to do honor to the
Deity . . . It has also directly prescribed laws for our mode of
thinking, feeling, and willing . . . While in Judaism only actions
were commanded, the Christian church goes farther and com-
mands feelings, a contradiction in terms."[16]

A crucial point at which Jesus succumbed to the Jewish
spirit was his willingness to let religion be a private matter. This
failure of nerve opened the door to one of the worst forms of
dualism, the separation of religious and political life. The disci-
ples are to some degree responsible, since it was they who "had
no interest in the state like that which a citizen of a free republic
takes in his fatherland" to whom the founding of the church
was entrusted.[17] But Jesus himself is not innocent. When he
told the young man to sell all he had and give it to the poor he
showed "how much [he] was concerned in his teaching only
with the education and perfection of the individual man, and
how little this was extended to society at large."[18] And when he
said, "Render unto Caesar the things that are Caesar's," he an-
nounced that Christianity was a religion of inwardness which
could co-exist with all forms of political alienation. It does not
require that dimension of freedom which for Hegel is the pre-
requisite of an "association of beauty." Rather it is an association of private persons submitting passively to a hostile state.
Since it is obviously not a kingdom of this world, its only recourse is "separation from the world, and flight from it into
heaven; restoration in the ideal world of the life which this
world turned away empty handed."[19] Thus the whole Jewish
tradition of Messianic and apocalyptic ideas comes into play.

Heaven and the church take the place of fatherland and a free state.[20]

This separation of religious from political life, however, is but one of the dualisms which constitute Christian culture. *The Spirit of Christianity and Its Fate* concludes with a more complete account of the ways in which Christian consciousness is separated from actual life: "In all the forms of the Christian religion which have developed themselves in the advancing fate of the ages, there lies this fundamental characteristic of opposition in the divine, which is supposed to be present only in consciousness, never in life ... And it is its fate, that church and state, worship and life, piety and virtue, spiritual and worldly action, can never dissolve into one."[21]

In starkest contrast to the spirit of Judeo-Christian culture is the harmonious and happy humanism of Greece. The religion of Hellenic folk culture was the spontaneous creation of free men, and it stood in intimate relation to the whole of life. Man lived in a whole which was at once religious, ethical, and political, and the individual felt himself to be an inherent part of that whole. His religion stemmed from the traditions of his people, and expressed itself in their folksongs, their monuments of art, their daily religious rites, and their periodic festivals, all of which were public. His faith in the gods was "interwoven by a thousand threads" into the web of daily life. No feelings of life were excluded, but the prevailing atmosphere was that of joy and ecstasy. Thus even the bacchanalia were sacred to the gods. "If the imagination of the Greek priestesses of Bacchus slipped over into madness and to the wildest eruption of anarchic drunkenness in order to see the divinity himself present, still this was an enthusiasm of joy and jubilation, an enthusiasm which soon returned again to common life."[22]

To the terror and awe of Sinai and Calvary this beauty and joy of Olympus bear no resemblance. The Jewish cultus was a reminder of "the nothingness of man and the littleness of an existence maintained by favor" and of an emancipation which the people did not accomplish for themselves but passively received with a "most slavelike demeanor." The Christian sacrament in turn was the reminder of a Lord no longer present, a cold and lifeless private exercise and by no means a celebration of delight in society. But Greek festivals celebrated the solidarity of the people with their gods and with nature, expressing their exuberance for life.[23] Whereas the Germans, "who never were a nation," have only Luther for a national hero and celebrate his Reformation only with the wearisome annual reading of the Augsburg Confession and the dull sermon which follows, "anyone who did not know the history of the city, the culture, and the laws of Athens could almost have learned them from the festivals if he had lived a year within its gates."[24] Not surprisingly the important religious concept of sacrifice comes to radically different forms of expression as well. On the one hand there is the Judeo-Christian concept grounded in the notions of sin, punishment, and regaining the lost favor of one's supreme Lord. On the other is a softer and milder conception grounded in cheerfulness, thanks, and good will directed toward the being who, though he transcends man, does not despise whatever man may bring as an offering and needs no appeasing.[25]

Hegel's enthusiasm for the Greeks belongs to the larger story which has been told by E.M. Butler as *The Tyranny of Greece over Germany* and by Henry Hatfield as *Aesthetic Paganism in German Literature*. Like the literary figures they discuss, he was influenced by Winckelmann's idealization of Greek experience, particularly through the mediation of Goethe and Schiller. But these influences came to soil already well prepared. Hegel began his reading of Homer, Euripides, and Sophocles, as well as Plato and Aristotle, during his gymnasium years. His sister tells us that during his student years the Greek tragedies were his favorite reading, and of these, Sophocles, whom he read uninterruptedly for several years and translated as well, his favorite author, and *Antigone* his favorite play. His high school papers include one on the religion of the Greeks and Romans and another on the characteristic distinctions of the ancient poets.[26]

This interest continued through his seminary days at Tübingen, where his friendship with Hölderlin only served to intensify it. The translation of Sophocles continued, and when he had to spend some time at home due to illness, he spent it reading the tragedians. He even presented a revised version of his last high school paper on the ancient poets.[27] He tells us himself that he went to seminary at his parents' wish and insofar as he pursued theological studies of his own accord it was due to their connection with classical literature and philosophy. So it was natural that his seminary training led him, vocationally, not to the parish but to the academy, where he could devote himself to ancient literature and philosophy. The choice of philosophy over literature, incidentally, coincided with his Jena appointment.[28]

In the earliest fragments of the early theological writings, which probably date from Hegel's last year in Tübingen, his name for the Greek experience is folk religion. His references to the simplicity or naivete of their customs [*Einfalt der Sitten*] foreshadows the term he came to use instead of folk religion during the Jena period, *Sittlichkeit* or Ethical Life, an important term in the *Phenomenology*.[29] It is in terms of the first of these that he formulates the basic question of the Bern and Frankfurt period: "What are the requirements of a folk religion . . . Do we meet with them in the Christian religion?"[30]

There is no need for further comment on Hegel's answer to the second part of the question, except to note that by the time he comes to write the *Phenomenology* his view is less one sided. While he continues to link the Christian religion with the alienation pervading modern culture, he also finds it to be integrally bound up with the possibility of a new cultural harmony.

It is the answer to the first part of the question which reveals the principles at work in his admiration of the Greeks. The requirements for folk religion are three:

"I.   Its doctrines must be grounded on universal reason.
II.   Imagination, the heart, and sensuousness [*Sinnlichkeit*] must not be left empty handed by it.
III. It must be so constituted that all needs of life, including the public acts of state, belong to it."[31]

To the first requirement belongs the distinction between autonomy and heteronomy. It is precisely the acceptance of political, ethical, and religious heteronomy which leads Hegel to label Judeo-Christian culture a slave culture. By autonomy, on the other hand, Hegel does not mean that a genuine folk religion would stay within the limits of mere reason, for such an attempt leaves only lifeless abstractions. Rather, its teachings should be "so human that they are suited to the stage of

spiritual culture and morality which a people have reached."
Both will gradually develop together.[32] The important thing is
not that there be nothing historically conditioned and particular in the religion, as opposed to the timelessly universal, but
that there be nothing which has to be imposed on the people by
theologians rather than arising from the people themselves.[33]
The contrast between heteronomy and autonomy resides in the
difference between "forcible institutions" and the "common
life" with its "spontaneous interest," between what is "given
throughout" and what is "given as something free to be freely
received."[34]

To the third requirement belongs the contrast which Hegel
gradually develops between Ethical Life [*Sittlichkeit*] and
Morality [*Moralität*], so crucial to the *Phenomenology's* sixth chapter. Folk religion is a public matter, and much of the meaning
of Ethical Life derives from its contrast with the connotation of
Morality as a private and personal affair. But Morality is not
only private; it is also abstracted from other dimensions of life,
the religious, and legal, and the traditional [*die Sitten*]. Ethical
Life and folk religion, by contrast, represent that simplicity of
customs in which these separations have not yet been made.
Man is not yet divided into moral and legal, religious and
worldly, rational and emotional, theoretical and practical components. In short, the conclusion of *The Spirit of Christianity and
Its Fate* (see note 21 above) serves as a negative definition of
Hegel's folk religion-Ethical Life ideal.

Where then does the second requirement of a folk religion
fit in—the demand that the heart, imagination, and feelings be
satisfied and not starved? The important thing here is not so
much Hegel's repeated emphasis on the role of an indigenous
imagery growing out of a people's history and traditions in
achieving this goal, as his making this goal the end to which the
first and third requirements serve as means.[35] The reason why
a people's religion should be autonomous, public, and inte-
grated with all of life is that human experience should not be
what Hegel finds it to be in his Preface, "so poor that, like a
wanderer in the desert who languishes for a simple drink of
water, it seems to crave for its refreshment merely the bare feeling of the divine in general. By that which suffices Spirit one
can measure the extent of its loss."[36]

We have indeed returned to our point of departure for this discussion of Hegel's Greek ideal, his diagnosis of the present standpoint of Spirit. The irrationalism against which he proposes his concept of philosophy as Science, the "prophetic talk [*prophetische Reden*, Schleiermacher, et.al.]" which "deliberately keeps its distance from the concept and from necessity as if they were the reflection that makes its home in the finite,"[37] and which seeks to respond directly to the demand of the age for edification, ecstasy, and fermenting enthusiasm—this irrationalism is not wholly unwarranted, even if it is not to be accepted. For it recognizes the present position of Spirit as one in which the non-rational (better: non-theoretical) components of man have been starved, and it accepts the responsibility of addressing hungry and thristy men, not transcendental egos. It is this same recognition and acceptance which started Hegel on his diagnosis of the present situation as the loss of substantial life and the sense of the divine presence. Although the story of his love for the Greeks can be told in much more detail, this brief sketch is enough to give some initial understanding of his otherwise all too cryptic diagnosis.

2B. The Life-World of Critical Philosophy

Assuming that the text supports this reading of the Preface, there can be no further question about the existential import of the Phenomenology. At issue is nothing less than the meaning of human life, especially in its social and religious dimensions. But a new question arises. By now the phrase 'task of the *Phenomenology*' seems to designate nothing unambiguously. Are there two accounts of its purpose, an epistemological one in the Introduction and a cultural-existential one in the Preface? Something like this is implied by Haering and those who follow him in arguing that the *Phenomenology* is non-organic due to the way it was written. It is argued that the original intention was to break off somewhere in the section entitled "Reason" and make a direct transition to the Logic. The entire second half of the text, Chapters Six through Eight, in which the central concept of Spirit is developed, was added in the process of writing, for some reason, and the Logic was relegated to a separate work.

Of these two parts the first is quite easily related to the epistemic orientation of the Introduction, but because the last three chapters or so venture off in new directions, Hegel had to write a Preface oriented primarily to them. In other words, the *Phenomenology* began as a reply to Kant and company, but this concern fell into the background as Hegel felt impelled to get his philosophy of Spirit into print. Having lost sight of his original purpose he abandoned the debate with critical finitism, which had occupied him at Jena, and returned to the religious and social concerns of his days as tutor in Bern and Frankfurt.[38]

But even if Hegel did not have the entire plan for his book in mind when he began to write, it does not follow that the final product is a piece of patchwork. Hegel himself rejects this interpretation, since the Preface clearly reaffirms the noetic concerns of the Introduction and develops many of them as well. Nor can he mean that he will first deal with the critical philosophy and then, putting on another hat as it were, deal with cultural crisis, folk religion, etc. We have already seen from the earliest Jena writings that he refuses to separate the epistemic and the existential in this way. We have also seen that in the Preface he prescribes "the concept" as the genuine cure for the present cultural malaise. In other words, the issues discussed in critical philosophy are intimately related to the possibility of experiencing folk religion. The Introduction and the Preface are correlative descriptions of the task of the *Phenomenology.*

I have argued in another place that Kant's dualism and finitism are the expression of a religious world-view, since the thing-in-itself is so clearly defined as the thing-for-God.[39] If this is true, we will have to conclude that as the problem of the *Phenomenology* developed and took on dimensions transcending the narrowly epistemological, Hegel moved closer to the spirit of Kant and to real engagement with his thought. For both of them the question of knowledge becomes the question of man in relation to God.

The Preface is Hegel's bold attempt to relate this enlarged concept of his undertaking to the permanent noetic orientation of one for whom "humanity exists only in the accomplished community of consciousness," though animals are able to communicate only through feeling.[40] The phrase 'community of consciousness' itself contains the implication that human consciousness or knowledge can never be wholly independent of human social life.

Both these dimensions are involved in Hegel's answer to the question around which the Preface moves, What is Science? If one asks about its form and content the answer is given exclusively in terms of knowledge. Formally, Science is mediated, organized, systematic knowledge. Its subject matter [*die Sache selbst*] is substance as subject. Form and content are internally related, since the form is required by the content it seeks to express. The union of the two is crucial to Hegel's idealism. "That the true is actual only as system, or that substance is essentially subject, is expressed in the conception which speaks of the Absolute as Spirit . . ."[41]

But all this is directly related to the more concrete concerns on which the Preface dwells, for the passage just quoted continues, "This is the most sublime concept, and it belongs to the modern age and its religion." The knowledge which is Science belongs to a new religion, one which no doubt involves the restoration of substantial life and a sense of the divine presence. Science not only has a form and content which can be described in noetic terms; it has a purpose and result which break through the limits of any narrowly theoretical conception of knowledge. This two-fold but unified nature of the Preface and of the *Phenomenology* itself is elegantly summarized at the conclusion of the paragraph whose opening has just been cited. "Spirit, when it knows itself developed in this way as Spirit, is Science. Science is the actuality of Spirit and the kingdom which it builds for itself in its own element." Science is the kingdom? What kingdom? Since we have to do here with the new age and its religion it may well be the Kingdom of God which Hegel has in mind. The full confirmation of this can only come in the long journey through the text, but we do know that such an identification of Science and the Kingdom of God can be found as early as a 1795 letter to Schelling and as late as the 1816 inaugural lecture at Heidelberg.[42]

It is not enough, however, for Hegel simply to assert this unity of his project. He must give us some indication of how such a unity is possible, especially since we, like his original readers, are more inclined to separate what he insists on uniting. To find Hegel's response to this demand we need only backtrack to the point at which he began reflecting on "the present standpoint of Spirit" (his heading for the second section of the Preface), its loss of substantial life and sense of the divine presence. What motivates this discussion? First, it is Hegel's awareness that the "conviction of the age" is not in sympathy with his conception of the scientific system as the true form in which the truth exists, and that the demand of the age is not for "the concept" but for feeling and intuition. Second, and this is the crucial move, is the suggestion that such a demand should be "considered in its more general context," which is to say that "one should see what stage self-conscious Spirit occupies at present."[43]

The point is that Hegel's description of the present standpoint of Spirit is given precisely as the context out of which arises "such a demand." But such a demand has the critical philosophy for its basis, whether in the romantic form here described with reference to intuition and feeling, or in the earlier form described in *Faith and Knowledge* as faith-philosophy. Hegel makes no distinction between a Kant, Jacobi, or Fichte telling us that he has denied knowledge in order to make room for faith, and a Schelling, Schleiermacher, or Schlegel telling us that we must abandon conceptual knowledge for feeling and intuition. Nor need he, since the negations of critical finitism are presupposed by both of these traditions.

Now if "such a demand" is made on the basis of critical philosophy and Hegel's investigation of the "present standpoint of Spirit" concerns the context from which such a demand arises, it is nothing less than an inquiry into the nature of the life-world in which critical philosophy can flourish. Such a procedure assumes that abstract and theoretical thought is not autonomous but is intimately related to everyday life with its familiar and obvious contours. It only deceives itself in thinking it dwells in its own isolated and insulated medium. More concretely, Hegel is suggesting that what comes to expression in the *Critique of Pure Reason* is nothing less than society's loss of substantial life and of a sense of the divine presence.[44]

Hegel knows that reflection on the life-world out of which critical philosophy arises does not refute that philosophy. It may help to explain it, but never to explain it away. The juxtaposition of the critical philosophy with an analysis of how "the times are out of joint" reminds us that the deficiencies of the former are not simply theoretical. More importantly, it warns us that any possibility of genuinely transcending the critical-sceptical point of view depends upon getting the times back in joint.

It follows that when Hegel tells us that "the time has come for the elevation of philosophy to a science,"[45] he means this in a very strong sense. It is not that others have tried their hand at such a task and done it clumsily, so that it's now time to quit fooling around and do it right. It is rather that "the present standpoint of Spirit" is undergoing a change, that a new soil is being prepared in which new philosophical flora can thrive.

At times Hegel can speak as bitingly as Kierkegaard about "the almighty age and its culture," which he sees as a kind of spiritual sickness. At the same time, however, he is persuaded that "our age is an age of birth and transition to a new period. Spirit has broken with what was hitherto the world of its existence and ideas and . . . is at work giving itself a new form."[46] In Baillie's rendering of *der bisherigen Welt seines Daseins and Vorstellens* Spirit's break is with "the old order of things hitherto prevailing, and with the old ways of thinking." This is perhaps a rather free translation, but it is entirely in the spirit of the passage, for Hegel's point is the correlation between thought and the world from which it arises.

What Hegel sees happening in his time is a comprehensive cultural revolution. The period of preparation in which Spirit "matures slowly and quietly toward the new form, dissolving one particle of the edifice of its previous world after another," is nothing less than "a far-reaching revolution in ever so many forms of culture."[47] By culture [*Bildung*] Hegel does not mean simply the fine arts, the theater, and the *New York Review of Books*. He includes the most basic and original transcendence of man's natural life by means of ideas [*Gedanke*] which achieve some form of universality. Beyond the mere presence of language, the catechisms and proverbs of a people are examples of culture in this sense, for they are the wisdom which even a young child possesses and by which he is socialized into the spiritual world to which he was born. "Children are to be seen and not heard," "In Adam's fall we sinned all." "I pledge allegiance to the flag . . ."

After the gradual and largely invisible revolution of culture the appearance of the new world of Spirit is as sudden as lightning or the birth of a child after months of gestation. Like the newborn child, the new world is not fully developed at the beginning. It takes still more time for it to develop its "perfect actuality," just as it takes time for an acorn to become an oak. Only then can Science, "the crown of a world of Spirit," itself be complete and anything more than an unfulfilled promise.[49] But of course, at the top (crown) of an oak tree one will find acorns and not pine cones. Just the same, at the crown of a world from which substantial life and a sense of the divine presence have departed one will not find Science as the systematic, actual knowledge of the Absolute. Since the "unsurpassable horizon [*feste Standpunkt*] which the almighty age and its culture have fixed for philosophy is that of a sense bound reason, such philosophy can proceed to know, not God, but what is called man."[50] Note well! The notion of reason as finite is not something which philsophy seeks to impose on its age but something which is given to philosophy by its age. It is as if critical philosophy were the dreams and symptoms in which the collective unconscious of the age comes to the light of day. We are reminded of Hegel's later formulations of the idea that philosophy is its age comprehended in thought.[51]

In his Jena essay on natural right Hegel had already developed this motif in direct connection with the concept of Ethical Life. Science, he says, is the empirical condition of the world reflected in the mirror of thought [*ideelen Spiegel*]. The form of Ethical Life in which a people develop themselves is bound by the limits of their geographical-climatic and world-historical location, just as the life of fish and birds is bound to the elements of water and air. As these elements condition the development of a people's life together, so that life in turn conditions the higher levels of spiritual expression, not excluding philosophy. It too must learn to honor its necessity and to overcome the individuality and contingency of its world by penetrating and enlivening it, not by fleeing from it.[52]

The reason for this is the organic character of spiritual life, expressed in the Preface by the metaphors of the oak tree and the newborn child.[53] Not only is there continuity of development in time, such that each stage must be seen as part of the whole process, but at any given stage of development the parts

are organically related to one another in the whole. Thus the
Germans, who (in 1803) are "a dissolved people" whose political
institutions are only the "dead husks" of a form of life no longer
present, live in political heteronomy and untruth. But since
such an untruth is an "inner untruth of the whole" one cannot
expect to find truth anywhere among them, in their social life,
their religion, or their philosophy.[54]

What we have before us is a full-fledged theory of ideology, which can hardly be said to have originated with Marx. For
it was Hegel to whom we owe the discovery that "a radical
critique of knowledge is possible only as social theory."[55]
Habermas, whose formulation this is, argues that Hegel was too
much in the grip of the philosophy of identity to carry out such
a program consistently or even formulate it clearly. Whether
the *Phenomenology* carries out such a program consistently we
cannot tell without reading it. But that Hegel failed to formulate such a program clearly, giving it as the standard by which
his work is to be measured, does not seem to be a fair reading of
his Preface against the background of his earlier writings.

Of course this is not a materialist theory of ideology. One
will look in vain for any consistent ordering of the various elements as basis and superstructure. A careful examination of
Hegel's usage will turn up more than enough evidence to make
him into Marx or Weber, but only as long as the contradictory
evidence is ignored. His practice, which suggests the model of
mutual interaction within an organism, is consistent with his
earliest formulation: "The spirit of a people, their history, religion, and level of political freedom should not be considered in
isolation from either their influence on one another or their
own constitution. They are interwoven into a single cord."
Perhaps with reference to his friendship with Schelling and
Hölderlin at Tübingen, Hegel compares the different moments
to three colleagues each of whom can do nothing on his own
apart from what he has incorporated from the others.[56]

Now it is no longer puzzling why Hegel should think that
"the seriousness of the concept" presupposes "the seriousness
of that fulness of life which leads to the experience of the Absolute [*die Sache selbst,* used in this context repeatedly for the subject matter of philosophy]."[57] Nor is it puzzling that the heart of
his philosophy, the concept of the Absolute as Spirit, should be-

long to "the new age and its religion;"[58] that epistemological discussions about the relation of thought to actuality should involve "all important human interests," especially the effort to achieve a harmonious human life;[59] that Science and the Kingdom of God should be so intimately connected;[60] that the difference between religious autonomy and heteronomy should be so closely bound to the difference between political freedom and slavery;[61] that the faith-philosophy of Kant, Jacobi, and Fichte is a fundamentally Protestant form of thought, whose discussions about finite and infinite, real and ideal, sensible and supersensible, etc., belong to the ongoing debate over faith, as positive religion, and reason;[62] and that the metaphysical discussion of finite and infinite is identical with the theological question of nature and grace.[63]

2C. The Medical Function of Philosophy:
a) Midwifery

At the heart of the idea of ideology is the claim that theoretical thought is not autonomous, that our ideas are conditioned by our interests and our situation. In the twentieth century this has come to be almost taken for granted. While the term 'ideology' is used only in special contexts, the basic insight finds some sort of expression in almost every philosophical tradition. It is, of course, fundamental to Marxism and pragmatism. It is implicit in Wittgenstein's suggestion that language is a form of life, and it underlies the turn from "ideal language" philosophy to "ordinary language" philosophy. It has received detailed development in the phenomenological tradition, and a whole new discipline, the sociology of knowledge has arisen on its foundation. Especially in these last two traditions insight into the social and existential conditioning of thought, including philosophical thought, entailing "the historically changing nature of mind," has brought with it "the vertigo of relativity."[64] Whether it is called historicism, psychologism, perspectivism, or whatever; and whether it is seen as a peril to be avoided at all costs, as a fate to be courageously accepted, or as a tough question to be sidestepped so that research can continue—relativity is the shadow under which the heteronomy of theory is dis-

cussed. Platonism is alive and well in our day, at least in its assumption that truth and becoming make poor bedfellows.

Hegel sees things, if the expression may be forgiven, from
a different perspective. He too, as we have seen, recognizes the
dependence of thought on its life-world, and he does not seek
to escape the consequence of this, the historically particular nature of all theory. As Merleau-Ponty puts it, "There is not one
of our ideas or one of our reflexions which does not carry a
date." Even the thought of the philosopher is "not without
roots," but "is always situated and always individuated."[65] But
Hegel is not embarrassed by this fact and he is not smitten by
"the vertigo of relativity." In contrast to the Platonism of our
contemporaries, his thought, at least on this point, can be described as biblical, for he finds history to be the medium for divine revelation. So rather than focusing on the timelessness
which philosophy cannot have and should not seek, he directs
us to the timeliness it can and should achieve if it is willing to
think its present world rather than trying to be the formal-
dehyde in which a passing form of life is preserved. Rather
than asking whether thought can ever be absolute in being unconditioned by life, he asks whether the human existence which
ever comes to expression in thought can itself become absolute
by becoming the Kingdom of God. After all, the relativity of
thought conditioned by a world which is the Kingdom of God is
a relativity which even the most ardent Platonist might be willing to accept.

The question, then, is where the Kingdom of God is breaking into human history. Hegel did not view the Holy Roman
Empire during the last years of its existence as that Kingdom.
So he said of his analysis of its internal contradictions, "The
thoughts contained in this essay cannot have any other aim or effect upon publication than the understanding of that which is,
and thus to promote calmer contemplation as well as the ability
to endure it . . ."[66] But he does not believe that calm endurance
is the appropriate reaction to every possible state of affairs.
Rosenkranz gives us a fragment from the Jena period in which
Hegel looks forward to a new, post-Protestant religion "in
which the infinite pain and the entire weight of Spirit's disharmony is acknowledged but at the same time serenely and purely
dissolved, if there should be a free people and reason's reality

should be born again as an ethical [*sittlichen*] Spirit which can have the audacity to take its pure form from its own soil and its own majesty." If individuals are not to participate in this new spiritual life blindly, they require a knowledge of what is going on. "This knowledge which comprehends the whole energy of the suffering and disharmony which has ruled the world and all forms of its cultural development for some thousand years and at the same time rises above it—this knowledge philosophy alone can provide."[67]

Philosophy's immersion in history does not mean that it can create the new religion and the free people *ex nihilo*, giving birth itself to the Kingdom of God. Rather, its role is to provide insight instead of blindness before the historical process, which does not proceed at the philosopher's beck and call. It brings the new age and its religion to the form of the concept.[68] But in this instance the result of an "understanding of that which is" cannot be calm endurance. The knowledge which philosophy provides at such a moment of birth does not exclude the memory of morning sickness and labor pains with all their agony. But its keynote is the joyous realization, "Unto us a son is born."

By giving insight into historical developments philosophy serves in a Socratic way. The historical process is an organic development which continually gives birth to new forms of life and thought. In the difficult and even unhappy times of birth,[69] philosophy assists as midwife, not as the giver of life. As Socrates examines the newly born thoughts of individuals to see whether they are genuine or spurious ($\alpha\lambda\eta\theta\eta\varsigma$ or $\psi\epsilon\upsilon\delta\eta\varsigma$), and, as he tells Theaetetus, if he finds them to be but phantoms ($\epsilon\check{\iota}\delta\omega\lambda\sigma$), "I take the abortion from you and cast it away," so Hegel sees philosophy as examining the new offspring of the age to see whether they are viable forms of human life, whether the appropriate response is endurance or enthusiasm, whether they should be nourished or starved.[70] In this way philosophy can serve its contemporaries, needing neither to flee from its time nor to succumb to it.

Fichte had reintroduced this motif into philosophy when, decrying the shallowness of the age, he described the current form of the Kantian philosophy as "the most fantastic abortion that has ever been produced by the human imagination."[71] In *Faith and Knowledge* Hegel suggests the same verdict for Kant

himself, not just the Kantians, along with Jacobi and Fichte.[72]
Then in the Preface he not only announces that "our time is a
time of birth and transition to a new period," indicating that a
genuine birth has taken place; he also practices his art of critical
midwifery on those romantic enthusaists who flee conceptual
thought and believe themselves to be "His beloved to whom
God gives wisdom in sleep. What they thus conceive and give
birth to in sleep are, naturally, dreams."[73] In other words, to
the age which gave birth to both critical finitism and romantic
irrationalism his message is that of Socrates, "I take these abortions from you and cast them away."

2D. The Medical Function of Philosophy:
b) Socioanalysis

Midwifery can be a dangerous art, as Socrates discovered.
Like a bear robbed of her whelps the age is likely to turn on any
midwife who does not treat all its offspring as a campaigning
politician would. Yet Hegel knows he has no choice but to rely
on the one weapon which failed Socrates, persuasion. Like all
the arts, this one requires knowledge; but unlike most arts, this
one cannot be practiced unless it can be taught. That is, the
philosophical midwife can perform his services only by implant-
ing in the patient his own understanding of the situation.

Psychoanalysis is such an art. We are reminded that in the
Introduction Hegel seemed to commit himself to something
like a psychoanalysis of the anxiety critical finitism displays
about its capacity to be in touch with the Absolute. It is now
clear that this depth diagnosis of the age will be absolutely essential to the practice of philosophical midwifery espoused in
the Preface, though it now looks as if socioanalysis would be a
better name for the process. Here the Introduction and Preface
are united. Coming from the direction of the Introduction and
its epistemological concerns, the necessity for socioanalysis is
linked to the task of deepening the reflections of transcendental philosophy. Coming from the direction of the Preface and its concerns about the historical crisis of the era, this
necessity derives from the responsibility of philosophy to serve
its times without simply being their child. But there is only a

single task—to show the age its sickness, freeing it from its doting on the phantoms and dreams it takes to be glorious progeny, thereby freeing it for something better.

Hegel has one enormous advantage over Socrates, who, in his famous ignorance found nothing but abortions in the Athenian wisdom. Hegel has bad news for his contemporaries too, but like John the Baptist he calls them to repentance out of the persuasion that the Kingdom of God is at hand.

Only the sketchiest glimpse of this Kingdom which Hegel announces is available to us before we plunge into the text; but a more nearly complete picture of the diagnosis which grounds his call to repentance can be given. Its elements are already before us, though not in the form of a systematic answer to the Introduction's question about the deepest roots of contemporary scepticism.

The life-world of critical philosophy is structured by Judeo-Christian religious traditions and the newer traditions of the modern scientific revolution. The linking of critical philosophy to these two factors is an echo in the Preface of the argument of *Faith and Knowledge*. Critical finitism is there described as the systematic expression of a culture of common sense [*gemeiner Menschenverstand*],[74] a culture in turn repeatedly described as, on the one hand, Protestant, and on the other, a Lockean-Humean culture, i.e., one intoxicated with the exploits of Newton.

A third dimension of the same world has also been uncovered, present but less conspicuous than the other two in both the Preface and *Faith and Knowledge*. It is the political-social sphere, without which neither Hegel's conception of substantial life nor his idea of the divine presence can be understood. This is because politics and religion are not independent variables for Hegel, but are like the convex and concave sides of an arc.

In these terms we can summarize Hegel's view of the old modernity quite simply. It was structured by protestant Christianity, the new scientific outlook, and a political perspective best described as privatism. What remains is to indicate how each of these elements contributes to the social neurosis Hegel seeks to diagnose.

If we ask what sort of religious life would come to philosophical expression as an anxiety about the remoteness of the Absolute and the possible inability of reason to grasp it, the answer is easy. Any form of religious heteronomy is likely to do so. By the time Hegel wrote the *Phenomenology* he had come to view Christianity as reconciling rather than alienating in its essence. But he still retained the view, so outspoken in his earlier writings, that both its original and subsequent historical manifestations had the form of extreme heteronomy.

On this score Protestantism is seen as an intensification of the heteronomous elements of Christianity. Catholicism at least borrowed some of the beautiful elements of paganism.[75] In its concern for orthodoxy, Protestantism enforced correct belief from above, by the theologians if possible, by the police and army if necessary.[76] In this respect there was an equality of heteronomy, but only a formal one. Materially there was an important difference. On Hegel's view the inner motif which makes the enforcement of orthodoxy necessary to Protestantism is bound up with one of its most fundamental distinctives, its view of nature and grace. It is the total depravity of man and his total dependence on divine grace which requires his particular dependence on divine revelation for knowing God and the good.[77] For Hegel (as for Luther) no aspect of Protestantism is more prominent or distinctive than man's sinful impotence before God and his complete dependence on divine mercy. "Theological prejudices about a congenital depravity of human nature," which are derived from "artful exegesis," are "constantly pounded into the memory and conscience of the common man," with the result that what is healthy, powerful, and active in him is destroyed.[78] As the life-world becomes Protestant human self-confidence is undermined and God becomes *Deus absconditus,* the Wholly Other.

This is why Hegel sees the *Critique of Pure Reason* as a palimpsest on which Luther's experience of guilt and grace can still be read beneath arguments about synthetic a priori judgments. After all, the epistemological implications of Protestantism did not have to await Kant for their formulation. Luther himself drew them in his own scathing denunciations of human reason. The peculiarity of Kant's position, on this view, is that he accepts Protestantism's bad news about the capacities of human reason without accepting the corresponding good news about revelation and grace.

The political and social character of the modern world can scarcely be unrelated in Hegel's mind to this religious character. At Jena this is put in terms of Ethical Life rather than folk religion, but the point is the same. The living customs of a people should be expressed both in universal form as their laws and institutions, and in particular form as the God of the people, who is intuited and worshipped in their cultic life. But when a nation is losing its spiritual life and "is not able to sense and enjoy the image of divinity in itself, but places this outside itself . . . then vassalage and bondage have absolute truth, and this condition is the one possible form of Ethical Life, and thus the necessary, the right, and the ethical [*sittliche*] form."[79]

It is this same correlation which had earlier enabled Hegel to explain the triumph of Christianity as a slave religion over the pagan religions of free men in terms of the disappearance of political freedom and participation under the despotism of the Roman emperors. The loss of public virtue among the Romans, together with the corresponding success of Christianity, mean that private life comes to be all important for the individual, the security and expansion of his property his major worldly project.[80]

Since the triumph of private over public, of independence over participation, has this economic dimension, political despotism is not its only possible origin. It can arise directly from economic conditions, and in the modern world it is the rise of the bourgeoisie which Hegel pinpoints as the source of that individualism which dissolves a people into the war of all against all; though at times he simplistically blames the "stubborness" of the German character, which has always defined freedom as independence rather than participation. In making this analysis he does not neglect to mention the happy harmony between bourgeois economic privatism and Protestant religious inwardness.[81]

What this dimension of the life-world contributes to critical finitism should not be too hard to see. The altogether finite individual pursuing his private economic advantage does so at the mercy of two impersonal, remote, and at times apparently hostile powers, the Market and the State. They are the infinite whose workings are neither comprehensible nor controllable, especially during the period under consideration. The lesson of religious humility which was taught on Sunday was reinforced by a lesson of political-economic humility during the rest of the week. Not even economic success worked to counteract this. It was more natural to see this too in terms of the grace of God.

There is another, possibly more important consideration. If, as Hegel suggests, the divine is simply the living customs of a people or their national genius intuited in the form of particularity, then the replacement of common participation in public life by competition in private life can hardly increase man's sense of the divine presence. The absence of the divine becomes less a religious teaching than an everyday experience. Such experience might well take epistemic form as a theory of knowledge as the instrument for grasping a recalcitrant Absolute not already with us from the start; all the more so if the gradual rationalizing of economic life, in Weber's sense, involves an everyday familiarity with a thoroughly instrumental sort of economic know-how.

Finally, if the value of instrumental knowledge belongs to what is taken for granted in the economic zones of the early modern world, this is even more true in the scientific realm. For Hegel there is a strong link between modern science and Protestantism, viewed as a religion of the heart, of feeling, of yearning after an absent God. And why is God absent? At least in part because his intuition has been denied by the understanding, which knows what is intuited only as a thing, the sacred grove only a timber. [82] Timber is very useful in countless ways, and the reason understanding can see the forest only as timber and not as a sacred grove is that it is that form of man's intellectual capacity which has learned to understand things in terms of their usefulness, to produce the kind of knowledge which will extend man's power over nature.

This instrumentalism is only part of what Hegel is getting at here. He is equally concerned about what we would call positivism, the view which makes the natural sciences the paradigm of knowing and tends to discredit all knowledge claims which cannot be assimilated to that model. In this context it is man's power and accomplishments rather than his weakness and finitude which are front and center. The results of the exact sciences are so impressive in their clarity, their certainty, and their usefulness, that they are easily taken to be the highest use of reason. When this happens a reality that is finite and a knowing that is empirical tend to be absolutized. It is no wonder then, that the sacred grove is reduced to timber, a potentially useful object of empirical knowledge. When it is a question of knowing what is infinite, for which empirical methods are demonstrably unsuited, it is natural that there should be a fear that this might not be possible; and it is just as natural that this fear should become the dogmatic conviction that whatever cannot be known by the application of knowledge as a formal instrument (categories, logical-mathematical calculi, etc.) to a sensible subject matter is unreal, and that all other attempts at knowing are sophistry.[83]

It may be that "the eye of the Spirit had to be directed forcibly to the things of this earth and kept there," and that the scientific revolution took a long time to make itself felt in common sense.[84] It is not easy to get people to live in the cave once "the significance of all that is" has derived from "the thread of light that tied it to heaven." But when people have lived in the cave long enough to make it their home and have learned how to furnish it with an ever increasing standard of living, we know how they will respond to anyone who challenges the cave's ultimacy by, e.g., seeking to develop another form of knowing in terms of the ontological argument or claiming that nature is not only *natura naturata* but also *natura naturans.*[85]

Humility before God, the Market, and the State. Confidence concerning the certainty and usefulness of instrumental knowledge in economics and natural science. Such in brief is Hegel's view of the old modernity he bids his contemporaries abandon in favor of the new modernity whose John the Baptist he purports to be. The old modernity is the Protestant, bourgeois, scientific life-world out of which critical philosophy arose. Its critique can only be the examination of this life-world, and its transcendence can only come about through the actual transcendence of this life-world. When Fackenheim claims that the Hegelian philosophy assumes the ultimacy of "the modern bourgeois Protestant world," and views this as "in principle final and indestructible," the seminal form of the Kingdom of God, we shall ask whether this is intended to apply to the *Phenomenology.*[86] As we come to the main body of the text we have every reason to expect that it is precisely as the modern world is becoming post-Protestant and post-bourgeois (as well as post-positivist) that Hegel is able to detect any seminal ultimacy in it.

The stages of Hegel's argument follow from this analysis. First, there will be an analysis of natural scientific knowledge to see whether the imperialistic majesty attributed to it is justified. (Chapters Three and Four) There will follow an examination of man's political and social life to see whether community and freedom are as irreconcilable in essence as they have come to be in fact. The religious dimension of social life will emerge in this examination. (Chapters Five and Six) Finally, there will be a description of religious life itself, not neglecting its social dimensions, and the implications of the whole project for philosophy will be drawn. (Chapters Seven and Eight) Only if a new life-world has shown itself to be in the making can there be any promise of a new philosophy in the system to which the reader is introduced by the *Phenomenology.*

If all goes as planned the three examinations which lead to whatever conclusions we find at the end will not be carried out by either Hegel or the reader. "Consciousness examines itself." In other words, Hegel will only be calling our attention to things that are happening in the modern world. Our contribution is simply to watch carefully in order to see what is there to be seen.

NOTES

1. PhG, VI/12/70.
2. PhG, XXXV/27/90.
3. PhG, XLII-XLIV/32-33/96-97.
4. Kroner, *Von Kant bis Hegel,* Tübingen, 1961, II, 374. Marcuse, *Reason and Revolution,* Boston, 1960, p. 23.
5. PhG, VIII/13/71-72. In this paragraph Hegel uses both *das Wesen* and *der Substanz* as synonyms for the Absolute. For a similar use of the former see *Volksreligion,* HTJ, 3, 5, 25, and Fragment #3, HTJ, 361.
6. PhG, X-XI/14/73.
7. PhG, IX/13/72. When Hegel speaks of "the concept" he does not mean any particular concept in the usual sense, but the whole of Science, conceptual knowledge of what truly is.
8. *The Crisis of European Sciences and Transcendental Phenomenology,* tr. Carr, Evanston, 1970, pp. 2, 12, 14.
9. *Glauben,* GW, 4:360.
10. *Differenz,* GW, 4:12-14.
11. PCR I, HTJ, 223-24/156-58. cf. *Volksreligion,* HTJ, 71.
12. PCR I, HTJ, 177/101.
13. PCR II, HTJ, 148-50/178-80.
14. SC, HTJ, 253-54/196, 260/204-05.
15. Fragment #2, HTJ, 359.
16. PCR I, HTJ, 208-09/139-40.
17. PCR I, HTJ, 163/82.
18. Fragment #2, HTJ, 360.
19. SC, HTJ, 327-29/283-87.
20. PCR I, HTJ, 227/162. cf. 224-25/158-59.
21. SC, HTJ, 341-42/301.
22. PCR I, HTJ, 220/152; *Volksreligion,* HTJ, 26-27, 54; Fragment #1, HTJ, 357.
23. SC, HTJ, 249-51/190-92; *Volksreligion,* HTJ, 26.
24. PCR I, HTJ, 215/146-47. cf. Fragment #2, HTJ, 359.
25. *Volksreligion,* HTJ, 24-25; Fragment #1, HTJ, 355.
26. Rosenkranz, *Georg Wilhelm Friedrich Hegels Leben,* Darmstadt, 1963, pp. 10 f. For the letter from Hegel's sister see Kaufmann (as cited in Ch. 1, n. 61), p. 299.
27. Rosenkranz, *op. cit.,* pp. 11, 25-27.
28. From the *Lebenslauf (curriculum vitae)* submitted by Hegel in

1804 for his promotion at Jena. The text appears in HTJ, IX, and in *Briefe von und an Hegel,* IV, 91-92.

29. The development of the Greek ideal at Jena comes primarily in *Naturrecht* and *Sittlichkeit.* As a technical term *Sittlichkeit* comes to be practically synonymous with Hegel's whole view of the Greek experience, at least during the Jena period. This whole section (2A) can be taken as its extended contextual definition, especially the sentence on p. 32. "Man lived in a whole which was at once religious, ethical, and political, and the individual felt himself to be an inherent part of that whole."

30. *Volksreligion,* HTJ, 62.

31. *Volksreligion,* HTJ, 20.

32. *Volksreligion,* HTJ, 14, 21, 23. cf. all of PCR II.

33. PCR I, HTJ, 194-95/122-23.

34. PCR II, HTJ, 139-44/167-74.

35. *Volksreligion,* HTJ, 26,39.

36. PhG, XI/14/73. See note 6 above.

37. PhG, XI-XII/15/74.

38. For a brief discussion see the editor's introduction to Hoffmeister's edition of the PhG. Though he quarrels with the specifics of this Haering-Hoffmeister thesis, Otto Pöggeler gives, if anything, more emphasis to the tension between the Introduction and the Preface. See *"Zur Deutung der Phänomenologie des Geistes,"* Hegel-Studien, Band 1, 1961, and *"Die Komposition der Phänomenologie des Geistes,"* Hegel-Studien, Beiheft 3, 1966.

39. See Ch. 1, n. 25.

40. PhG, LXXXVII/56/127.

41. PhG, XXVIII/24/85-86.

42. *Briefe von und an Hegel,* I, 18; HP, SW, 17:20/I, XII.

43. PhG, VI-VIII/12-13/70-71.

44. In the title essay of *Traditionelle und kritische Theorie,* Hamburg, 1968, Max Horkheimer writes of the Kantian philosophy that in it *"die gesellschaftliche Aktivität erscheint als transzendentale Macht, das heisst als Inbegriff geistiger Faktoren . . . Das Zusammenwirken der Menschen in der Gesellschaft ist die Existenzweise ihrer Vernunft . . ."* pp. 24-25.

45. PhG, VI-VIII/12-13/70-71.

46. *Glauben,* GW, 4:323 and PhG, XIII/15/75. This theme of a new age was expressed in Hegel's final Jena lecture. "We stand at the gates of an important epoch, a time of ferment, when Spirit moves forward in a leap, transcends its previous shape and takes on a new one. All the

mass of previous representations, concepts, and bonds linking our world together, are dissolving and collapsing like a dream picture. A new phase of the Spirit is preparing itself. Philosophy especially has to welcome its appearance and acknowledge it, while others, who oppose it impotently, cling to the past." As he returned to university life ten years later, this theme was much on his mind. In an address from 1815 we read, "We must oppose this mood which always uselessly misses the past and yearns for it. That which is old is not to be deemed excellent just because it is old . . . The world has given birth to a great epoch." In 1816 Hegel writes to Niethammer, "I stand by my belief that the world spirit has given [our] time the order to advance. This order is being obeyed." And in an essay on the proceedings of the Württemberg Estates, published in 1817, Hegel writes, "One might say of the Württemberg Estates what has been said of the returned French emigres: they have forgotten nothing and learnt nothing. They seem to have slept through the last twenty-five years, possibly the richest that world history has had, and for us the most instructive, because it is to them that our world and our ideas belong." Quoted from Schlomo Avineri, *Hegel's Theory of the Modern State,* Cambridge, 1972, pp. 64, 71, 72, and 74.

47. PhG, XIII-XVII/15-17/75-77. For both aspects at once, see the conclusion of the Preface, LXXXVIII-XC/57-58/128-29.

48. PhG, VI/11/70, LXXXIV-LXXXVI/55-56/125-27. cf. XXXIX/30/94.

49. PhG, XIV/16/76.

50. *Glauben,* GW, 4:323.

51. See the Preface to *The Philosophy of Right* and HP, SW, 17:82-86/I, 51-55.

52. *Naturrecht,* GW, 4:419, 479.

53. PhG, III-IV/10/68.

54. *Naturrecht,* GW, 4:483.

55. Jürgen Habermas, *Knowledge and Human Interests,* tr. Shapiro, Boston, 1971, p. VII.

56. *Volksreligion,* HTJ, 27.

57. PhG, VI/12/70.

58. See note 41 above.

59. See note 10 above.

60. See notes 41 and 42 above.

61. See the first section of this chapter.

62. *Glauben,* Introduction.

63. PCR II, HTJ, 146/175-76.

64. Karl Mannheim, *Ideology and Utopia*, tr. Wirth and Shils, New York, 1936, p. 67, and Peter Berger and Thomas Luckman, *The Social Construction of Reality*, Garden City, 1966, p. 5. These are two important works in the sociology of knowledge. From the phenomenological tradition perhaps the most important works are Heidegger's *Being and Time*, especially sections 12-16 and 29-33, Husserl's *Crisis*, and Merleau-Ponty's essay, "The Primacy of Perception" (see following note).

65. *The Primacy of Perception and Other Essays*, ed. Edie, Evanston, 1964, pp. 41, 48, 51.

66. *The German Constitution, Werke*, I, 463/145. For this translation see Kaufmann (as cited in Ch. 1, n. 61), p. 107.

67. Rosenkranz, *op. cit.*, p. 141.

68. See note 41 above.

69. *Naturrecht*, GW, 4:484.

70. *Theaetetus*, 149a-151c, Cornford translation.

71. *First Introduction to the Science of Knowledge*, in Fichte (as cited in Ch. 1, n. 32), 12n., *Werke*, I, 430n.

72. *Glauben*, GW, 4:315.

73. PhG, XII-XIII/15/74-75.

74. *Glauben*, GW, 4:322.

75. Fragment #1, HTJ, 359.

76. *Volksreligion*, HTJ, 42; Fragment #1, HTJ, 356; PCR I, HTJ, 194-95/122.

77. PCR I, HTJ, 161-62/79-80.

78. *Volksreligion*, HTJ, 43. cf. pp. 63-69; PCR I, HTJ, 157/74, 205-10/135-42; *Glauben*, GW, 4:405-08. All this sounds as if Hegel had been subjected to the strenuous sort of religious upbringing which Kierkegaard received, filled with intense emotional crises in childhood and adolescence. The evidence is quite to the contrary.

79. *Naturrecht*, GW, 4:470, 480; *Sittlichkeit*, pp. 54-55.

80. *Volksreligion*, HTJ, 70-71; PCR I, HTJ, 219-230/151-65; SC, HTJ, 273/221, 327/284; "Fragment of a System," HTJ, 349/315; *Naturrecht*, GW, 4:456-57. Note especially the quotation from Gibbon in this last reference.

81. *Naturrecht*, GW, 4:458, 468; *The German Constitution, Werke*, I, 516-17/189-90.

82. *Glauben*, GW, 4:316-17.

83. This is the heart of Hegel's argument in *Glauben* and *Skepticismus.*

84. See note 6 above.

85. *Glauben,* GW, 4:35-38; *Skepticismus,* GW, 4:223.

86. Emil Fackenheim, *The Religious Dimension in Hegel's Thought,* Bloomington, 1967, pp. 232-33.

CHAPTER THREE

The Knowledge of Nature:

3A. "The Truth is the Whole" as Hermeneutical Guide

In view of the scope and boldness of the phenomenological task as described in the Introduction and Preface it is surprising that Hegel's book should be as short as it is. It is, nevertheless, a very long book, and it is not surprising that the old saw about Mom's hash being so good because "She put everything she had into it" could so easily be used to caricature comments frequently directed against the *Phenomenology*. Hegel made hash out of what might have been a good book, so the story goes, because under pressure of the imminent disruption of life at Jena by Napoleon's armies, he threw into one book just about everything he was thinking about at the time.

But Hegel's claim is that "the truth is the whole." This means not only that his philosophy can only supersede other philosophies by including them, but also that philosophy as such can validate its truth claims only by including those non-philosophical forms of experience which make a claim on the truth.[1] Just as the truth about the plant is neither the bud, nor the blossom, nor even the fruit by itself, but rather the whole process in which each plays its necessary part, thereby retaining its radical difference from the others, so the whole truth about knowledge may turn out to be quite complex.[2] It may have to include not only the discussion of such obvious topics as sense perception and physical science, but even the analysis of "the madness of Diderot's musician . . . [and] the fanaticism of Marat and Robespierre."[3]

We can at least be thankful that Hegel begins where we would expect a treatise on knowledge to begin, with sense perception and our knowledge of the external world. But even here we run into the problem of totality and inclusion; for there is more philosophy going on in the three chapters collectively entitled Consciousness than the reader can possibly dream of in a single reading. To begin with, at least three major moments in the history of philosophy are narrated here simultaneously. Each of them provides a different but indispensable perspective for understanding the significance of Hegel's descriptions.

One way of reading these chapters is as a re-telling of Plato's *Theaetetus*. The parallel is threefold. With natural consciousness in the role of Theaetetus, Hegel's method is that of Socratic dialogue. At least his claim would be that "the arguments never come out of me, they always come from the person I am talking with. I am only at a slight advantage in having the skill to get some account of the matter for another's wisdom and entertain it with fair treatment . . . So I will have recourse to the wisdom of Theaetetus."[4] The result is equally Socratic. At the end of the chapters on Consciousness we can say that we have learned a lot, but not that we know what knowledge is, which was, of course, the question at issue.

The final and most important parallel is that between the three answers given by Theaetetus to the question What is knowledge? and the three answers given by natural consciousness under Hegel's questioning. When Theaetetus says first that knowledge is perception he means to identify knowledge with the direct and unreflected having or enjoying of the rich, concrete, sensory content given in perception. It is such a view which Hegel describes as Sense Certainty. When Theaetetus is reminded that such a view makes it impossible to preserve the connection between knowledge and truth, since one can "see" what isn't there, he replies that knowledge is true judgment. Already this implies that knowledge is complex enough to involve the difference between subject and predicate, referring and describing, substance and quality. It is no longer the passive having of sheer sensations, but involves the active discrimination by the knower of features in the field of knowledge. It is this view of knowledge which Hegel calls Perception. Finally, Theaetetus is led to see knowledge as true judgment with the addition of an account or reason [λογος]. Merely to assert the truth is not to know, for that can happen quite by accident. To know is to be able to ground one's correct judgments, to recognize their truth by relating them to other truths, thus weaving them into the whole fabric of truth. This is the project Hegel calls Understanding.

To follow only these clues, however, would be to miss entirely another story that Hegel is here re-telling. This is the story of modern natural science. The transition from Perception to Understanding highlights the way scientific knowledge is rooted in our everyday perception of the external world, which perception it in turn uproots. The development within Understanding traces the replacing of the Aristotelian physics of forces with the Galilean-Newtonian physics of laws. An integral part of this story is its first philosophical telling by Bacon and Descartes, Locke and Hume. In this tradition epistemology becomes identical with philosophy of science. For the question—What is knowledge?—is answered not so much by establishing the claim of the exact natural sciences to be knowledge as by assuming them to be and simply analyzing their method. The question about knowledge becomes the question—How is science possible?

By recapitulating this tradition Hegel is led, as the wording of the last question suggests, to a third story which Hegel wants us to re-hear, the one about Kant and his Copernican Revolution. The analysis of the Here, the Now, and the I of Sense Certainty can be read as another deduction of space, time, and the transcendental unity of apperception as a priori conditions of the possibility of experience. The constitution of objects in space and time by and for the transcendental ego, and particularly the role of the category of substance in this constitution are the Kantian themes underlying the discussion of "things" and their "properties" in the chapter on Perception. Then the chapter on Understanding restates Kant's discovery of the importance of rules and the concept of nature in general for the way we experience objects. It can thus be read as a further deduction of the categories of cause and reciprocity.

The dialogue between Hegel and natural consciousness in the section on Consciousness is not identical with any one of these three stories, but it can be read fruitfully from the standpoint of each, for each is included in that dialogue. In fact, since for Hegel the truth is the whole, we will understand these chapters as he wants them understood, only if we somehow manage to see them from all three standpoints at once.[5]

This is not, however, the only demand made of the reader

by Hegel's principle of totality. It is not loosely that his narrative is described as a dialogue, for it represents both the experience of natural consciousness and the meta-experience which occurs "for us" as "we" observe the dialectical movement of natural consciousness. To grasp the totality of Hegel's account we must recognize the different levels on which it operates, grasping not only their discreteness but also their interrelation.

Two passages from the Preface throw light on this requirement. Both contrast the movement of natural consciousness, even in some of its highest forms, with another movement of thought which can only be that of the philosophical observer. "The beginning of culture [*Bildung*] and of the struggle to pass out of the immediacy of substantial life has always to be made by acquiring knowledge of universal principles and perspectives, by first working oneself up to the thought of the subject matter in general. It is equally important to support or refute these thoughts with reasons, to grasp the concrete and rich fullness in its determinateness, and to know how to furnish an orderly account and a serious judgment about it."[6]

This movement of thought from original immediacy to the knowledge which grasps its object through the mediation of universals, i.e., in judgment, and then goes on to support its judgments with reasons is the movement of natural consciousness as traced in the *Theaetetus*. Hegel stresses its abstractness. Since thought's labor is *herausarbeiten* and *heraufarbeiten*, thought's movement to the thought of the subject matter in general, *die Sache überhaupt*, is a movement away from *die Sache selbst*, away from the concrete and rich fullness which it set out to think.

"This beginning of culture will, however, very soon make way for the seriousness of life in its fulness, which leads to the experience of the subject matter itself [*die Sache selbst*], and when in addition the seriousness of the concept descends into the depths of the subject matter, knowledge and judgment of the previous kind will keep their due place in conversation."

Over against the thought which owes its achievements to its abstractness there inevitably arises the appeal to concrete experience, to immediacy, to intuition, etc., in the name of seriousness. Enlightenment and Romanticism always go together. But there is another seriousness which distinguishes itself from both. It claims to be more serious than romantic seriousness, for it recognizes the deficiencies of the first attempt to think without assuming that this exhausts the possibilities of conceptual thought. This seriousness of the concept acknowledges the genuineness of the appeal to "the experience of the subject matter itself," but it boldly claims that it is just this experience and this subject matter which it will think. Since it is on the phenomenological path of doubt and despair that the seriousness of the concept is born, it will already begin to appear alongside various modes of natural consciousness. The insights which "we" derive from observing natural consciousness are the initial elements of a different level of conceptual achievement.

A second passage in which the same two modes of thought are contrasted gives a fuller indication of what the second, the seriousness of the concept, is like. Here the abstract mode of thought is attributed to antiquity. "The manner of study in ancient times is distinct from that of the modern world, in that the former was the development of natural consciousness. Testing life carefully at all points, philosophizing about everything it came across, the former created an experience permeated with universals. In modern times, however, an individual finds the abstract form ready made. In striving to grasp it and make it his own, he rather strives to bring forward the inner meaning alone without any process of mediation; the production of the universal is abridged instead of the universal arising out of the concreteness and multiplicity of existence."[7]

Hegel is not willing to rest with this antithesis between two modes of abstractness, the thinking which in its formality and universality abstracts from the subject matter it purports to think and the inevitable reaction which abstracts from conceptual thought in order to restore concrete encounter with the world. "Hence nowadays," he continues, "the task before us consists not so much in getting the individual clear of the stage of sensible immediacy, and making him a substance that thinks and is grasped in terms of thought, but rather the very opposite, namely by breaking down and superseding fixed and determinate thoughts to actualize the universal and infuse it with Spirit . . . Through this movement the pure thoughts become concepts and are then what they are in truth . . . that which is their substance, spiritual entities."

Hegel's remedy for sterile and lifeless thought is not to give up on reason but to transform it by moving from pure thought to concept, or, more specifically, from pure thought to Spirit. Hegel here coins the term *begeisten*. It is translated "enfuse with Spirit" because on the one hand it suggests *begeistern*, to animate, enthuse, or enliven, while on the other hand its own form is *be-Geist-en*. To enfuse the universal with Spirit is not only to enliven otherwise dead thought. It is to re-establish the connection between pure thought and its own living source by showing that pure thoughts belong to Spirit and are indeed *geistige Wesenheiten*, spiritual entities. Once again we must be able to move back and forth between two distinct levels of rational activity.

The full significance of this can only come with the development of the concept of Spirit (in Chapter Five below). But the following important implications are given in the paragraph already before us. "Thought determinations get their substance and the element of their existence from the ego," and "thoughts become fluent when pure thinking, this inner immediacy, knows itself as a moment, when pure certainty of self abstracts from itself. It does not 'abstract' in the sense of getting away from itself and setting itself on one side, but of surrendering the fixed quality of its self-affirmation, and giving up both the fixity of the purely concrete—which is the ego as contrasted with the variety of its content—and the fixity of all those distinctions, which are present in the element of pure thought and share that unconditionedness of the ego."[8]

This movement is twofold. First comes the Copernican Revolution, the discovery of the transcendental role of the thinking subject. The Cartesian ego, the "substance that thinks and is grasped in terms of thought," comes to know itself as a moment of its own knowledge, as the origin of the thought determinations which make its knowledge possible. But this is only half of what it means to *begeisten* the universal. When thought recognizes itself as a moment in the process of knowledge it also recognizes its own relativity. In abandoning the fixity of its self-affirmation both as the transcendental unity of apperception and as the determinate categories by which that unity is maintained, it abandons "that unconditionedness of the ego" which it claims for itself in the element of pure thought.

Just as the transcendental turn deprives the object of its fixity by showing that it is not simply given, this second move is the discovery that the subject is not simply self-posited.

In this sense one can ask within the Hegelian context a question which is meaningless in the Cartesian, Kantian, and Fichtean context—*Who is the transcendental subject?* It is precisely the meaningfulness of this question which brings us to the realm of Spirit. At least part of the secret of this crucial but elusive concept is found in the idea that a phenomenology of Spirit will be a transcendental philosophy which sees the transcendental ego as conditioned. While it is too early to say that for Hegel "the achievements of the transcendental subject have their basis in the natural history of the human species,"[9] one can at least begin to see how some such formula might be necessary.

What these two passages indicate is that we must distinguish three different levels in Hegel's analysis of our knowledge of the external world. 1) There is the presentation of the different ways in which the object is grasped, first by pre-scientific everyday consciousness as the thing and its properties, and then by the two forms of scientific understanding as the interplay of forces and as the exemplification of universal laws. 2) There is then the reflective discovery of the active role of consciousness in all of that first order knowing. 3) Then there is the further reflective discovery of the contingent character of that transcendental activity, however necessary it may be in relation to the objects constituted by it.

These last two levels are what make up the "descent into the depths" which is the *Be-Geist-ung* of thought. Here thought overcomes the fallacy of misplaced concreteness and ceases to mistake the product of its own abstracting acts for the independently and genuinely real. It then learns to view those acts themselves concretely in the context from which they arise. These discoveries are, on the one hand, the introduction to the realm of Spirit; on the other hand, they are the scepticism of which the Introduction speaks, the "conscious insight into the untruth of phenomenal knowledge," and the "despair over notions, thoughts, and opinions which are called natural." The untruth of phenomenal knowledge is due to its incompleteness, whereas the truth is the whole. Everyday perception and natural science are genuine modes of knowing. But until they are seen as parts of the whole which makes them possible, they remain untrue from a philosophical point of view. Their object cannot be understood apart from their subject and their subject cannot be understood apart from the historical life of Spirit.

3B. The Mediated Character of Sense Perception

Sense Certainty has not yet learned any of these lessons, but Hegel's task is not exactly to teach. His "method" here as elsewhere is to observe the contradiction between the criterion by which a form of natural consciousness seeks to validate its knowledge and the actual knowledge which it produces. Such a contradiction comes to light in the first sentence on Sense Certainty. On the one hand it wishes to be "immediate knowledge." On the other it purports to be "knowledge of the immediate or of what is [*das Seinde*]." Having this object it claims to be the "richest" knowledge, for it has an infinite wealth of concrete content available to it, all that is to be seen, heard, smelled, tasted, and touched. The tree here, the house over there, and the whole world to which they belong—these are the riches of Sense Certainty.

At the same time Sense Certainty claims to be the "truest" knowledge and not only the "richest". For as immediate knowledge it has its object complete and unadulterated. Nothing has been added to it or taken from it by the knowing subject, to whom it is simply given. Since Sense Certainty is in this way the "truest" knowledge in relation to the riches of its content, it leaves no room for error and is also the "truest" with respect to form. That is, it is the most certain knowledge and deserves to be called Sense *Certainty*.[10]

But the criterion of immediacy by which Sense Certainty seeks to elevate sense perception to be both the truest knowledge in itself and the unshakable foundation of all other knowledge stands in sharpest contradiction to the richness of the actual knowledge which it takes to be its own. The knowledge which takes this criterion seriously is not the richest, but the "abstractest and poorest" knowledge of all. It can completely express itself by saying, It is. The rich content of its object has been reduced to its mere being, the most indeterminate of all predicates. Sense Certainty knows and can say *that* its object is, but not *what* it is. Any attempt to get beyond this indeterminacy runs afoul of the immediacy criterion, for every determination is a negation, and every negation is a mediation.[11]

Since Hegel seems to presuppose rather than deny that we sometimes do perceive trees, we may suppose that the "it" which "is" is a tree, and that it is perceived as a tree. But for the object of perception to be a tree, it has to have certain qualities which determine it as a tree and distinguish it from say, a computer or an igloo. But this is already to introduce mediation, for the tree can be a tree and not merely an "it is" only by virtue of its negative relation to other things. At the same time, to perceive the tree as a tree is to perceive it as not a computer and not an igloo. The determinate is given as such to consciousness only by the mediating act which distinguishes it from what it is not. Once again immediacy is lost.

This is not what Sense Certainty had intended. From its perspective, "I, this particular I, am certain of this thing, not because I develop myself as consciousness in relation to it and in manifold ways set thought to work on it; nor because the thing of which I am certain, in virtue of having a multitude of distinct qualities, is a copious relation to itself or a manifold relation to other things. Neither has anything to do with the truth of Sense Certainty. Neither the I nor the thing has in this domain the meaning of a multi-faceted mediation."[12] But the simple immediacy which avoids these mediations is only the "pure being" or the bare "it is" from which all content has departed. Such knowledge owes its certainty to its emptiness. As with the "knowledge is perception" thesis in the *Theaetetus,* the possibility of truth disappears with the possibility of error.[13]

The contradiction within Sense Certainty is a glaring one. It refutes itself in its opening statement. But just as Plato allows Protagoras to carry on a defense of the knowledge-as-perception view further than Theaetetus is able to, thereby developing his own argument in considerably more detail, so Hegel does not dispose of Sense Certainty without careful examination of its further attempts to extricate itself from the seeming contradiction involved in its claim to be simultaneously determinate and immediate. It suspects that it has let mediation get its nose in the tent by carelessly assuming that subject and object are equal partners in perception. In that case, "I have certainty through an other, namely the thing; and it is correspondingly in that certainty through an other, namely through the I." Both are thoroughly mediated through the other in perception. (What they may be outside of perception is, very importantly, not pertinent to the examination of Sense Certainty and its claim that *within* sense perception immediacy and determinacy can be combined.)[14]

Sense Certainty now seeks to avoid the previous difficulties by eliminating any suggestion of partnership between subject and object. In an asymmetrical relation in which one element is unessential and conditioned, the other might well be essential and unconditioned. In that case its presence in perception would not be mediated through the other. The realistic form of this defense is the first to be tried. It is the object which is to be the essential, conditioning, unmediated element of perception.

It is not realism as a metaphysical thesis which is here in question. The issue is not whether for a tree "to be is to be perceived," but only whether the suggested asymmetrical relation adequately describes the way the tree is present in sense perception for the perceiving subject. Since it is clear that to be present is to be here and now, we must ask what it means to be here and now for consciousness, or, in Hegel's locution, What is the Now? and What is the Here?[15]

Sense Certainty first discovers that the Now is not a particular, existing thing [*ein Seiendes*], but something negative, something which remains and preserves itself, something universal, and thus something mediated. What this means is not quite as forbidding as Hegel's language suggests, but in the background is the familiar argument of Kant's Transcendental Aesthetic.

For a thing to be present to consciousness now it must have a temporal location defined by its being later than some moments of time and earlier than others. More specifically, to locate the event of a thing's presentness as now is to place that event in a determinate relationship with the whole of time, the totality of moments to which the moment of this event belongs. The nowness of the perceptual event is not a function of a particular, the moment in which it occurs, but only of the totality within which this particular moment occurs and first becomes possible. The totality is neither this moment nor that one. One can say that it is the whole it is by virtue of its negative relation to its parts. It is what remains and maintains itself in and through the passing away of its moments. That Hegel should call this sort of negative, remaining, self-maintaining totality a universal sounds strange to modern usage for which the term is used to distinguish type from instance rather than whole from part. But that he should call the presentness of the object to perceptual consciousness something mediated can no longer be surprising, for the Here is evidently the same sort of universal as the Now, and together they are essential to perceptual experience. If we try to think of a perceptual content apart from the time and space which it normally occupies, to represent a perceptual foreground apart from its perceptual background, it is clear that we have abandoned what Sense Certainty wanted to talk about, our everyday perception of the tree here and the house over there, if indeed we are talking about anything at all.[16]

What has come to light in analyzing the here-and-nowness of the perceptual content is only slightly different from the discovery made in the preliminary examination of Sense Certainty. The principle there was that every determination is a negation, that for an object to be given in perception as determinate it must be taken as such, mediated by an act of consciousness which distinguishes it from what is not. Hegel's transition to the chapter on Perception is thus more than a pun on the term *Wahrnehmung*, for it succinctly locates the Achilles heel of Sense Certainty. "I point it out *as* a here which is a here among other heres . . . I take it *as* it is in truth, and instead of knowing something immediate, I take it truly [*nehme ich wahr*]."[17] There can be no unmediated givenness in perception, for to perceive is to take something *as* something. The analysis of the Now and the Here shows how this is true even for the least conceptual and most intuitive aspects of perception, for reference as well as description. In relation to space and time the logical principle that every determination is a negation becomes the explicitly perceptual principle—the object is always distinguished within perception as a foreground against a background. In both cases the result is the same. It is only by means of the judgmental act of the perceiving subject which takes the object as here and not there, now and not then, and, e.g., tree and not computer or igloo, that the object can be determinately given in perception.

Since Hegel is not here concerned with how mathematics is possible a priori his treatment of the transcendental character of space and time has a different emphasis from Kant's. It is not limited to the formal aspects of experience, but exemplifies a principle which applies to the content as well, to the greenness of the tree as well as its nowness.[18]

With this discovery of transcendental subjectivity Sense Certainty experiences a dialectical reversal, for the realistic asymmetry by which it sought to preserve immediacy with determinacy has turned into its opposite. "The object, which was to be the essential reality, is now the non-essential element of Sense Certainty; for the universal which it has become is no longer such as the object was to be for Sense Certainty. The certainty is now found to lie in the opposite element, namely in knowledge, which formerly was the non-essential element. The truth of Sense Certainty lies in the object as my [*meinem*] object, or in the intending [*Meinen*] of it. The object is because I know it."[19]

Again nothing can be inferred from the last sentence about the existence of unperceived trees, for the issue is still only the object as it is present in perception. But this also means that the subject, which is now taken to be the essential element, the unmediated giver of the given, cannot be deprived of its immediacy by reference to the physics of perception, for the impact of light waves on the retina is as inappropriate to the present discussion as is the existence of unperceived trees. In the language of later phenomenology, the natural standpoint has been bracketed. In the language of Anglo-Saxon empiricism the language of sense data has replaced that of physical objects. As Sense Certainty seeks to preserve itself "in the immediacy of my seeing, hearing, etc.," this no longer has reference to the relation of empirical subject to physical object.

Having been forced to withdraw from the familiar, everyday world in which it was completely at home to the rarefied atmosphere of sense data and noemata, Sense Certainty can now hope at best to salvage a highly qualified victory. But even this is not to be. Mediation raises its ugly head once again and forces Sense Certainty to one final desperate defense. The I, which is now taken to be the essential element, turns out to be the same sort of universal as the Now and the Here. The particular I which sees the tree and takes it to be a tree disappears and is replaced by another particular I which sees the house instead as the object present to consciousness. What does not disappear is the I as universal, the I which is not the particular seeing of any particular object but seeing in general, the totality of the perceptual capacity which makes possible the perceiving of both the tree and the house. Only the I which can also intend a house can intend a tree, for to intend an object as a tree is to intend it as not a house, as not the ground in which it grows, as not the birds who build their nests in it, and so forth. Hegel only says the obvious when he says that "Sense Certainty experiences in this connection the same dialectic as in the former case," i.e., as in the case of the realistic asymmetry. Both cases illustrate the contradiction which came to light in the opening sentences on Sense Certainty between its criterion of immediacy and the determinateness of its actual knowledge.

The final capitulation of Sense Certainty takes the form of one last desperate defense, the attempt to think a consciousness devoid of all the mediating universals which have come to light. It will be a consciousness whose Now and Here are unrelated to any other Nows and Heres and whose content is thus unrelated to any other content, if that makes any sense. As intentional act it will not relate itself to any other intentional act. In short, it will have the character of what is sometimes called the solipsism of the present moment. Loewenberg has tried to describe it in this way: "A consciousness dominated by an intense sensation completely withdraws from all distinctions and all relations. While the sensation lasts, the content present and the self aware of it constitute a miniature world."[20] One must hasten to add that the distinction between the self and the content of its awareness is one of the distinctions from which this consciousness has completely withdrawn.

Something like this minature world can occur during the moment of transition from fainting to fully regained consciousness.[21] There is no sense of personal identity or of location in space and time. Only after the "experience" and not during it is the "I think" able to accompany it. But in spite of this

complete lack of orientation, there is a feeling which can subsequently be vaguely described as a pressure or a pain. These
determinations of the "experience" as mine and as of pain are
absent from the "experience" itself. For a moment I become a
pure feeling, unowned, unlocated, and indescribable. As this
"experience" gradually becomes my experience of pain it completely changes its character. As Hegel says, "Were we to concern ourselves afterwards with this truth, or stand at a distance
from it, it would have no meaning at all, for that would do away
with the immediacy which it essentially is."[22]

In attempting to think a consciousness like Loewenberg's
minature world or this not quite conscious consciousness, Sense
Certainty concedes the untenability of its position. In thinking a
consciousness which strictly adheres to its criterion of immediacy it shows how fully indeterminate and empty that consciousness must be, if it can legitimately be called consciousness at all.
If such a consciousness could speak, absurd as such a supposi-
tion is, its assertion "It is" would sound, if anything, like an
exaggerated account of its experience.

That such states of pure immediacy exist, in infancy, in
semi-consciousness, in mystic trances, and so on, Hegel does
not deny. That they are as devoid of truth as of falsity, since
they lack all determinate content, Hegel does not need to affirm. Sense Certainty has discovered this for itself. It will return
to the world of everyday perception, whose richness remains,
quite unchanged by the now completed dialogue. Sense Certainty, however, has changed so radically in abandoning its immediacy criterion, that it is no longer Sense Certainty, but what
Hegel calls Perception.

3C. Language, Sense Certainty, and Feuerbach's
Critique

It is too soon, however, to turn to the chapter on Perception, for what is most often taken to be the heart of the chapter
on Sense Certainty has been completely overlooked to this
point, namely the discussion of language in relation to sense
perception and the notorious claim that we cannot say what we
mean. That this can hardly be the key to Sense Certainty's self-

refutation should be clear from the foregoing, where that self-refutation occurs without so much as a reference to the three passages where the so-called argument from language is found.

The first and most important of these passages is the following paragraph, which occurs between the analysis of the Now and that of the Here: "It is *also* as a universal that we express [*aussprechen*] the sensible. What we say is, This, i.e., the universal this. Or we say, It is, i.e., being in general. Of course we do not have in mind [*vorstellen*] the universal this or being in general when we speak in this way, but we express what is universal. In other words, we simply do not say what we mean in this Sense Certainty. But language, as we see, is truer than our meaning or intention [*Meinung*], which we ourselves immediately refute when we speak. And, *since the universal is the truth of Sense Certainty, and language merely expresses this truth,* it is not possible at all for us to express in words any sensible particular [*sinnliches Sein*] which we mean."[23]

For the understanding of this paragraph it is crucial whether we take the (italicized) protasis of its last sentence or its apodasis as our point of departure. The latter calls attention to the *discrepancy* between what we mean and what we say. The italicized statement, by contrast, points to the striking *congruity* between language and perception, thereby echoing the "also" of the paragraph's first sentence. That the universal is the truth of Sense Certainty is the discovery of the preceding paragraph in which the Now is found to be a universal. That we *also express* the sensible as universal and now wish to discover the consequences of this (in the last sentence of the paragraph) indicates first, that the self-refutation of Sense Certainty occurs in the discussion of the Now (and subsequently of the Here and the I) rather than here in the discussion of language, and second, that we are here concerned with expanding our understanding of those other parts of the dialogue. For example, it might be intended that from the isomorphism of language and perception, together with the discovery that we cannot say what we mean, we should draw the conclusion that we also cannot even perceive what we mean.

This intriguing possibility could be uninterruptedly pursued at this point only by ignoring the loud protest from Feuerbach. Not entirely unlike Thrasymachus in the *Republic,* he insists that Hegel has made a farce out of dialectic by reducing what should be a dialogue between Speculation and Empiricism to a monologue between Speculation and itself in the form of a pseudo-defender of Empiricism who presupposes the results of Speculation and is entirely unable to get inside the perspective of Sense Certainty and think the way it thinks. Feuerbach volunteers to act as the advocate of Sense Certainty, and promises to play a real *Du* to Hegel's *Ich*. He promises not to capitulate obediently as the previous defenders of Sense Certainty have done in the face of Hegel's all too Socratic word games.[24]

If only because Feuerbach's critique has been so regularly repeated, wittingly or unwittingly, down to the present day, it is worthy of examination. His point of departure is the apodasis of the final sentence of the paragraph cited above. Thus he finds the heart of Hegel's critique of Sense Certainty in the claim that we cannot say what we mean, that verbal expression never adequately captures the unique particularity of the sensible particular.

This leads to a double misunderstanding of Hegel's text. The first concerns the criterion by which Sense Certainty is to be examined. Feuerbach reminds Hegel that it is a nominalistic consciousness which knows that "language by no means belongs to its object . . . How then should sensible consciousness find itself to be refuted or actually be refuted by the fact that the particular does not allow itself to be said? Sensible consciousness rather finds in just this fact a refutation of language."[25] If Hegel thinks that Sense Certainty is refuted by showing that we cannot say what we mean, this can only be because he attributes to it the claim that we can say what we mean. Feuerbach's point is that Sense Certainty need not make such a claim, and that Hegel's refutation rests on tricking some pseudo-representative of Sense Certainty into making that claim and then showing the absurdity of his position. What Feuerbach fails to notice, largely because of his almost exclusive focus on the discussion of language, is that it is quite a different criterion by which Sense Certainty is examined, namely that of immediacy, and that its refutation takes place in those analyses of the Now, and Here, and the I to which he pays almost no attention. It is not Sense Certainty in Hegel's critique, but Hegel in Feuerbach's who is judged by a criterion imposed from without.

The curious phrase "refutation of language" expresses Feuerbach's second and equally basic misunderstanding. What does it mean for language to be refuted? Feuerbach finds the *Phenomenology* to begin with the contradiction between word as universal and thing as particular. "But no more than the word is the thing as spoken or thought being actual being." This actual being to which language and thought are opposed is "*Existenz*", and it is before its court that they are "refuted". For Feuerbach as for Kierkegaard the term *Existenz* gathers around itself three interrelated themes: particularity inaccessible to thought, reality as opposed to mere possibility, and practical, or as we have come to put it, existential interest. These are the basic categories of Feuerbach's "existentialist" critique of Hegel on Sense Certainty.[26]

His point is clearest in the examples he gives. According to Hegel's critique the bread I eat may be "unsayable" because of its particularity, but it is a matter of life and death to me that I have the real unspeakable bread rather than the linguistic or logical bread which, just because it can be spoken cannot be eaten. Similarly, I have a brother named Johann Adolph. Since many other persons have that name, even his proper name does not distinguish him from them. "But does it follow from this that my Johann is unreal and that truth is found only in Johann-ness?"[27] Again, "This woman is, for example, my wife, this house my house, although everyone says the same thing about his house and wife that I say about mine: this house, this woman. But the indifference and absence of distinction which characterize the logical This is here broken through and transcended by the sense of right. If we were to apply the logical This in the realm of natural rights, we would come directly to the community of goods and wives where there is no difference between this and that . . . [but] right is grounded precisely on the reality of this distinction."

If it be objected that these examples introduce the realm of the practical whereas Hegel was only concerned with the theoretical, the reply is "that the practical standpoint is entirely in place here. The question of being is indeed a practical question, one in which our being has a share, a question of life and death."[28]

Feuerbach has located the decisive objection to his existentialist critique, for the practical point of view is surely out of place where the question of the independent reality of the objects of perception has deliberately been set aside so as to focus exclusively on the question of the way objects are present to consciousness in perception. As if to remind the reader of this Hegel does not end the chapter on Sense Certainty without an anticipatory reference to his own upcoming discussions in which eating and drinking as well as life and death will be considered. And as if to refute Feuerbach's interpretation directly Hegel indicates here that what he means by the unreality of the sensible particular is illustrated and confirmed by the phenomenon of eating.[29]

Feuerbach knows all this, but objects that it is illegitimate to postpone the practical perspective when it is a question of being. Perhaps so. But Hegel is not here discussing the question of being, only the very limited question of the being of something for consciousness in perception. Such reflection in no way implies the unreality of Feuerbach's brother or his bread; and far from implying that he is suddenly unable to distinguish his wife from other men's wives, it stresses the determinateness of the perceptual object and assumes that we can at least distinguish trees from houses. Rather than denying our capacity to refer to individuals, Hegel is asking how it is possible for us to do so.

Actually Feuerbach is a better Hegelian than he knows, for he ends up arguing for rather than against the two major results of Hegel's dialogue with Sense Certainty: the mediated character of sense perception and the concrete humanity of the perceiving subject.[30] We have already seen that the mediated character of sense perception is the heart of Hegel's analysis of Sense Certainty. Similarly Feuerbach sees a double mediation in sense perception. Our certainty of the existence of external objects is mediated through our dialogue with other persons, and the way in which we perceive them is a function of the expectations and hopes we bring with us, which in turn are a function of our degree of culture and of our historical context. Any "immediate" sensible intuition could only be the result of a purification of these factors and thus an abstraction. It would thus be what Hegel calls "that immediacy which does not leave mediation outside itself but which is mediation itself."[31] This means that man is distinguished from the animals in his whole being, including the senses, that "even the lowliest senses, smell and taste, rise up in man to perform spiritual, scientific acts."[32]

This is already to affirm the concrete humanity of the perceiving subject. Idealism had asked, "What are the eyes without consciousness?"[33] Feuerbach now answers with idealism, Animal eyes, not human eyes. But if sense cannot be abstracted from consciousness, consciousness or thought must not be treated as an abstraction either. From the principle that "Man thinks, not the I," Feuerbach derives the following categorical imperative: "Don't think as a thinker . . . think as a living, actual being . . . think in *Existenz,* in the world as a member of the world . . ."[34]

That Hegel also wishes to go beyond the abstract ego of earlier transcendental philosophy to something like Feuerbach's "Man thinks, not the I," is indicated clearly in the Preface (see sections 2B. and 3A. above). But that he does so in the dialogue with Sense Certainty, that we are to learn from it that it is man who perceives, not the senses, or even the Kantian tandem of senses and transcendental ego, intuitions and concepts—this is not yet clear. It is necessary to return to the question of language and ask what its contribution to the chapter may be, since the refutation of Sense Certainty has proven not to be its task.

Prior to the Feuerbachian interruption the hypothesis had been developed that since language and perception are isomorphic in that "the universal is the truth of Sense Certainty, and language merely expresses this truth," and since on the linguistic side this means that "it is not possible at all for us to express in words any sensible particular which we mean," it would seem to follow that on the perceptual side we also cannot even perceive what we mean. Does this make any sense?

It is usually not noticed that every time Hegel says we cannot say what we mean he reaffirms the obvious fact that in sense perception we mean, intend, or refer to the particular. In this sense, namely as intended or referred to, the particular is present to perception. To say that we cannot perceive what we mean is only to say that this intention is never completely fulfilled, that this reference is never completely unambiguous. The object we mean is a fully determinate particular, but in and for perception it is never more than partly determined, partly determinable. In this respect the perceived object and the spoken object are alike. When Urban says that "poetry says what it means, but it does not say all that it means,"[35] what he says may be true not only of language as such, but, *mutatis mutandis,* of perception as well. After pragmatism and the debate over phenomenalism this discovery can hardly be said to be the esoteric possession of either Hegelian or twentieth century phenomenology.

Such a reflection on the isomorphism between language and perception completes two of the three moments described at the conclusion of section 3A. above. As far as the object is concerned, Hegel has first stressed its determinacy and now its indeterminacy. This determinate-indeterminate object is precisely the thing and its properties of the chapter on Perception. The thing is the fully determinate and thus fully particular object we intend. Its properties are the many different and incomplete ways in which it is determinate for consciousness. The difficulties of Perception are simply that the gap between the thing and its properties, its oneness and its manyness, its determinacy and its indeterminacy is never actually bridged in Perception.

The determinate-indeterminate character of the perceptual object has this further consequence, that as a mode of knowledge sense perception is both uncertain and incomplete. The attempt to maintain immediacy was from the start an attempt to maintain or regain certainty, and the inability of Sense Certainty to sustain its claim to immediacy has cost it its claim to certainty. On the other hand, the necessary indeterminacy of the object for perception means that this knowledge is never adequate to its object (as meant) and is thus essentially incomplete.

In the same process by which the nature of the perceptual object has been clarified, the active role of the perceiving subject has come to light. This object is only present to the consciousness which intends it in its full determinacy and particularity, permitting it to be given in actual perception by taking it to be what its various properties show it to be.

To this point, however, no insight has been gained concerning the third moment described in 3A., the manner in which the essential acts of perceiving consciousness may themselves be conditioned. It is not yet clear who the transcendental subject may be. Along with this unanswered question there remains the unexamined phenomenon of the isomorphism of language and perception. Reflection on the "fact" of this isomorphism has helped to clarify the indeterminacy of the perceptual object, but the "fact" itself, the structural similarity of perception and language, has not been discussed. Is it merely a fact, an accident, that we *also* express the sensible as universal, that we can and do say what we see, even if we cannot say what we mean?

When this unexamined phenomenon is juxtaposed to the unanswered question about the identity of the transcendental subject, an hypothesis suggests itself. The transcendental subject is the speaker of a language. This in turn suggests that the relation of language to perception may not be an accidental one, that for the human perceiver it is above all his language which makes possible his perception, which enables him to intend the particulars he intends and to take them in the way he does as variously determined. This would be a special way of saying that it is man who perceives, neither the animal senses, nor the transcendental ego, nor the two in conjunction. For man distinguishes himself from the animals by language, and language is always a language, carrying with it its own history and tradition, structuring the expectations and hopes we bring with us to perception.

None of this is explicit in the text. Sense Certainty has long since moved on to Perception and is about to become Understanding. Since it is still an unsophisticated form of natural consciousness it keeps all its attention on the object, and so far from worrying about who the transcendental subject may be, it forgets about transcendental subjectivity altogether as quickly as possible. Fully resubmerged in its object, it employs a whole variety of categories which it does not recognize as such. When philosophy tries to reflect on them and win some sort of mastery over them, perceptual common sense reproaches it for wasting its time on mere lifeless thoughts. It does not realize that it is tossed about like the prey and plaything of these *Gedankendinge,* which it takes to be unreal abstractions. Since it never becomes aware "that there are such simple realities operating within it and dominating its activity," it remains a thoroughly alienated, false, pre-Copernican consciousness.[36]

But we who observe the experience which consciousness makes are supposed to see what goes on behind its back and need not close our eyes to what is going on right before them. Nor did Hegel. The hypothesis which suggests itself more or less between the lines of the *Phenomenology* is one which he had already developed with some care just previously in the Jena *Realphilosophie*.[37]

3D. Language and the Double Mediation of Theoretical Consciousness

Man's mastery over nature is both theoretical (ideal) and practical (real). To deal with either in isolation from the other and from the context of social interaction in which they take place, that of family and people [*Volk*], is to deal with an abstraction. For, to take the case at hand, the speaking perceiver of theoretical consciousness is always at the same time a member of a family and society who shares in their socially organized labor. When Marx, for example, insists that the abolition of private property has implications for sense perception he is simply refusing to treat theoretical consciousness in abstraction from the rest of man.[38]

It is just such abstractions with which natural consciousness feels most at home. It assumes that the distinction between theoretical and practical as well as that between sense and intellect is fixed and immoveable. In seeking to lead natural consciousness to see that it is man who perceives and not the senses, Hegel must begin where natural consciousness is, with theoretical activity abstracted from the total man. He must think it so concretely that the rigid distinctions of natural consciousness break down. This is the strategy in both the *Phenomenology* and the *Realphilosophie*.

Natural consciousness is proud of man's superiority over the animals. But at the theoretical level it tends to conceive of this as the pasting together of sub-human animal sensation with a formal ego which is too abstract to be human. In the *Realphilosophie* Hegel wants to show that the mediation which humanizes pure sensation is not that of the ego, which he describes as a formal universal, but that of Spirit, which is truly universal since it contains the particular within it. To do this he develops the linguistic character of perception, for language is "the true being of Spirit as Spirit in general."[39]

A two-fold mediation is involved here, between subject and object and within the subject itself, conceived of as Spirit. We have first to observe "how Spirit intends the thing," that is, "how the object comes to be something universal for it, or how it makes it to be what it is, intends it as what it is." At the same time we are to see that "Spirit is that which is self-mediating. It exists only as withdrawing from and thus transcending what it immediately is." In language this self-mediation of Spirit has its extremes in the individual consciousness and the universal consciousness which contains the individual consciousness within it and comes to expression by means of it.[40]

In both cases "the middle is the essential"—neither subject nor object, individual nor universal consciousness maintain their discrete and identifiable particularity. They rather become united in a third reality. Using the syllogism as a metaphor Hegel calls this third reality their middle, for like the middle term in a syllogism it so unites the other two terms that we can say that the one *is* the other (Socrates is mortal).[41] The mediation of subject and object is the process by which thing [*Ding*] becomes ego [*Ich*]. The mediation of individual and universal consciousness is that by which ego becomes thing, that is, takes on an empirical, objective character. At the heart of both processes lies language.

The first of these mediations corresponds to the analysis in the *Phenomenology* of the mediated character of sense perception, except that it makes explicit the linguistic character of perception. The "overcoming of the indeterminacy of sensation" is accomplished even in the child's apprehension of something as, e.g., a large nose.[42] Already this involves language and its presuppositions, imagination and memory. In imagination the original intuition becomes the object of consciousness. The image is "being as mine, as transcended." Like the first stage of experience within Plato's cave, the realm of images can only be compared to night-time, dreaming consciousness. Waking consciousness involves the "power to call up images out of this night or to leave them submerged in it." Through this mastery which consciousness wins over the realm of its images, the image becomes a sign which refers back to the original object, which, in the process, "has come under the mastery of the self and has lost the significance of being immediate and independent." This image-sign, which has become the essence [*Inner-*

lichkeit] of the thing does not remain wholly inner. It becomes a thing itself and wins outward existence as language when the subject names the thing. The perceptual process completes itself only in this bond between name and image made possible by the cooperation of imagination and memory. It is what Kant called the schema.[43]

This is a kind of linguistic idealism. But it is not the "laughable idealism" which opposes itself to realism. Both parties to this irrational conflict, about which there is nothing rational to say, assume that subject and object sustain themselves unchanged in perception, that no mediation takes place. But perception is "a synthesis of object and self, of content and ego." The essence is their middle, and it does not make sense to ask what the contribution of each party may be. The truth is the whole and the human perception of a large nose belongs to the totality from which sensation (passivity) and naming (activity) cannot be isolated as discrete realities.[44] It is to counteract the crude realism of common sense that Hegel invokes idealistic language to make his point; as when he says the thing becomes ego, or more specifically, "Thus it is through the name that the ego gives birth to the object as the thing it is. This is the first creative power which Spirit exercises. Adam gave all things names. This is . . . the creation of nature out of Spirit. λογος is reason, the essence of things and of speech, of telling and of what is told [*Sache und Sage*]. In short, reason is category. Man speaks to things as to his own and lives in a spiritual nature, in his own world, and this is the being of the object."[45]

We are brought in this way to the second mediation, that of Spirit with itself. For while transcendental subjectivity has just regained the spotlight, the linguistic character of its presentation in the Jena lectures leads directly to reflection on the identity of this transcendental ego, the "bearer, space, and substance" of names, which creates the world in which man lives.[46] Language as the namegiving power is "the true being of Spirit as Spirit in general" because "it is there as the unity of two free selves." It takes two (or more) to play a language game. This clarifies Hegel's claim that in seeing how the thing is intended we get beyond the formal universality of the transcendental ego to Spirit as the true, self-mediating universality which contains the particular within itself.[47] Again universality signifies whole in relation to part rather than type in relation to instance. The perceiving subject is the player of many language games. Since each of these involves living interaction with at least one other human individual, the speaking-perceiving subject stands in relation not only to the object of his perception but also to the linguistic community of which he is a part. This community is the universal consciousness which stands over against the individual consciousness. But language is the middle in which the two are united and lose their abstract opposition to one another. Just as there is no language without an individual who speaks, so no individual speaks except in a language already there, given to him and imposed on him by his society.

When one asks, against the background of the linguistic character of perception, Who is the transcendental subject?—the most accurate answer would be, Language. For the perceiver who intends the object of perception does so as the speaker of a language. This means that he is not the abstract, ahistorical transcendental ego of Kantian thought, but the concrete, historically conditioned bearer of a given language and all of the cumulative tradition built into the language.[48] This concreteness of transcendental subjectivity is neither that of the empirical ego as a discrete, isolable individual nor of a social totality somehow distinct from the individuals which make it up. For, to repeat, the essence of language is the middle where the individual is simultaneously master and slave of his linguistic tradition, where a people's linguistic self-expression is servant to and served by the speaking individual.[49]

The socialization process by which the individual becomes the bearer of this historically specific transcendental subjectivity is described by Hegel in his own inimitable way: the ego becomes thing. The formal possibility of the ego to be the "I think" by which experience is possible becomes a concrete actuality as the ego becomes determinate and in this respect thinglike. The namegiving power was free and arbitrary for Adam, but we are confronted by a relatively fixed "order of names." Transcendental subjectivity is thus the result of the historical process in which consciousness "forms itself and constitutes itself as Spirit existing for itself and withdrawing itself from nature." The ego becomes thing not by relapsing into nature, but by taking to itself a second nature which is itself the product of human activity. Hegel calls this man's unorganic nature to distinguish the socially-historically conditioned aspect from the biologically given aspect of his nature.[50] For him as for Marx, "the nature which comes to be in human history, in the activity which founds human society, is the actual nature of man."[51] For both of them this means that "the education of the five senses is a work of all previous world history."[52]

In this way theoretical consciousness is denied autonomy. Both the subject, as Spirit, and its relation to the object, have a history . Furthermore, consciousness does not preside over that history but plays a servant role. As Hegel puts it in a Jena fragment, "Through consciousness Spirit intervenes in the way the world is ruled."[53]

3E. Sense Certainty and the Phenomenology as a Whole

The truth is the whole for Hegel, and it follows that the part is the false so far as it is merely part. But the part is also true in the degree that it expresses in its own limited way the whole. It is legitimate to ask in what ways, if any, the whole of the *Phenomenology* is expressed in its first chapter. The question is a timely reminder that Hegel is not simply trying to develop a theory of perception but is engaged in the complicated task described in the Introduction and Preface.

The first such reflection of the whole in the part concerns the unity of the transcendental and historical perspectives, the epistemic and the existential. Whereas Haym and so many others following him have been able to see only a hopelessly confused mixture of two thoroughly distinct types of investigation, the preceding analysis of Sense Certainty shows exactly how the transcendental and historical perspectives arise simultaneously and how only an artificially abstract transcendentalism can avoid reflection on Spirit and its history.

No doubt it would have helped if Hegel had made these connections as explicitly in the *Phenomenology* as in the *Realphilosophie.* He seems to have ignored his own advice that the successful phenomenology cannot be a hurried one but must be willing to take its time over each moment.[54] But when the chap-

ter on Sense Certainty is read against the background of the lecture materials it is possible to see one of the ways in which
Hegel discovered "that a radical critique of knowledge is possible only as social theory."[55]

The first and central theme about Sense Certainty, however, is not the linguistic nature of perception but its mediated
character. It seems likely that the silencing of immediacy also
has a significance for the work as a whole, especially since so
much of the Preface is devoted to an attack on the appeal to
immediacy at the highest levels of religious and philosophical
knowledge. It doesn't matter whether our immediate knowledge of the Absolute is entitled intellectual intuition, as in
Fichte and Schelling, faith, as in Jacobi, or feeling, as in
Schleiermacher. In each case "beyond Kant" means "back to the
immediate itself."

We have already seen Hegel's analysis of this. Kant's destruction of traditional metaphysics is the authentic expression
of an age which "has passed beyond the substantial life that it
formerly led in the element of thought—beyond this immediacy of its faith, beyond the satisfaction and security of the certainty which consciousness possessed about its reconciliation
with the divine . . ."[56] This is not a loss Spirit can dispassionately
observe. When it becomes conscious of this loss, as it did so
forcefully in Kant, as the price for its movement beyond the
immediacy of its faith, it is not surprising that a "back to immediacy" cry should be raised. Philosophy is now asked to come
to the rescue "not by returning the chaotic consciousness to the
order of thought and the simplicity of the concept, but rather
by confounding the distinctions of thought, by suppressing the
discriminating concept, and by establishing the feeling of the
divine, granting not so much insight as edification."[57]

This "suppressing" [*unterdrücken*] is an almost psycho-
analytic concept, and Hegel's interpretation suggests that it is
indeed a defense mechanism. Similarly, the appeal to immediacy has the form of a wish-fulfilling illusion. It is not only an act
determined more by interest than by insight. It also involves
systematic self-deception.

To see this we must begin again with Kant. He not only
undermined traditional metaphysics. He also generalized the
negative character of thought. "Our age is, in especial degree,

the age of criticism, and to criticism everything must submit. Religion through its sanctity, and law-giving through its majesty, may seek to exempt themselves from it. But they then awaken just suspicion . . ."[58] Kant's everything was no hyperbole. It became all too clear that the foundations were being shaken, not only of the world beyond, but of this world as well.

Such a situation generates not only the hope for instant metaphysics but also a sudden fondness for the familiar. It is then possible for the appeal to immediacy to function as an absolutizing of the familiar in the following manner. The accomplishments of the people and tradition to which the individual belongs at first confront him as external and objectively given. But socialization is a process of "acquiring what is thus given to him [das Vorhandene], digesting his unorganic nature, and taking possession of it for himself." This inheritance includes what is here called das Aufheben of existence and was previously called "the thought of the subject matter in general." In other words, mediation has already taken place. But "existence, taken back into the substance, has merely been transposed immediately by this first negation into the element of the self. This possession which the self has acquired thus still has the same character of uncomprehended immediacy and unmoved indifference as does existence itself . . . At the same time it is thus something familiar, something that the existing Spirit has mastered so that its activity and interest no longer abide in it . . . But knowledge is directed against the way of thinking that arises in this way, against this familiarity. It is the activity of the universal self and the interest of thinking. What is familiar is not known simply because it is familiar."[59]

Ignoring Hegel's warning, natural consciousness takes what is familiar in this way to be self-evident truth. It is essentially a dogmatic form of thought, for it rests upon unexamined presuppositions. The contingency of the familiar is hidden from natural consciousness by its very familiarity, its relative immediacy to consciousness. Consequently the appeal to the immediate often ends up as an attempt to go beyond criticism by returning to dogmatism. In this absolutizing of the familiar what began as wish-fulfillment ends up as ideology.[60]

The irony of the situation is not noticed by natural consciousness. The conservative substance of the appeal to immediacy is masked by its radical appearance. Described as a return to nature it sounds like a return to the primal and archetypal, the overcoming of the disharmonies of mediated existence by return to the original harmony. But when this nature is seen to be only what has contingently become man's second nature at a given stage of historical development within a particular society, and when immediacy is seen to designate the familiar rather than the primordial, the whole project is condemned by its own criterion. It claims to capture the archetypal and absolute. It only dogmatizes the consequent and contingent.

Hegel's Science, to which the *Phenomenology* belongs, can be more than merely an alternative to this project of his contemporaries only if he can show it to be self-refuting. He cannot appeal to external criteria. Here lies the significance of the critique of Sense Certainty for the whole of the *Phenomenology*. For like Sense Certainty all the contemporary philosophies of immediacy claim to unite a rich content with the form of immediacy. When the lessons of Sense Certainty are applied to these philosophies of intellectual intuition, faith, and feeling they can be shown that their content comes from the familiar, which is only relatively immediate. A philosophy which took its own immediacy criterion seriously would be utterly silenced. It would expose itself as sheer emptiness, "the night in which all cows are black," the "monochromatic absolute painting," which drowns all the distinctions of reflection "in the emptiness of the Absolute," and whose masterpiece is "pure identity, formless whiteness."[61]

The only alternative would be to acknowledge that whatever content consciousness possesses has been historically mediated. This brings with it the anxiety that what is familiar and relied upon will turn out to be abortions that should be cast away. But it also opens the door of hope—openness to the possibility that somewhere in the historical process one will encounter something new and unfamiliar which deserves to be called the Kingdom of God.

NOTES

1. It is thus an Hegelian principle which Feuerbach directs against Hegel when he writes, "The philosopher must include in the text of philosophy what Hegel reduced to only a footnote, that in man which does not philosophize, but is rather against philosophy and opposed to abstract thought." *Vorläufige Thesen zur Reform der Philosophie,* in *Kleine Schriften* (henceforth KS), ed. Karl Löwith, Frankfurt, 1966, p. 135.

2. PhG, III-IV/10/68.

3. Rudolf Haym, *Hegel und seine Zeit,* Berlin, 1857, p. 241. The reference is to Section B of Chapter Six.

4. Theaetetus, 161b-162b, Cornford translation.

5. Hints of the Kantian story are already found in the Theaetetus at 184d ff. One of the rocks on which the knowledge-is-perception thesis founders is the discovery that in knowing we employ concepts which are not derived from sense experience.

6. PhG, VI/11-12/70.

7. PhG, XL-XLI/30-31/94-95.

8. Hegel often uses the adjectives *fest* and *fix* when describing unexamined presuppositions which are dogmatically taken to be self-evident, eternal truths. Here the fixity, *das Fixe,* which is to be replaced is the assumption that the a priori or categoreal features of experience are such self-evident, eternal structures, free of all historical conditioning. Kant is the primary, if not the only target of these remarks.

9. Jürgen Habermas, "Knowledge and Human Interests: A General Perspective," (Frankfurt inaugural address of June, 1965) translated by J. Shapiro in *Knowledge and Human Interests,* Boston, 1971, p. 312.

10. PhG, 22/79/149. cf. 43/93/166.

11. For this and the following paragraph, PhG, 23/79-80/149-50. In the *Science of Logic* the first category, Being, is defined as the indeterminate immediate, indicating that Hegel is speaking of immediacy in its absolute sense and not in the relative sense which neither precludes mediation nor determinacy. The familiar is immediate in this latter sense. See section 3E. below.

12. *Idem.* Baillie's rather free translation of part of the next sentence is right to the point. " . . . the I here does not think."

13. This provides a helpful commentary on Hegel's identification of the fear of error with the fear of truth in the Introduction.

14. For this and the following paragraph, PhG, 24-25/80-81/150-51.

15. For this and the following paragraph, PhG, 25-27/81-82/151-52.

16. See Introduction, 12/69/138. "With the intending of something individual the beyond is also intended, even when it is only next to what is limited, as in spatial intuition."

17. PhG, 37/89/160, italics mine. This same discovery leads in the *Theaetetus* to the thesis that knowledge is true belief or judgment. Kant's identification of experience with empirical knowledge also expresses the judgmental character of perception. Much of what contemporary phenomenology discusses under the rubric 'intentionality' is treated in the Wittgensteinian tradition in terms of 'seeing as'. Where the former is chosen over the latter in what follows this is for stylistic and not philosophical reasons.

18. In this respect the theory of transcendental subjectivity which emerges from the discussion of the Now and the Here is, in spite of its obvious Kantian overtones, closer to the Husserlian principle of strict correlation between intentional act and intentional object, of noesis and noema.

19. For this and the following two paragraphs, PhG, 28-29/83-84/153-54.

20. J. Loewenberg, *Hegel's Phenomenology: Dialogues on the Life of Mind*, LaSalle, 1965, p. 33.

21. I am trying here to describe an "experience" I have had on several occasions.

22. PhG, 31/85/156.

23. PhG, 26-27/82/152, my italics.

24. Ludwig Feuerbach, *Zur Kritik der Hegelschen Philosophie* (henceforth *Kritik*), KS, 99, 104-07. cf. *Grundsätze der Philosophie der Zukunft* (henceforth *Grundsätze*), #62, KS, 218.

25. *Kritik*, KS, 105.

26. *Grundsätze*, #28, KS, 187.

27. *Idem.* and *Kritik*, KS, 104-05.

28. *Grundsätze*, #28, KS, 186-87.

29. PhG, 34-35/87/158-59. cf. 25/81/151.

30. For the second of these see the next paragraph but one and ff. Agreement between Feuerbach and Hegel on these points does not establish their correctness. It is stressed only to indicate how deeply Feuerbach misunderstood Hegel, thereby rendering himself incapable of a cogent critique.

31. PhG, XL/30/94.

32. *Grundsätze*, #41 and #43, KS, 203-05; #53, KS, 214-15.

33. *Ibid.*, #17, KS, 169.

34. *Ibid.*, #50-51, KS, 212-13.

35. W. M. Urban, *Language and Reality*, London, 1939, p. 500.

36. PhG, 56-57/100-01/176-77.

37. In 1931-32 J. Hoffmeister edited and published in Felix Meiner's *Philosophische Bibliothek* series two volumes entitled *Jenenser Realphilosophie I* and *Jenenser Realphilosophie II*. The latter, which includes lecture manuscripts from Hegel's 1805-06 lectures on the philosophy of nature and Spirit was reprinted in 1967 with the simple title *Jenaer Realphilosophie* and is designated elsewhere in the present essay simply as *Realphilosophie*. The former was not reprinted, due to the discovery that Hegel gave separate lectures on the philosophy of nature and Spirit only in 1805-06 and that the first volume contains fragments mostly related to the 1803-04 lectures which included logic and metaphysics. For details see the essays by Heinz Kimmerle in *Hegel-Studien*, Volume 4. Since these materials come from the Jena period their exact date and setting is not crucial for the use to which I am putting them. I shall draw on both volumes and, for the following section only (3D.), designate them simply as I and II.

38. Karl Marx, from the 1844 Paris manuscripts, *Die Frühschriften*, ed. Landshut, Stuttgart, 1968, pp. 239-45. An English translation is available in *Karl Marx: Early Writings*, Bottomore, trans., New York, 1964, pp. 159-64.

39. II, 179, 183.

40. II, 179.

41. II, 192; I, 213.

42. II, 188.

43. II, 179-83. cf. I, 207-12. Careful study of these passages shows that Hegel is blending Aristotelian and Kantian accounts of perception.

44. I, 213-16; II, 182.

45. II, 183. cf. I, 211. A similar linking of categories and language is found in *Theaetetus*, 185-86, where Plato describes the mind as "the faculty that works through the tongue." For discussion in the PhG of the thing becoming ego, see 168/179/277 and 174-76/183-84/281-83.

46. II, 185.

47. See note 39 above.

48. This is true even if there is a deep structure which is common to all languages.

49. Cf. I, 200-02, 206.

50. I, 197. For discussion in the PhG of man's unorganic nature, see XXXIII-XXXVI/26-28/89-91 and 240-42/225-27/333-36.

51. Marx makes this statement, interestingly enough, at the conclusion of the spectacular and often quoted passage in which he discusses the implications for *sense perception* of the abolition of private property. *Die Frühschriften,* pp. 239-45; Bottomore, pp. 159-64. He distinguishes not only human from non-human eyes, but also emancipated human eyes from not yet emancipated ones.

52. *Die Frühschriften,* p. 242; Bottomore, p. 161.

53. Quoted in Schlomo Avineri, *Hegel's Theory of the Modern State,* Cambridge, 1972, p. 64.

54. PhG, XXXV/27/90-91. cf. Kant, *Critique of Pure Reason,* A xviii-xix. "If the size of a volume be measured not by the number of pages but by the time required for mastering it, it can be said of many a book, that it would be much shorter if it were not so short."

55. Habermas, *op. cit.,* p. VII. See Ch. 2, n. 55.

56. PhG, VIII/13/71-72. cf. Ch. 2, n. 5.

57. PhG, IX/13/72.

58. *Critique of Pure Reason,* note to A xi.

59. PhG, XXXIV-XXXVI/27-28/90-92. cf. n. 6 above. Perhaps Hegel is thinking of Augustine's comment on time. "What, then, is time? I know well enough what it is, provided that nobody asks me; but if I am asked what it is and try to explain, I am baffled." *Confessions,* XI, 14, Pine-Coffin translation. The discussion of scepticism in 1B. above and of surprise in 1C. are both pertinent to Hegel's attitude toward the familiar.

60. Hegel returns to this theme in its political overtones in the Preface to the *Philosophy of Right,* where he writes that truly rational thought "does not remain stationary at the given, whether the given be upheld by the external positive authority of the state or the agreement of mankind, or by the authority of inward feeling and emotion and by the 'witness of the spirit' which directly concurs with it . . . The unsophisticated heart takes the simple line of adhering with trustful conviction to what is publicly accepted as true [*die öffentlich bekannte Wahrheit*] . . ."

61. PhG, XIX/19/79 and LXII/43/110/ cf. 74/112/192 on absolute darkness and pure light. These passages form a helpful commentary on the treatment of Being and Nothing in the Logic.

CHAPTER FOUR: The Knowledge of Nature:

B) Natural Science

4A. Preliminary Sketch of Hegel's Phenomenological Philosophy of Science

The movement of the first two chapters of the *Phenomenology* is not so much from Sense Certainty to Perception as it is the discovery that consciousness is always inescapably at the level of Perception. Sense Certainty is an unreal abstraction. Our knowledge of the external world does not begin in the rarefied atmosphere of pure sensation but in the everyday world of things and their properties.

But if all our knowledge begins in the familiar world of Perception, it does not follow that our knowledge always stays at home. "Spirit exists only as transcending that which it immediately is, stepping back from it;" and since its life is "not the life that shrinks from death and keeps itself undefiled by devastation, but the life which endures and preserves itself through death" and "gains its truth only by finding itself in absolute dismemberment,"[1] everyday life is not immune to the wanderlust which calls it to find new life through self-destruction. It is in the natural sciences that our knowledge of the external world finds its most impressive new form of life. After the previous chapter we are eager to move on from the theoretical to the practical and from the transcendental to the historical. But Hegel will linger long enough to examine this new form of theoretical consciousness. Since its description will inevitably involve transcendental reflection, the question will become, How is science possible?

The question has a Kantian ring, but Hegel's understanding of Understanding differs in two important ways from Kant's. The first is expressed in Dilthey's description of Wilhelm Scherer: "He was a modern man, and the world of our ancestors was no longer the *home* of his spirit and his heart but his historical *object*."[2] Though it is the *Geisteswissenschaften* which are here in question, the issue is their enthrallment with the methodology of the natural sciences, especially as formulated by Mill. For it was the natural sciences which first achieved the methodological dismemberment of the everyday world by which nature ceased to be man's home and became his object.

The story is told brilliantly by Descartes.[3] Probably no more dramatic reminder of the gulf between the world of common sense and nature as conceived by modern science is to be found than his analysis of the piece of wax in the Second Meditation. Kant's tribute to the scientific revolution retains the Cartesian emphasis on method in one of its most elegant expressions. The scientific revolutionaries "learned that reason has insight only into that which it produces after a plan of its own, and that it must not allow itself to be kept, as it were, in nature's leading-strings, but must itself show the way . . . constraining nature to give answer to questions of reason's own determining."[4]

Implicit in this formulation is Dilthey's contrast between nature as home and as object. But Kant tended to equate the question—How is science possible?—with the question—How is experience possible? The result was to narrow the concept of experience, and, perhaps even more important, to blur the difference between the life-world and science. Correspondingly, when in the Jena Logic (1804-05) Hegel treats essentially the same materials as belong to Perception and Understanding in the *Phenomenology* as a discussion of the Kantian categories of relation (substance, cause, reciprocity), the same merging of science and everyday perception occurs.

But in the *Phenomenology* the fuller Cartesian perspective is restored. The difference between Perception and Understanding is not that the former operates with the category of substance while the latter thinks in terms of cause and reciprocity. The two are rather entirely different forms of consciousness. Taking his cue from Descartes, Hegel makes the point with considerable rhetorical flourish. Substituting a cube of salt for the piece of wax, he distinguishes the sensible world of ordinary perception from what he calls the supersensible world of the natural sciences. The sensible salt is the familiar salt which we sprinkle on our food and on icy sidewalks. The supersensible salt is, most simply, NaCl, an object which does not directly appear to sense perception. Dilthey's contrast between home and object expresses Hegel's perspective most succinctly.[5]

Having stressed the mediated character of Perception over against the claims of Sense Certainty, Hegel is now stressing the immediate character of Perception in contrast to the mediated and indirect relation of Understanding to its object. We have here a splendid example of the relativity of immediacy and mediation in Hegel's usage. In this contrast Hegel's affirmation of the primacy of Perception is enriched. It becomes clear that Perception is not only the inescapable and irreducible starting point for natural consciousness, but also that when it leaves this home for the new world of Understanding it does not really leave the latter behind. For its presence to the supersensible world of scientific explanations is always mediated through its immediate presence in the world of everyday Perception.[6]

There is a second important difference between the Kantian and Hegelian ways of asking, How is science possible? This one is expressed in Gadamer's comment that "for Helmholtz the methodical character of the natural sciences required neither an historical derivation nor an epistemological restriction."[7] For Hegel (as for Husserl, Gadamer, and Whitehead after him) the triumph of method which gave birth to the scientific revolution was doubly finite, for it was both an historical accomplishment and an epistemological restriction. This brings to focus a question which lies at the heart of Hegel's philosophy of science, Is method the way to truth? or does one pay too high a price for its services?

It is just by keeping the gap between science and our everyday perspectives that this question is not lost sight of. It is not possible to ask how science is possible without beginning on the road to transcendental philosophy. But it is possible to leave this road quite quickly. Already in Kant's "Appendix to the Transcendental Dialectic" this transformation of the transcendental question into the methodological question—How does one go about doing science?—begins to take place. Neo-Kantianism and positivism are but the heirs of this tendency in Kant.

When, however, science is recognized as a radical demolition of and withdrawal from natural consciousness' home in its pre-scientific sensible world, the question of the possibility of science cannot be reduced to the how-to-do-it question of a methodologically oriented philosophy of science. The method

question becomes less important than the motive question, and
instead of asking how to do science we ask how it comes about
that science occurs. For to see science as both an historical accomplishment and an epistemological restriction is to see it as
praxis, as a special form of human behavior. This raises questions about the purpose and results of this activity in relation to
other human behavior. What is it that inspires consciousness to
claim its inheritance and set out from its father's house seeking
fame and fortune in a far country? Will consciousness turn out
to be a prodigal son indeed, forced to return from the husks of
the supersensible to the father's house once scornfully abandoned?[8]

Here as in the analysis of Sense Certainty transcendental
philosophy is led beyond itself and the boundary between the
theoretical and the practical is blurred. "We", at least, are to see
that the transcendental perspective in the Kantian sense is an
unstable one, either relapsing into methodology, thereby reducing knowledge to know-how, or transcending itself by reflecting on the historical derivation and epistemological restriction involved in the human activity called science. As the question about the possibility of science becomes the question—Why
and with what results does consciousness abandon nature as its
home in order to make nature its object?—the whole network
of issues is brought into play which in the previous chapter
were summarized by the question—Who is the transcendental
subject? In this way Hegel seeks to discredit, not science, but
those philosophical perspectives which are overawed by science
and have come to worship it.

We have now to see that this preliminary sketch actually
describes what is found in Hegel's text, briefly in the transition
from Perception to Understanding, then in the analysis of
Understanding (Hegel's Chapter Three) and Observing Reason (Chapter Five-A). That it is scientific consciousness which is
described in Chapter Three is clear from the detailed account
of the postulation of forces and the search for laws, in spite of
Hegel's allusions to similarities between scientific consciousness
and other forms, particularly Platonic and religious, and in
spite of the fact that in other writings Hegel often uses the term
Understanding in distinction from Reason to characterize a
genus of thought which has science as only one of its species.

The inclusion of Chapter Five-A at this point is more problematic. Apart from the Kantian tradition which sharply distinguishes Understanding from Reason, it at first appears as if any joint treatment of Understanding and Observing Reason involves excessive violence to Hegel's own format, in which the two are separated by all of Chapter Four on Self-Consciousness. In the process the realistic attitude of Understanding has been replaced by the idealism of Reason. It is nevertheless neither desirable nor necessary to separate the two. It is undesirable because so much of the latter is a repetition of the former, or rather, the application of the same insights to new illustrative material. This is especially clear in relation to the search for laws of nature, which characterizes both Understanding and Observing Reason. It is unnecessary because the theoretical differences between realistic Understanding and idealistic Reason actually play no significant role in the analysis of science. Observing Reason is repeatedly described as merely the instinct of Reason, a description equally appropriate to Understanding.[9]

4B. The Supersensible Character of Scientific Thought

Since he is seeking to lead natural consciousness to understand its own self-transcending tendencies, Hegel takes the bold step of reformulating the question—How is science possible?—by asking instead—Why is science necessary? Is it a mere accident that Perception becomes Understanding? Or is there something about the former that somehow generates the latter? Most of the chapter on Perception is devoted to showing how the answer to this last question must be affirmative.

Hegel directs our attention to a cube of salt, just as Descartes directed it to a piece of wax. Both these familiar objects are used to illustrate the movement of consciousness to the world of scientific thought. It is entirely typical of Hegel that while Descartes points out the changeability of the wax in our *sensory* experience of it, he focuses on the volatility of our attempts to *think* the salt. It is not the changing appearance of the salt from one moment to the next but its contradictory character at any given moment which drives consciousness beyond Perception.[10]

The cube of salt is the determinate-indeterminate object which emerged in the discussion of Sense Certainty. As intended in its full determinateness it is an entirely unique particular. As actually present to consciousness, however, it is only partially determined in a process of determination which is never completed. In precisely these two aspects it is the thing and its properties, the former as intended, the latter as actually intuited. There seems to be no contradiction here, for the determinacy and indeterminacy of the object are parcelled out to different aspects, namely to the in-so-far-as-intended and the in-so-far-as-intuited. It is in fact the function of the category, thing-and-properties, to avoid contradiction by distinguishing respects in this way.

This distinguishing of respects is crucial. For contradiction arises when conflicting predictions can be made of the same subject matter at the same time and in the same respect, and the salt is clearly at the same time *qua* thing something one and simple and *qua* properties something manifold and diverse.[11] If it should turn out that there is a single respect in virtue of which the object both is a thing and has its properties, Perception would be in trouble. Thinghood and property having would be revealed as not genuinely different aspects of the object, but simply the artificial attempt of natural consciousness to hide the contradiction between the thing's oneness and its manyness, its determinacy and its indeterminacy. This would be fatal to Perception, whose criterion Hegel discovers to be self-sameness or self-consistency [*Sichselbstgleichheit*], by which he means to say simply that for common sense a thing is what it is and not another thing.[12]

Hegel finds that there is indeed a single respect by means of which the perceptual object is a thing and has its properties. The very determinacy which distinguishes Perception from Sense Certainty is now its Achilles' heel. For the object is the one thing it is just in so far as it is determinate, while it is also the many properties it "has" just in so far as it is determinate. "Healthy common sense" is here betrayed by the very "in so far" that it uses to preserve the integrity of its objects. Since it is in respect to its determinateness that the object is a thing and has properties, is one and many, Hegel finds a genuine contradiction. "The object is rather *in one and the same respect* the opposite of itself: for itself in so far as it is for another, and for another in so far as it is for itself."[13]

Since consciousness "experiences"[14] this contradiction between its criterion and its actual knowledge, though without knowing exactly what is happening, it develops itself into another form of consciousness. Perception is distinguished from Sense Certainty by the universality of its object, i.e., by its mediated character in a variety of whole-part contexts.[15] "But this universal, since it is derived from sense, is essentially conditioned by it, and hence is, in general, not a genuine self-identical [*sich selbstgleich*] universality, but one affected with opposition." Consciousness therefore seeks for the "unconditioned absolute universality" in opposition to this "merely sensible universality."[16]

Typically for Hegel the adequate statement of the problem practically provides its own solution. The trouble with the things of Perception is that they can neither be nor be understood apart from their relation to other things. They are in this sense both mediated and conditioned. Their full comprehension can only come through grasping the whole of which they are a part. This whole is the unconditioned universal which can both be and be understood in terms of itself. It is mediated and therefore both real and determinate, but it is self-mediated and therefore intelligible in itself. It is Spinoza's substance, or what Kant calls the concept of nature in general.[17] It is clearly an object of thought, for this sort of totality is not given in sense experience.

This distinction between conditioned, sensible universality and unconditioned universality, free from the limits of sense, is clearly a categoreal issue. It involves the basic conceptual framework within which the object of consciousness is determined. But the transition is not simply from the category of substance to those of cause and reciprocity, as the parallel sections in the Jena Logic would suggest.[18] Still less is the difference between empirical concepts and a priori categories, for it is already clear that 'thing-and-properties' is no less categoreal than such concepts as force and law. The transition from the sensible to the supersensible world is one from the categoreal framework appropriate to everyday perceptual experience to a system of categories which systematically reinterprets that experience. Descartes' wax becomes matter in motion, Hegel's salt NaCl.

Hegel's task is now to describe two different but closely related modes in which Understanding ascends to its supersensible world, force postulating science and law formulating science. The former corresponds roughly to Aristotelian science, the latter to Galilean-Newtonian science. The boundary between them is not sharp, since the concept of force did not die out quickly but continued to play an important role even for Newton.

When consciousness begins to think in terms of forces and their expression (whether these be Aristotelian entelechies or gravitational and magnetic forces) instead of in terms of things and their properties, "the unconditioned universal emerges as the unobjective or inner aspect of things."[19] Since it is the universal aspect of things in Hegel's own distinctive sense which is their truth or essence, the truth of things is no longer their immediate, familiar presence to everyday perception, but something related to this presence as inner reality to outer experience. Remember Descartes' wax. Baillie is quite justified here in introducing "unperceived" as a gloss on "inner".

Hegel stresses the indirect and non-perceptual relation of consciousness to what is now its object. "This true being of things has here the characteristic of not existing immediately for consciousness; rather consciousness has a mediated relation to the inner and as Understanding looks through this middle, the play of forces, into the true background of things. The middle [die Mitte] which unites the two extremes, Understanding and the inner of things, is the developed being of force, which Understanding itself now takes to be that which disappears. It is therefore called appearance [Erscheinung] . . . The being of the object is mediated for consciousness through the movement of appearance, in which the world of Perception and sensible objects in general have only the negative significance that consciousness thus reflects itself out of the sensible into itself as the true, but as consciousness makes this truth into an objective inner realm . . . an extreme over against it . . . It is only in this inner realm of truth, as the absolute universal . . . that a supersensible world now opens up as the true world above the sensible world of appearance, the permanent beyond [das *bleibende Jenseits*] above the disappearing present [*das verschwindende Diesseits*], an in itself which is the first and therefore incomplete appearance of Reason."[20]

It is no different when Understanding seeks to discover laws of nature. Such a law is the "changeless image of changing appearance. The supersensible world is in this way a peaceful kingdom of laws, no doubt beyond the world of Perception, for this exhibits the law only through constant change, but likewise present in it and its immediate unmoving image."[21] This definition of laws as the unchanging or unmoving image of the temporal flux is a deliberate inversion of Plato's definition of time as the moving image of eternity. For Hegel as for the neo-Kantian, the law formulating scientist is a kind of Platonist.

The analysis of the quest for laws in Chapter Five repeats these motifs with special emphasis on the link between scientific method and the abandonment of the everyday life-world. Scientific consciousness is anything but a passive receptacle to whom experience happens. "Here it settles itself the observations to be made and the experience to be had." Nature must answer questions of Reason's own determining. Science thus consciously takes the perceptual world as *aufgehoben*. It claims to know the truth about the "things" of that world, bits of wax and salt, for example. In doing so "it transforms their sensibility into concepts, i.e., precisely into the kind of being as thought [*gedachtes Sein*] and asserts in fact that things have truth only as concepts." For this reason the perception of a penknife lying beside a snuffbox does not count as a scientific observation, nor do the tradesman and housewife express a law of nature when they complain that it always rains at the fair and on washday.[22]

What these forms of everyday knowledge lack is the experimental procedure by which reason "purifies the law and its moments and makes them concepts. It puts the law to the test of experiment. As the law first appears, it presents itself impurely, enveloped in particular, sensible being, and the concept which constitutes its nature is submerged in empirical subject matter." In experiment "the law seems only to be plunged still deeper into sensible being, but instead it is the sensible aspect which is lost in the experiment . . . As the truth of this experimenting consciousness we see that pure law which is freed from sensible being. We see it as a concept, which while present in sense, op-

erates there independently and unrestrained, while sunk in
sense is free from it and is simple concept."[23] This purification
of law takes place primarily as the purification of its moments,
i.e., by the development of such concepts as positive and negative electricity, acid and base. The object is to be understood not
in terms of the features it immediately offers to everyday perception, but in terms of precisely defined concepts developed
for the purpose of making nature answer questions of Reason's
own determining. In this way scientific method replaces the
sensible with the supersensible object.[24]

4C. The Tautological Character of Scientific
Explanation

In spite of its supersensible character science is at least as
worldly as the original Prodigal Son. For its interest in the
supersensible world is nothing but the desire to make sense of
the sensible world, or, as it is often put, to explain it.[25] The examination of science's claim to be paradigmatic knowledge now
takes the form of testing its explanatory power. As in the Jena
Logic, the thesis which emerges is that scientific explanations
are tautologies.[26]

A sense of the explanatory emptiness of Aristotelian science contributed significantly to the rise of modern science in
the sixteenth and seventeenth centuries. The developing
critique of its substantial forms as occult causes was effectively
summed up by Molière's witticism about opium causing sleep
by means of its dormitive virtue. This translates into the rather
unilluminating assertion that opium causes sleep by means of
its capacity to cause sleep.

That Hegel's critique of force is directed against Aristotelian science is particularly clear in the Jena Logic where the link
between the category 'force-and-its-expression' and the category 'actuality-potentiality' is explicit. In that context he even
gives his own version of Molière. "That the stone falls to the
ground, i.e., posits itself as one with the ground, is not expressed by scientific explanation by saying that it posits itself as
one with the ground because it posits itself as one with it, but
rather by saying that a force in the stone posits it as one, namely

the force which posits it as one with the ground." Nor does explanation describe a magnet by saying "that the magnet orients itself to north and south because it orients itself that way, attracts iron filings because it attracts them, and repels its like poles because it repels them; rather because in the substance which shows itself in this way there is something else than itself, namely a magnetic force, and this magnetic force has the power to orient the substance in this way, to attract such filings to it and to repel like poles."[27] In this way the tautology is hidden.

Modern science did not immediately abandon the concept of force, however. Even Newton, the prime target of Chapter Three, was not entirely of one mind about the matter. At times he speaks of the "deduction" of forces, while at other times his concern is for descriptive laws, accompanied by an agnosticism about any causal forces behind the regularities described. Compare the following:

1a) By the propositions mathematically demonstrated in the first book, we then derive from the celestial phenomena the forces of gravity with which bodies tend to the sun and the several planets.

1b) But hitherto I have been unable to discover the cause of those properties of gravity from phenomena, and I frame no hypotheses.

2a) By this way of analysis we may proceed from compounds to ingredients and from motions to the forces producing them; and in general, from effects to causes.

2b) To tell that every species of things is endowed with an occult specific quality by which it acts and produces manifest effects is to tell us nothing. But to derive two or three general principles of motion from phenomena, and afterwards to tell us how the properties and actions of all corporeal things follow from those manifest principles, would be a great step in philosophy, though the causes of those principles were not yet discovered.[28]

These passages express a movement of thought which Hegel takes up in the *Phenomenology*, an ambivalence in modern science. On the one hand squeamishness about occult causes leads from force to law as the principle scientific category. On the other hand the distinction between the expression of force appearing as effect and force proper as hidden inner cause is not abandoned. Instead it is simply maintained that "the inner being of things cannot be known." To be sure, Hegel replies, there can be no knowledge of the inner, so conceived, "but not because reason is too shortsighted or limited . . . but because of the nature of the matter itself, namely that in the void there is nothing known, or to put it from the other side, because the inner is determined precisely as that which lies beyond consciousness."[29] In other words, the unknowability of the inner realm is as tautological as the previous claim to explanation by reference to it. Having defined the inner as unknowable, Understanding wisely frames no hypotheses and confesses that the substance of things is "something I know not what."

That which explains nothing and is itself unknowable seems to be more than useless. But rather than seeking to reduce the concept of force to absurdity, a la Molière, Hegel seeks to understand it.[30] The problem is that the distinction of force proper from its expression "exists only in thought" so that "the truth of force thus remains only the thought of force." In this way "consciousness has reflected itself out of the world of Perception and sensible objects and into itself as the true . . ." But consciousness doesn't realize this and so "it again makes this truth an objective inner reality . . ."[31]

Hegel's point is fairly simple. Consciousness begins with substances externally related to each other, the things of Perception. In seeking to think these things it develops a concept, force, in which the processes of the perceptual world are conceived in terms of a distinction between two internally related moments, force proper and its expression. But consciousness forgets that its thinking has not left the perceptual world unchanged, and it takes its own conceptual distinction of internally related elements for a distinction of externally related substances. It then treats force proper as a cause and its expression as an effect. At first this results in pseudo-explanation; then, as the explanatory claim is withdrawn, it results in the idea of an unknowable inner world hidden behind the appearances which somehow both conceal and reveal it. Lacking self-consciousness, Understanding is snared by what Whitehead calls the fallacy of misplaced concreteness. That is to say, when it finds certain conceptual devices useful for some purpose it immediately and without further ado takes these for the definitive expression of the real. While it is proud of its radical transformation of the perceptual world, it continues to treat its newly developed concepts as if they belonged to that long since abandoned sensible world. It is all too half-hearted about leaving home.

There is nothing very original in this critique of Aristotelian science and its residual presence in Newtonian science. Where Hegel's discussion of science is untimely, relative to "the present standpoint of Spirit," is in the discovery that law formulating science as such is plagued by the same problems as force postulating science. Understanding claims that in uncovering the laws of nature it achieves a genuine, non-tautological form of explanation. Hegel finds this to be a delusion just because "Understanding has not yet transcended the process of framing laws."[32]

Rather than impose an external criterion on science, Hegel compares the actual laws of nature it puts forth with the "pure concept of law" (which he curiously wants to identify with Newton's universal law of gravitation) and finds a contradiction. Science does not conform to its own criterion, and "the concept of law is turned against the law itself." The variables related in the law are to be, in Hegel's language, "mutually indifferent and inherently real entities." But at the same time "the pure concept of law . . . must, to get its true significance, be so apprehended that in it as something absolutely simple, the variables [*Unterschiede*] which are present in the law as such return again themselves into the inner as simple unity. This unity is the inner necessity of the law."[33] Had Hegel mentioned Hume here as he does in a similar passage in the Jena Logic, it would have been easier to see that this is his way of posing the problem of finding any necessary connection between independently specifiable variables.

If the two components of the concept of law, independent specifiability and necessary connection, are as incompatible as they seem to be, science can only vacillate between them. Its laws will either possess necessity without independence or independence without necessity. But it will no more be able to combine both in the same law than Sense Certainty was able to combine genuine immediacy with determinacy. This is what Hegel finds, though his formula is once again less than Humean in its lucidity. "Either the universal, force, is indifferent to the division into elements which is found in the law, or the variables, the elements of the law are indifferent toward each other."[34]

Fortunately there are examples. Electricity is used to illustrate the first case, where the force in question is said to be indifferent to the analysis used in formulating laws. Since it represents a series of phenomena to be caught in a nomological network, it may be spoken of as a force distinct from the laws which describe it. It is analyzed into positive and negative electricity, and the laws about the relation of these two elements seem to express a necessary connection. But such necessity is "an empty word," for there is no necessity that electricity should be analyzed in this way. To reply that this is the way electricity is defined is to let the cat out of the bag. It is to confess that necessity has been purchased at the cost of independent specifiability. Within the context of a certain analysis positive and negative electricity are necessarily related to one another in various ways, but this necessity is a function of the theory, not of anything in nature. For there is no reason apparent to Hegel why electricity should be conceptualized in this way.[35]

In the second case the elements into which a phenomenon naturally divides are seen as indifferent to one another. The division of motion, for example, into spatial and temporal determinations, distance and velocity, belongs to the subject matter in a way in which positive and negative do not belong to electricity. But these elements are indifferent to one another and resist the attempt to discover any necessary connection between them. This is not to deny that Understanding can observe regularities in nature. It is only the reminder that observed regularity is one thing, necessary connection quite another. Hegel's point is the same as Hume's, even if the style is not.

Laws of nature, then, pose this dilemma: either they achieve the necessity their concept calls for, only to discover that it is a definitional necessity and "it is thus only its own necessity to which Understanding gives expression," or they fail to find that necessity and are reduced to summarizing empirical data. "While explanation makes as if it would say something different from what is already said, it really says nothing at all, but merely repeats the same thing over again."³⁶ When a law-like statement must be interpreted as merely a summary of the data on which it is asserted, it loses the nomological, as opposed to the accidental universality, which is required of a law of nature. It can no longer support subjunctive conditionals. To do so and thus to conform to the idea of a law of nature some sort of necessity would have to be regained. But the only available necessity is tautological.

The materials with which Hegel illustrates this dilemma in Chapter Five are obscure for historical reasons, but not hopelessly so. The horn of the dilemma on which only contingency and indifference are to be found is illustrated at great length in the discussion of Physiognomy and Phrenology. They represent extreme cases of Observation coming upon a genuinely indifferent subject matter and becoming ludicrous in the attempt to extract necessity from it.

On the other hand, when Observation turns to an organic subject matter or to the relation of individual human personality to its environment, it is dealing with a subject matter where genuinely internal relations are present. But here where the parts have their meaning only within the process of the whole and are not thus indifferent to one another, "the law wants to grasp and express the opposed elements as independent variables [*ruhende Seiten*] and to give them in their independence the determinacy which is their relation to one another . . . [The moments] lose their organic significance in being kept apart in this way. And at the bottom of the idea of law lies just this, that each of its two aspects should have a subsistence on its own account indifferent to the other."³⁷ For Hegel this means simply that we murder to explain, that Observation can apply its method to a living subject matter only by first turning it into a cadaver. For Observation it means that all hope of finding non-tautological necessity is lost. It is in this context that Hegel calls special attention to the quantifying dimension of scientific method.

One example from this domain of the organic is of particular interest. It concerns the analysis of organisms into three systems: sensibility, irritability, and reproduction. Irritability, the strange looking member of the trio, is simply the power of an organism to respond to stimuli. Structurally it refers to the muscular system, while functionally it is the complement of sensibility, the capacity to receive stimuli. When observation seeks to formulate laws about the relation of these functions it may seek to quantify the qualitatively complementary elements of sensibility and irritability and come up with a neat looking inverse proportion, "Sensibility and irritability stand in inverse quantitative relations." Hegel's opinion of this is expressed in the parallel he suggests, "The size of a hole increases the more we decrease what it is filled with." The tautological character of these affirmations lies in the fact that the two elements are so related conceptually in each case that "the one has any significance at all only in so far as the other is present." Like north and south poles of a magnet, positive and negative electricity, acid and base, one element is defined by its relation to the other. Hence the tautological character of the necessity discovered.[38]

It is not impossible, of course, to define the organic functions independently of one another. This would be necessary for finding a non-tautological law. But at the same time all hope of finding necessity is lost. The functions then become indifferent to one another and "defy the attempt to reduce them to law. For their character as sensible being consists in existing in complete indifference to one another . . . in exhibiting nature's irrational way of playing up and down the scale of contingent quantity . . ."

Here again is the dilemma of contingency and tautological necessity. But this time the two horns are represented by one and the same subject matter, not by different fields of scientific endeavor. Here Observation vacillates in its treatment of a single phenomenon between finding its variables contingently related and finding them necessarily related, though the latter is possible, in Carnapian language, only because the proper meaning postulates have been added to the system.

The witticisms which Hegel sprinkles throughout his analysis of science will suggest to some that in this area he was reduced to ridiculing what he could not understand. But the problems he pinpoints have merited serious discussion in our own century quite outside Hegelian circles. What he calls the supersensible character of scientific thought lies at the heart of the problematic of Whitehead's *Science and the Modern World* as well as Husserl's *Crisis*. At the same time contemporary philosophy of science concerns itself with what he calls the tautological character of scientific explanation. We take it to be a law of nature that copper is a good electrical conductor, that if equal weights are placed at the extremities of a homogeneous rigid bar suspended in the middle the lever is in equilibrium, and that a body moving without the influence of external forces maintains a constant velocity. But while these laws were at first asserted on experimental grounds and were presumably falsifiable by counter evidence, they now most often function as logically necessary truths, expressing in whole or in part the definitions of copper, equal weights, and freely moving bodies.[39] Similarly, when the conservation of energy was challenged by beta-ray decay, instead of taking the law to be refuted, it was "saved" by positing the neutrino. When this sort of thing happens, "we are along the road to transforming the meaning of some of the terms employed in the premise, so that its empirical content is gradually absorbed into the meaning of those terms."[40]

Hegel's critique of the quest for Laws of nature can be summarized as follows:

1) Science is not able to find the necessity it seeks for its laws, for the concept of law requires that the related elements be independently specifiable whereas necessity resides in internal relations. Where science comes upon internal relations, it first destroys them by its mathematical analysis, and then bemoans the problem of natural necessity.

2) What necessity science does profess is only apparent or tautological. It comes from identifying nature with its own conceptual framework, where all necessity is definitional.

3) These difficulties and the consequent vacillation between contingency and tautology result from science's attempt to force nature to answer its own questions, to impose its own purposes on the world.

This last way of putting it indicates that the time has come to move on from the pre-transcendental analysis of the object of science, nature as the interplay of forces and the realm of lawful processes, to consideration of the transcendental and post-transcendental insights which have come to light "for us."[41]

4D. The Transcendental Source of Science's Supersensible Tautologies

We have already noted the naive objectivism of Perception. Its object and the process of perceiving it stand in strictest correlation. "The object is in its essential nature the same as the process." But healthy common sense, instead of being aware of the categories by which its own activity is carried out and thereby coming to master them, is unconscious of them and is thus tossed about as their plaything and prey.[42]

Understanding resembles its common sense counterpart in this respect. "We" who watch its object emerge out of the world of Perception see that it "has arisen through the movement of consciousness in such a way that consciousness is implicated in its development, and the reflection on both sides is the same, i.e., there is only one reflection. Intentional act and intentional object are inseparable. The given is what is taken. Understanding, however, is still consciousness, focused on its object, not self-consciousness, aware of itself. Its transcendental subjectivity is hidden from it and "it does not know itself in that reflected object," i.e., in the object developed by the systematic reinterpretation of the perceptual world.[43] This recurring assertion from Chapters Three and Five-A that science doesn't know itself in its object or that it finds itself there but doesn't recognize itself means simply that Understanding is a systematically false consciousness. Not recognizing its own creative activity in its own products, it becomes enslaved to them as if they were independently and eternally given.[44]

This objectivism is not merely the absence of a certain self-awareness. It involves a mistaken self-image on the part of Understanding. In taking its object [*Gegenstand*] to be something objective [*gegenständlich*] it not only views the object as simply given. It views itself as having no role in the result of the knowing process. It merely looks on and mirrors [*ihr nur zusieht und sie rein auffasst*].[45] There is no quarrel here between Hegel and the Understanding about the criterion to be invoked. Hegel, too, knows that "scientific knowledge, however, demands precisely that we surrender to the life of the object or, and this is the same, that we confront and express its inner necessity." The only question is whether science adheres to this criterion sufficiently to be genuinely scientific, or whether it is the kind of knowing which "instead of abiding in the subject matter and forgetting itself in it . . . always reaches out for something else and really remains preoccupied with itself instead of sticking to and devoting itself to the subject matter." Hegel finds it to be the latter, the kind of formal understanding which "instead of entering into the immanent content of the matter always looks over the whole and stands above the individual existence of which it speaks, i.e., it simply overlooks it."[46]

At issue here is the significance of scientific method. Science claims to be objective in an honorific sense because it has a method which frees its knowledge from private and collective prejudice and provides it with intersubjective verifiability. Hegel, on the contrary, finds that it is precisely science's method which precludes its giving itself in a listening way to its subject matter and results in its imposing itself on its subject matter. Its questions and its categories determine the way in which the world can be given to Understanding. It is not nature who offers herself as a network of necessary connections between independent variables. It is scientific method which requires that she appear that way. Being unaware of all this, Understanding is objective in a pejorative sense. The phenomenological task is to assist natural consciousness in this stage of its development by bringing to light the transcendental subjectivity without which scientific explanation is impossible.

It is not that Understanding is entirely unreflective. But its philosophy of science, like Hume and unlike Kant, recognizes problems like that of necessary connection without winning its way through to an explicit and systematic transcendental self-consciousness. Like the early Wittgenstein it recognizes the difficulty of developing a language which is isomorphic with reality, but unlike the late Wittgenstein it doesn't see that language constitutes the world and is no mere attempt to mirror it. Understanding must first be brought to the Kantian or transcendental perspective and then to the late Wittgensteinian or post-transcendental perspective. In this latter perspective language is recognized as a form of life, theory as a form of praxis. There it is possible to see science as both an historical accomplishment and an epistemological limit, and, in seeing both together, to transcend the positivistic tendencies of Kantian transcendentalism.

Hegel returns to the problem of necessity in laws of nature. The spatial and temporal variables dealt with there, distance, velocity, etc., are indifferent to one another and sustain no necessary relation. But in the law they are *begeistet*, and assume, like positive and negative electricity, a necessary relation. In the process of explanation Understanding transcends the independence of the variables and posits them in necessary relation. But the movement and necessity here is that of Understanding. This is why "there is so much satisfaction in explanation, because consciousness, being there, so to speak, in conversation with itself, enjoys only itself. No doubt it seems to be occupied with something else, but in fact *it fools around only with itself.*"[47] The moments of the law may be abstractions in the sense of being products of the activity by which Understanding deliberately withdraws from the perceptual world. "By its way of looking at the matter, Observation transforms the opposition into one which conforms and is *adapted to its own point of view.*"[48]

With this insight "we see that in the inner world over against appearance Understanding experiences nothing other than appearance itself," but in such a way that at the same time it "in fact only experiences itself. Raised above Perception, consciousness reveals itself united and bound up with the supersensible world through the mediating agency of the world of appearance, through which it gazes into the background. The two extremes, the pure inner world and the inner world which looks into this first inner are now merged together . . . In this way the curtain of appearance no longer hides the inner world, which, instead, is present to the gaze of the other inner world . . . It is manifest that behind the so-called curtain which is to hide the inner world there is nothing to be seen unless we ourselves go behind it, as much in order that we may thereby see as that there may be something behind there which can be seen."[49]

Hegel is entitled to speak of "inner" worlds here for one very simple reason: he is talking about what is not given in the "outer" world of Perception where consciousness first makes its home. It is only by transcending this patent and palpable world of outward sensory awareness that consciousness discovers the two inner worlds which here unite. The first is the world of theoretical entities and laws postulated by science. The second is the world of scientific intelligence whose theorizing brings the first to light. To say that these two "are now merged together" and that in experiencing the first inner world consciousness "in fact only experiences itself," i.e., the second inner world, is to say that the two belong inextricably together. Hegel's way of putting it suggests a fictionalist or conventionalist account of scientific theory. But his point is not so much to settle the ontological status of science's objects as to call epistemological attention to the importance of science's activity. The totality of nature as the object of scientific theory turns out not to be the unconditioned universal after all, for in its presence to consciousness it is thoroughly conditioned by consciousness itself. The totality which could claim to be a genuinely unconditioned universal will have to include not only the object of consciousness but consciousness as well, in all the modes of its active encounter with its object. It follows that the knowledge of nature cannot be Absolute Knowledge, for it does not include the conditions of its own possibility.

This is the result of the whole dialogue with Sense Certainty, Perception, and Understanding, a movement from Consciousness to Self-Consciousness. Its full meaning has yet to be disclosed, for it is only a transcendental perspective which has here been achieved, and the post-transcendental attitude for which Hegel has been preparing us has not yet emerged. We have reached a half-way house between the simple and sophisticated forms of objectivist consciousness with which we began and the standpoint of Spirit to which Hegel wants to lead us.

The Idealism whose description prefaces Chapter Five is a permanent resident of this half-way house. It has achieved transcendental self-consciousness and knows that the "I am I" or the transcendental unity of apperception is the foundation of all knowledge. But having forgotten the path by which this insight has been achieved and the evidence which could support its claim, it not only cannot go further but comes on the scene as a dogmatic and unintelligible assurance.[50]

An even more serious consequence of this forgetfulness is that this Idealism (Hegel seems to have Fichte in mind more than Kant) does not fully understand its own insight and cannot even articulate its full meaning. What needs to be unfolded and developed is the claim that "all objects are in a deep sense *mine.*"[51] But it is only in a very shallow sense that this newborn

Idealism is able to see all objects as its own. "Its first declaration is merely this abstract, empty phrase that everything is its own . . . Reason knowing itself in this sense in its object is what finds expression in abstract, empty Idealism, which only grasps reason as it appears at first, and by pointing out this pure mine [*Mein*] of consciousness in all being [*Sein*] . . . it fancies it has shown that mine to be complete reality. It is bound, therefore, to be at the same time absolute empiricism, because for the filling of this empty mine . . . its reason needs an impact [*Anstoss*] from without in which alone lies the diverse content of sensing or representing. This idealism is thus just such a self-contradictory equivocation as scepticism."[52]

In identifying this Idealism with empiricism and scepticism and discussing it simply as a preface to the description of Observing Reason, Hegel gives us part of the socio-analysis of critical finitism which was called for by the Introduction.[53] That finitism, with which Idealism is here associated, sees clearly that a knowing which consists of bringing together highly formal (mathematical-logical) a priori categories with sensibly given subject matter cannot know the Absolute. Yet it absolutizes this finite knowing because it is so bedazzled by its spectacular achievements as natural science. It claims to be philosophy but is overawed by a knowledge it knows cannot fulfill philosophy's task. Had it pursued its transcendental insights more doggedly it would have avoided dogmatically absolutizing a mode of knowledge whose method bars it from the truth.[54]

This empirical, sceptical Idealism has learned with Kant that the "I think" must be able to accompany all my representations, and that they are all in this sense mine. And it has learned with Descartes that I, who think, am a thinking being. But it has not reflected deeply enough on the Cartesian question, What am I, in so far as I am a thinking being, *res cogitans*? In the Third Meditation Descartes' answer is that a thinking being is one who, among other things, doubts, believes, imagines, and chooses. While transcendental analysis of these activities can be given, it is important to notice that the transcendental ego never doubts, believes, imagines, or chooses anything. Hegel's account reminds us that only concrete persons do these things, and that how they do them depends at least in part on where they stand in history. "Consciousness will determine its relation to otherness or its object in various ways, according as it is at one or another stage in the development of World Spirit to self-consciousness. How the World Spirit immediately finds and determines itself and its object, or how consciousness is for itself, depends on what World Spirit has already come to be . . ."[55]

This is to suggest that the transcendental ego must be placed in the context of Spirit and its history. Spirit is not Aristotle's Unmoved Mover which thinks itself outside of any relation to the processes of our world and its history. Its self-consciousness is not immediate, but mediated through its own external expressions. What Hegel says of individual Spirit is no less true of universal Spirit. "Language and labor are expressions [*Äusserungen*] in which the individual no longer retains possession of himself, but lets the inner get completely outside of him and exposes and abandons it to another." This has the consequence that "in order to know what a specific individual is in himself" one must acknowledge the wisdom of Solon, "who thought it possible to know this only from and after the course of one's whole life."[56] Spirit is known through the interpretation of its words and deeds, i.e., through historical understanding.

To place transcendental subjectivity in this context is to adopt the post-transcendental perspective. It is to talk about the history of intentionality, of how consciousness takes what is given, thereby bridging the alleged gulf between the transcendental and historical points of view. This calls for an explicit development of the concept of Spirit and a comprehensive interpretation of its history.

NOTES

1. *Realphilosophie,* 179 and PhG, XXXVIII/29-30/93. This latter passage comes in the context of Hegel's critique of the familiar.

2. Quoted from Hans-Georg Gadamer, *Wahrheit und Methode,* 2nd ed., Tübingen, 1965, p. 4. My italics.

3. Also see the opening chapters of E.A. Burtt, *The Metaphysical Foundations of Modern Science,* and of A. N. Whitehead, *Science and the Modern World.*

4. *Critique of Pure Reason,* B xiii.

5. So does Heidegger's distinction between *Zuhandenheit* and *Vorhandenheit.*

6. The importance of this dependence has been developed with great subtlety as a major theme of twentieth century phenomenology, not only in the work of Merleau-Ponty, from whom the phrase "primacy of perception" is borrowed, but earlier in Heidegger's *Being and Time* and Husserl's *Crisis.*

7. *op. cit.,* p. 3.

8. It is in the Preface that Hegel himself invokes the image of the Prodigal Son while describing the poverty of Spirit underlying the reversion to immediacy. In the following paragraph he relates this directly to the scientific revolution. See section 2A. above. The metaphor is particularly apt, since he seeks to show that like the original prodigal, scientific consciousness comes by itself to recognize its poverty and to return home from the far country. This return is at first without repentance, however, since it appeals to an immediacy which absolutizes the familiar, i.e., tries to act as if nothing had happened.

9. See note 20 below.

10. An explicitly practical "deduction" would not be in place here, since the form of natural consciousness which is our object here has not yet come to question the rigid boundary between theory and praxis. That science is not pure theory but a form of behavior is something which "we" are to see in the course of the description.

11. PhG, 41/91/164. *zugleich.*

12. PhG, 44/93/167.

13. PhG, 54-56/99-100/175-76. Hegel italicizes the phrase here in italics as well as the remainder of the sentence. In this context "for itself" implies oneness, "for another" manyness.

14. In both the Introduction and the Preface Hegel develops the

concept of "the experience which consciousness makes" to refer to its transitions from one form to another rather than to its life within each form. This sense of "experience" is developed more explicitly in the chapters on Perception and Understanding than anywhere else in the *Phenomenology*.

15. On the link between universality and mediation, see PhG, 39-40/90/163-64.

16. PhG, 54-55/99-100/175-76.

17. Spinoza defines substance as "that which is in itself and is conceived through itself." *Ethics*, Part I, Definition III, Elwes translation. In terms of the Kantian categories of quantity, Hegel is here looking for the Totality which will keep Unity and Plurality from falling apart.

18. GW, 7:38-75. For Kant the category of substance is already a determination of the whole, of nature in general.

19. PhG, 65/106/185.

20. PhG, 71-73/110-11/190-91.

21. PhG, 78/114-15/195.

22. PhG, 174-77/183-85/281-84. cf. Ch. 3, n. 45 and 256/236/349.

23. PhG, 186-89/191-93/291-93.

24. This discussion should be read in conjunction with C.G. Hempel, *Fundamentals of Concept Formation in Empirical Science*. Although Hegel almost expresses the notion of operational definitions here, he ignores the important role of quantification and calculation in concept formation until a later passage. See note 37 below.

25. See Ch. 2, n. 6.

26. GW, 7:48-50, 58-61.

27. *Ibid.*, pp. 59-60.

28. Quoted from E.A. Burtt, *The Metaphysical Foundations of Modern Science*, Garden City, 1932, pp. 210, 226, 225, and 223. The first pair is from *The Mathematical Principles of Natural Philosophy*, the second from the *Opticks*. Burtt does not call attention to the striking ambivalence of these passages, widely separated in the former work, but only four pages apart in the second.

29. PhG, 74/112/192. Though Hegel may be alluding to a poem of A. v. Haller, Book III of Locke's *Essay* and Newton's refusal to hypothesize are the original formulations of the position in question. Haller's poem from 1730 includes the lines, "*Ins innre der Natur dringt kein erschaffner Geist,/ Zu glücklich, wenn sie noch die äussre Schale weist!*" See GW, 7:372, note to page 63.

30. The contemporary reader can appreciate Hegel's patience in

dwelling with this form of scientific consciousness. Science has turned back on itself, and the once despised practice of an ontologically oriented science has returned in new dress. See J.J.C. Smart, *Philosophy and Scientific Realism*. So much is this the case that Wilfrid Sellars is able to define the scientific outlook not in terms of the quest for laws, which he sees as merely a sophisticated form of common sense, but in terms of the postulation of imperceivable entities. See "Philosophy and the Scientific Image of Man," in *Science, Perception, and Reality*. Whether the postulating of theoretical entities in this sense can be said to provide an explanation of phenomena which is non-tautological is the discussion of a long essay by C.G. Hempel, "The Theoretician's Dilemma," *Minnesota Studies in the Philosophy of Science*, Vol. II, edited by Feigl, Scriven, and Maxwell.

31. PhG, 63-72/105-11/183-90.

32. See quotation 2b) from Newton above, and PhG, 214-15/209/313.

33. PhG, 80-81/116/197. cf. 183-89/189-92/288-93 and GW, 7:47-51.

34. PhG, 84/118/200.

35. PhG, 81-82/117/198-99. cf. GW, 7:61.

36. PhG, 84-86/119/200-01. The parallel between the former alternative and Poincaré's conventionalism on the one hand, and between the latter alternative and the Mill-Mach economy theory of scientific laws is striking.

37. PhG, 210-15/206-09/309-13. On quantification see 216-21/210-17/313-23. On human personality and its environment see 240-42/225-27/333-36.

38. For this and the next paragraph, see PhG, 202-09/201-05/303-08.

39. Ernest Nagel, *The Structure of Science*, London, 1961, Ch. 4. For similar discussions see N.R. Hanson, *Patterns of Discovery*, Cambridge, 1961, Ch. 5, and T.S. Kuhn, *The Structure of Scientific Revolutions*, Chicago, 1962, pp. 78, 132.

40. Nagel, *op. cit.*, pp. 66-67. Also see the Hempel essay cited in n. 30 above and Quine's essay, "Two Dogmas of Empiricism," in *From a Logical Point of View*.

41. See section 3A. above.

42. PhG, 38/89/162, 56-58/100-02/176-78. cf. Ch. 3, n. 36.

43. PhG, 59-60/103/180-81.

44. While this language suggests Marx, one could also use Freud-

ian metaphors; for the neurotic is enslaved to processes going on within him largely because he is unaware of them. In PhG, 193-96/ 195-97/296-99 and 231/220/326 these formulas about knowing oneself or finding oneself in the object have a different meaning and belong more to the philosophy of nature than the philosophy of science.

45. See note 43 above.

46. PhG, V/11/69 and LXVI/45/112. These passages from the Preface deal with philosophical thought, but they express Hegel's view of science and its method most succinctly. This is true of the entire second half of the Preface and is especially clear in the critique of pure mathematics. For similar passages dealing directly with science, see notes 47 and 48 below.

47. PhG, 93-97/124-27/207-10, my italics.

48. PhG, 183/189/288 and 198/198/300, my italics.

49. PhG, 99-100/128-29/211-13.

50. PhG, 164-65/176-77/273-75.

51. J. N. Findlay, *Hegel: A Re-Examination,* New York, 1962, p. 101, his italics.

52. PhG, 170-71/180-81/279.

53. See section 1B. above.

54. This critique is developed at length in *Glauben* and *Skepticismus.*

55. PhG, 166/178/275-76. Some editions would substitute "World Spirit" for the last mention of consciousness in the quotation, reading *er* instead of *es.* I have followed the first edition, which is retained by Hoffmeister. The "correction" by earlier editors doesn't significantly change the meaning, but it tends to underplay the interplay between individual and universal consciousness which comes to expression, for example, in the following passage: " . . . consciousness takes as the middle term between universal Spirit and its individuation in sensible consciousness the system of the forms of consciousness, as a life of Spirit which orders itself to totality [*zum Ganzen*],—the system which is dealt with in this treatise and which has its objective existence as world history." PhG, 231/220/326.

56. PhG, 246-49/229-31/340-42. The link between *Äusserung* in this passage and *Entäusserung* in Chapter Eight is crucial for the entire *Phenomenology.*

CHAPTER FIVE: The Concept of Spirit

5A. The Official Introduction to Spirit

It is not uncommon that we become acquainted with someone and learn to interact with him in various ways without ever being officially introduced. This does not always render such an introduction wholly useless. Indeed, when it finally comes it can significantly alter the relationship which has developed. Hegel's reader has by this time developed some such acquaintance with Spirit, but the time for an official introduction has clearly come. We'd love a simple definition. But Hegel insists upon a long and detailed derivation designed to defend the definition he ultimately gives us from the charge of being merely stipulative. The procedure by which Hegel derives the concept of Spirit is so thoroughly Kantian that it could usefully be called the transcendental deduction of Spirit. The point of contact with Kant's famous deduction is not merely procedural but also substantive. For Hegel wants to lead natural consciousness to an understanding of Spirit through a deepened reflection on self-consciousness as foundational to all our experience.

Having completed his description of the forms of consciousness collectively entitled Consciousness, Hegel has two apparently quite different tasks to perform. Most immediately his task is to develop the insight that "consciousness of an other, of an object in general, is indeed itself self-consciousness." This is the lesson which natural consciousness has derived from its experience at the end of Chapter Three. "The necessary advance from the previous forms of consciousness, which found their true content to be a thing, something other than themselves, brings to light this very fact, that not merely is consciousness of a thing only possible for a self-consciousness, but that this self-consciousness alone is the truth of those forms."[1]

The other task rests on Hegel's earlier promise to overcome the severe abstraction of theoretical from practical consciousness which characterizes the reflections on Consciousness.[2] It is clear from the way this promise is made that he does not mean practical reason in the Kantian sense, but rather a

phenomenological orientation to desire.[3] The philosophy of
Spirit cannot begin with Spirit. Its highest principle must be its
developed result, not its presupposed starting point. Just as the
analysis of theoretical consciousness begins with sense perception, that of practical consciousness begins with desire. In both
cases, and here Hegel is thoroughly Aristotelian, perhaps even
Feuerbachian, the starting point is not man as rational but man
as animal, as embodied. The task is to discover what is distinctively human in human perception and desire, never to find
Spirit by disembodying man. From the perspective of the
Phenomenology idealism is a philosophy of Spirit incarnate. After
all, the guiding principle of Hegel's Jena work is that philosophy is to overcome such dualisms as that between mind and
body, reason and sense, freedom and nature, etc., not to initiate
them.[4]

It is through the combination of these two tasks that a distinctively Hegelian analysis of self-consciousness emerges. A
phenomenology of desire is to be built into the phenomenology
of self-consciousness. The fruitfulness of such a combination
for Hegel's project is immediately evident. It would provide an
initial answer to the question which he sought to evoke as a
question throughout the description of Consciousness—Who is
the transcendental subject? The transcendental subject is
(perhaps more but not less than) embodied desiring consciousness. The way we take the world is conditioned by those interests we have in it which are called desire. If the categories which
structure our intending of the world are the conditions for the
possibility of experience, our interest in the world is in turn the
condition for the possibility of those categories. What we are
likely to find in the world is not independent of what we are
looking for.

This would be the beginning of a meta-critical theory of
knowledge, one which achieves the transcendental standpoint
in such a way as immediately to transcend it by finding a larger
context for its insights. It is what Hegel has been preparing his
readers for.[5]

The question, then, is not the fruitfulness of combining the
two tasks before Hegel, but the possibility of such a combination. This possibility is already hinted at in Hegel's promise not
to abstract permanently from the practical. In the critique of

Sense Certainty he seeks to undercut the alleged "truth and certainty of the reality of the objects of sense," i.e., their absolute independence and dominance, by showing that they can be objects of sense only through the activity of consciousness. He finds a curious confirmation of this thesis in the phenomena of eating and drinking. In the mysteries of Ceres and Bacchus the initiate "not only comes to doubt the being of sensible things, but also to despair of it; and in dealing with them he partly himself brings about their nothingness, partly sees them bring about their own nothingness. Even animals are not shut off from this wisdom, but show themselves to be most deeply initiated into it. For they do not stand still before sensible things as if these had their being in themselves. Rather, in despair of this reality and in the full certainty of the nothingness of these things, they help themselves without ado and eat them up."[6]

The sense in which transcendental subjectivity and eating both undermine the independence of the object is formally expressed at the opening of Chapter Four. "In the kinds of certainty so far considered, consciousness takes the true to be something other than itself. The concept of this true, however, vanishes in the experience of it. Though the object was immediately [taken to be] in itself . . . it shows itself instead not to be this in truth. Rather, this in itself proves to be a way in which it is only for an other."[7] It is this abstract characteristic of being for another, of having its essential meaning in its relatedness rather than in its autonomy, that the intentional object shares with the eaten object.[8]

More than this formal similarity is implied, however, in the concept of a self-consciousness which a) is understood to be the truth of consciousness and b) at the same time is understood as desire. This implies some identity of intending consciousness with desiring consciousness such that desire can be said to be the truth or essence of intentionality.

That self-consciousness is the truth of consciousness is the result of Chapter Three. For Consciousness the object was something other than itself. But since it always showed itself to be for consciousness, attention is switched from it to a new "object," the consciousness before which the supposed autonomy [*Ansichsein*] of the first object always turned out to be a being-for-an-other [*für-ein-Anderes-Sein*]. Consciousness is thus no

longer knowledge of an other but knowledge of itself, and thus
Self-Consciousness, the successor not just of Understanding but
of the whole domain of Consciousness. The knowledge of nature, or more precisely, of the external world, has led beyond itself to another kind of knowledge. Because this new knowledge
is reflection in which the object is not alien to the subject but
identical with it, Hegel can say, "With Self-Consciousness then,
we have now passed into the native kingdom of truth." But far
from being at the end of our journey we have only really begun.
"We have to see how the form of Self-Consciousness first enters
the scene."9

Hegel now proceeds to show that Self-Consciousness is
only to be understood in terms of desire. It appears that Self-
Consciousness first enters the scene as the Kantian "I think,"
for it is a restatement of the deduction of the transcendental
unity of apperception which introduces it. But Kant's transcendental deduction is a two-edged sword which argues not
only that consciousness of an object is only possible for a self-
consciousness, but also the converse, that self-consciousness is
only possible through the consciousness of an object. For this
reason transcendental self-consciousness is not actual self-
consciousness. In the first flush of the discovery of self-
consciousness it is forgotten that self-consciousness is simply the
movement of reflection upon and out of object-
consciousness.10 For this reason it "seems" that the "essential
feature" of Consciousness has been lost, namely "the simple independent reality [selbständige Bestehen]" of its object. "But when
Self-Consciousness distinguishes only itself as itself from itself,
the distinction is immediately taken to be transcended
[aufgehoben] in so far as it involves otherness. The distinction is
not, and Self-Consciousness is only the motionless tautology, I
am I. When the distinction does not also have for Self-
Consciousness the form of being, it is not Self-Consciousness.
For Self-Consciousness then, otherness [Anderssein] is there in
the form of being [als ein Sein] or as a distinct moment. But the
unity of itself with this difference is also there for Self-
Consciousness as a second distinct moment. In that first moment Self-Consciousness has the form of Consciousness, and
the whole expanse of the sensible world is retained for it, but at
the same time, only as related to the second moment, the unity
of Self-Consciousness with itself. And consequently the sensible

world has for Self-Consciousness a reality [*Bestehen*] which, however, is only appearance [*Erscheinung*]. It is something distinct from consciousness which in itself has no being."[11]

Here again the truth is the whole. Self-Consciousness is neither of these moments alone but the two together, *Bestehen* and *Erscheinung,* the relation of consciousness to what is other and its relation to itself.[12] To hold the two together is to remember both lessons of Kant's transcendental deduction, the mutual interdependence of consciousness and self-consciousness. In the language of the Transcendental Aesthetic this means preserving not only the transcendental ideality but also the empirical reality of the objects of experience. Having devoted a major effort to analysis of the former in the description of Consciousness, Hegel urges us not to forget the latter just because it is not the whole truth.

Hegel is Kantian here not only in substance but also in method. The following description of Kant's method in the transcendental deduction applies as well to Hegel's procedure here. As opposed to the deduction of consequences entailed by the concept of self-consciousness, this method "specifies the presuppositions of the *possibility of the existence* of self-consciousness. But using this method, one can come to a knowledge of the conditions which, although they are not already given in the structure of self-consciousness itself, must precisely in virtue of this structure be presupposed if a self-consciousness is to become actual."[13]

But just at the point where Hegel is most Kantian he is suddenly beyond Kant. For he claims on the basis of strictly Kantian premises not only that transcendental apperception is only the idea of Self-Consciousness and not actual Self-Consciousness (to which Kant might agree in terms of his own distinction between transcendental and empirical apperception), but also that actual Self-Consciousness first enters the scene as desire.

The first conclusion is relatively simple and is already before us. Transcendental apperception is derived from the relation of consciousness to its object *as present to consciousness.*[14] In this relation it loses its character as radically other than consciousness, *Sein* as *Anderssein.* Self-Consciousness is therefore only the immediate and empty relation to self which Hegel calls a "motionless tautology." It is a tautology because it expresses identity without difference. It is motionless because the mediating process between self and other has been excluded. In support of his conclusion that Self-Consciousness can be actual only if mediated through an object genuinely other than itself, Hegel appeals not only to Kant's argument, but to his own phenomenological derivation of Self-Consciousness in which it is "the reflection out of the being [Sein] of the sensible and perceptual world and essentially the return out of otherness [Anderssein]."[15]

Somewhat less evident is the second thesis, the crucial one for going beyond transcendental philosophy, that it is in desire that Self-Consciousness is first actual. To begin with desire has the form of Self-Consciousness. It is the inseparable unity of self-relation and relation-to-another. That desire is actual Self-Consciousness in contrast to transcendental apperception means, as the foregoing indicates, that the moment of empirical reality, Sein as genuinely Anderssein, is retained in its experience of the object. This is exactly what Hegel finds to be true of desire. To desire an object is to experience its otherness. Desire is Self-Consciousness, since for it the object has "the significance of a non-entity [Character des Negativen]." Its own satisfaction is the essential thing; the object is merely a means to that end, material for its use. Desire is consequently that form of Self-Consciousness "which is absolutely for itself and immediately takes its object to have the significance of a non-entity," but which will at the same time "experience the independence of its object."[16] It is this dual experience of the object as there for consciousness yet independent of it which makes desire actual Self-Consciousness.

These two aspects of conscious desire are intimately intertwined. Desire is aware of the object as its own, as something for it. It is therefore "certain of itself only through dominating [das Aufheben] this other, which presents itself to Self-Consciousness as an independent living being . . . Certain of the nullity of this other, and taking the position that this nullity is the truth of this other, it annihilates the independent object and thereby gives itself the certainty of itself which is true certainty, a certainty which has won objective status." It is just this moment of satisfaction, however, in which the independence of the object is experienced. The self-certainty achieved in the satisfaction of desire is dependent on the object "for it exists through the dominating of this other. In order that this dominating may occur, this other must be there . . . It is in fact something other than Self-Consciousness, the essence of desire, and it is through this experience that Self-Consciousness learns this truth." Which is to say that Hegel knows as well as Feuerbach that one could starve on merely thought or imagined bread.[17]

It is in animal desire, then, the eating and drinking mentioned above,[18] that Self-Consciousness is an actual fact. But it is not fully actualized at this level. Animal desire is not the fully developed concept of Self-Consciousness, or, to speak more phenomenologically, desire is a richer phenomenon than the analysis of eating and drinking can reveal. What remains to be found if the *Phenomenology* is to proceed is not a form of Self-Consciousness independent of desire but a form of Self-Consciousness in which desire is distinctively human.

Hegel is simply seeking to interpret given phenomena here, not to deduce them *more geometrico*. But there is a principle suggested by his analysis which gives intelligibility not only to the movement just completed, from transcendental apperception to animal desire, but also to the movement now to be considered, from animal desire to human desire. Hegel states that principle this way: "The independence of the object of consciousness in itself is proportional to that of consciousness itself."[18] The object that is eaten is surely more independent than sense data. Still it has a relatively low grade of independence, and the Self-Consciousness of the eater achieves a rather minimal self-certainty from its triumph. Hegel actually calls it self-feeling rather than Self-Consciousness.[19] A higher grade of Self-Consciousness could only be achieved by victory over a more thoroughly independent object. In order to get a qualitative difference from the victory which depends on superior force, Hegel turns to the extreme case in which the object is so independent that desire can find satisfaction "only when this object itself carries out the negation of itself," i.e., offers itself for the sake of desire's happiness. This capacity for self-negation which the object incorporates into its independence means that it must itself be consciousness of some sort. In fact, since it relates to itself as self-negating while relating to the other for whose satisfaction it gives itself, it is Self-Consciousness. In the fullest sense "Self-Consciousness attains its satisfaction only in another Self-Consciousness."[20]

It is only as this new level, which Hegel calls the doubling of Self-Consciousness that Self-Consciousness is able to experience "the unity of itself in its other." In animal desire Self-Consciousness is actual, for its object has the genuine otherness of empirical reality. But the other of animal desire does not survive the negating act of Self-Consciousness. With its disappearance Self-Consciousness also ceases to be, and satisfaction must give way to a new desire for a new object in order constantly to renew the sense of self-certainty. Since the object has independence without permanence, Self-Consciousness can have no lasting experience of unity with its other. The object of desire whose empirical reality consists in its own ability to give or not to give itself for the other's satisfaction and self-certainty is different. It does not disappear in the moment of satisfaction. Since this satisfaction is a happy relation to otherness which is not self-destroying, Hegel says that Self-Consciousness can only here find "the unity of itself in its other."[21]

Hegel is about to turn to his famous description of Lordship and Bondage, an account of the difficulties involved in actualizing this satisfaction which is here but a conceptual possibility. But there are two reasons why we need not hurry on quite yet. The first is that the analysis of Lordship and Bondage only renders concrete the principles already contained in the preceding discussion. The inherently destructive nature of domination for the one who dominates is already before us. In such a project the other is reduced to the object of animal desire. He has no meaning other than the satisfaction of my desires and it is I who will bring about that satisfaction. The unsatisfactory nature of this kind of satisfaction is what moves the dialectic from animal desire to the doubling of Self-Consciousness. This move requires the qualitative transcendence of desire and domination, for at this new level satisfaction is something that can be given but not taken. Even at the purely human level *eros* must give way to *agape*.[22]

The second reason for not rushing right ahead is that Hegel himself lingers long enough to enlarge on the thesis that with Self-Consciousness in its fully developed form "we have now passed into the native kingdom of truth."[23] In doing so he informs us that we have also, without realizing it, been introduced to the concept of Spirit. In the analysis of Self-Consciousness "we already have before us the concept of Spirit. What remains for consciousness is the experience of what Spirit is—the absolute substance which is the unity of the distinct, self-existing [*für sich seiender*] self-conscious individuals in the perfect freedom and independence of their otherness to one another. Spirit is that I which is We and that We which is I. Consciousness first finds in Self-Consciousness as the concept of Spirit its turning point, where it leaves the colorful show of the sensible present [*Diesseits*] and the empty night of the supersensible beyond [*Jenseits*] to enter the spiritual daylight of the present."[24]

It may not be too bold to call this definition of Spirit *the* clue to the *Phenomenology*. The following distinctive characteristics of Spirit which it introduces are fundamental to the remainder of Hegel's argument:

1) Spirit is a social reality, a unity of individual human selves, not a timeless metaphysical reality akin to the world of Platonic forms or Aristotle's Unmoved Mover. It is something present, not a supersensible beyond. As the immediately following discussion of Lordship and Bondage shows, it is to a crude and primitive stage of human social experience that Hegel here applies the name of Spirit. Where the experience of I and We is to be found, there is Spirit.[25]

2) Yet Hegel speaks of Spirit, without having yet traced its development to its fulfillment, as absolute. The recurrence of such references to a determinate form of human social experience as absolute emphasizes both the temporal nature of Spirit and the fundamentally adjectival role of the term 'absolute' in the *Phenomenology*. One must not say with Royce, "The Absolute must be a self that by virtue of its inmost principle appears to itself as an interrelated unity of selves without being the less one self. From this point of view Hegel calls the Absolute *Geist.*"[26] While this is a valuable commentary on Hegel's talk about I and We, subject and predicate have been reversed. Spirit is that interrelated unity of selves which is at the same time one self, a We that is also an I, and in so far as this is the case Hegel speaks of Spirit as absolute.

3) Spirit is substance. This means that it must be understood as having such characteristics as self-sufficiency, permanence, and individuality in the sense of determinateness;
further, that it must be understood as the bearer of "attributes"
or "accidents," components which in isolation from the substance to which they belong do not themselves have the characteristics of substance just mentioned.

4) Yet Spirit needs to be for itself what it is in itself. Substance must become Subject. Not only must each I know itself
also as We, but the We must know itself as I. The social whole
must become conscious of itself.[27]

5) Finally, we have to do here with a turning point, an
entry into the native land of truth, in so far as the concept of
Spirit makes possible the treacherous voyage between the Scylla
of one dimensional this-worldliness and the Charybdis of an
appeal to the transcendent which flees to the emptiness of what
is wholly Wholly Other. In this thinly veiled allusion to the Enlightenment and Romanticism we have a reminder of the historical timeliness of a philosophy which takes Spirit for its central category. Our own time, too, knows the extreme worldli-
ness of scientific-technological rationality and the military-
industrial complex pitted against the extreme repudiations of
all that which we know somewhat too simply as "the Counter-
Culture." But we know little of what might mediate between
them. Perhaps we might learn something from Hegel.

5B. The Priority of Love Over Life and Labor.

Looked at in the context of Hegel's personal development
it is clear that the concept of Spirit is not only the attempt to
unify Kantian apperception with Aristotelian appetition; it is
also the fruition of his efforts at Frankfurt (1797-1800) to develop the concepts of love and life into fundamental
philosophical categories. Dieter Henrich has written, "Hegel's
system came forth without a break out of his assumption of love
as the key word of his reflection. This required only that the
theme of love be replaced, for reasons which can be specified,
with the richer structure of life and then again with that of
Spirit, which implies still more than life." The importance of

the first sentence can hardly be exaggerated, though the second is somewhat doubtful, as we shall see.

According to a fragment from 1797-98, "Where subject and object or freedom and nature are thought as so united that nature is freedom, that subject and object are not to be separated, there is the divine." But this ideal, which belongs to every religion, is not available to either theoretical or practical consciousness (the latter understood as simple desire). "The theoretical syntheses become fully objective, entirely opposed to the subject. Practical activity annihilates the object and is entirely subjective. *Only in love are we one with the object,* neither dominating it [*beherrschen*] nor dominated by it."[29] This phenomenon of love shows itself to be "a reciprocal giving and taking," but "the lover who takes is not thereby made richer than the other. He is enriched indeed, but only so much as the other is. So too the giver does not make himself poorer. By giving to the other he has to the same extent enhanced his own treasure. Juliet in *Romeo and Juliet:* the more I give to thee, the more I have, etc."[30]

Already the concept of Self-Consciousness in and through another self is present here, and Hegel is careful not to let the unity of those who love each other eliminate their difference. "The beloved is not opposed to us but is one with our essence. We see only ourselves in the beloved, whom we in turn, nevertheless, see as not ourselves—a wonder which we cannot comprehend."[31]

In the so-called "System Fragment" of 1800 Hegel suggests the following formula for such a relation: "the union of union and non-union."[32] Here, however, it is life rather than love which is the immediate subject of reflection. The first of the two surviving pages of this essay begins with the last three words of a sentence, " . . . absolute opposition prevails." Kroner's speculation that this refers to the realm of the dead makes good sense.[33] For Hegel maintains that the idea of the living individual "includes opposition against the infinite manifold [of other living beings] and union with this manifold. A human being is an individual life in so far as he is something other than all the elements and the infinity of individual lives outside himself. But he is only an individual life in so far as he is at one with all the elements, with all the infinity of life outside himself. He exists only in so far as the totality of life is divided into parts, he himself being one part and all the rest the other part; he exists only in so far as he is no part at all and nothing is separated from him. If we presuppose undivided life as fixed, then we can regard living beings as expressions or manifestations of that life ... If on the contrary we presuppose an individual life, namely ourselves as the observers, then that life which is posited outside our own limited life is an infinite life of infinite multiplicity, infinite opposition, infinite relation. As a plurality it is an infinite plurality of organizations or individuals. As a unity it is one unique organized whole, divided and unified in itself—Nature."[34]

Though this statement comes from the tradition of romantic philosophy of nature, if it is compared with the one in which Spirit is introduced in the *Phenomenology* it will come as no surprise that Hegel says of this infinite life that we can call it Spirit, "for Spirit is the living unity of the manifold ... an animating law in union with the manifold which is then itself animated."[35] Conversely, it is no surprise that in the *Phenomenology* Hegel should anticipate the concept of Spirit by devoting four paragraphs to the restatement of this concept of life, according to which "the independent members exist for themselves. This being for themselves, however, is really just as immediately their reflection into the unity as this unity is the breaking asunder into the independent forms. The unity is sundered because it is absolutely negative or infinite unity; and because it is what endures the members correspondingly have their independence only in it."[36]

Life so conceived serves as a conceptual model or metaphor for understanding Self-Consciousness as Spirit. But it can be no more than this, for while both are reflections of the same basic structure, the unity of what is distinguished, life simply is this unity while Self-Consciousness has this unity for itself. It knows itself to be this unity.[37] This means that of the two Frankfurt categories, love is more adequate to the concept of Spirit than life. For love is not simply the unconscious structure of Self-Consciousness. Those who love know themselves to be the unity of what nevertheless remains distinct, an incomprehensible wonder. Thus the unity which can be described as love can also be described as the substance which is also subject.

This privileged character of love over life is already to be seen in the Frankfurt period if one compares the "System Fragment" not just with the love fragments of 1797-98 but also with *The Spirit of Christianity and its Fate*. There love is every bit as sophisticated a category as life is in the "System Fragment," and one would not be tempted to call the latter the richer of the two. Both categories continue in the Jena period to be important ones, but with this important difference, which further establishes the priority of love: in the *Realphilosophie* life is relegated to the philosophy of nature, while, love, interpreted in terms of a new category, recognition, becomes the central category of the philosophy of Spirit.[38]

We use the term 'recognition' in two rather different senses. "I saw you sitting there some time ago but until just now I didn't recognize you." "It was not until just after his death that he finally won the recognition he deserved." In the first case recognition is simply a matter of properly identifying someone. In the second to recognize is to esteem, to value, to acknowledge a certain worth. It is always in this second sense that Hegel uses the term. According to the concept of Self-Consciousness human desire is fully satisfied only when the self "is in and for itself *for an other*."[39] To be in itself is to be autonomous, to be something independent of relation to an other. (For example, the Kantian thing in itself is the thing independent of its relation to our experience of it.) To be for itself is to preside over this autonomy, to have it as the active principle of self-maintaining and self-developing self-movement. To be something in and for itself for another is to be acknowledged by another self to be everything that 'in and for itself' connotes, or, as Hegel puts it simply, to be fully Self-Consciousness is to be recognized. It is not difficult to see why Hegel identifies recognition with love or to see the close connection between this concept and Kant's notion of the person as an end in himself.[40]

It is by means of this concept of recognition that Hegel returns in the *Phenomenology* from the pure concept of Self-Consciousness to the concrete experience for which that concept serves as criterion. The question is whether recognition is a reality and not just a fascinating concept, whether the consciousness in which this desire is at work can find the satisfaction it seeks.[41] The self wishes to be loved, to be acknowledged as an end in himself. He desires recognition. But this desire clearly cannot be satisfied as hunger is satisfied in annihilating the other. Here force is impotent. Satisfaction can only come about in so far as the other "itself carries out the negation of it-self," the negation involved in not taking himself to be the absolute end in itself.[42] But the independence of the other, so crucial to surpassing animal self-feeling, consists precisely in the power to recognize or not recognize. It is anything but automatic that Self-Consciousness in the fully developed sense of Spirit will be actualized in accordance with its concept. In fact, it is just the opposite that is phenomenologically more "natural".

In Sartrean language, love first appears only as the desire or demand to be loved. Both selves are so given to demanding love from each other that neither is in a position to give what the other demands. The lack which each self is, needing the other's love simply in order to be himself, makes of each self a primordial emptiness.[43] Two emptinesses encounter each other as the demand to be filled, but since there is no overflowing fullness anywhere on the scene, only a plurality of emptinesses, love turns out to be a useless passion. Out of reciprocal empti-ness there is no immediate path to reciprocal recognition.

This is what the celebrated life and death struggle which culminates in master-slave relationships is all about. The at-tempt to kill the other is fundamentally confused, for it rests on the assumption either that the desire for recognition can be satisfied like hunger through annihilating the other, or that the self-negation of the other can be coerced. Both assumptions are patently at odds with the concept of recognition, for it is clear that a dead man cannot recognize his conqueror and that a conquered man's coerced "recognition" of the conqueror is no genuine self-negation or love at all. For "there is no fear in love, but perfect love casts out fear . . . he who fears is not perfected in love."[44]

Hegel doesn't dwell much on the absurdity of the resort to violence in the attempt to extract recognition from the other. For him the more interesting (and more easily overlooked) as-pect of the struggle for recognition is the fact that each party risks his own life in seeking to take the life of the other. This brings to focus the distinctly human character of the desire for recognition in contrast to animal desire. The desire which con-

sciously risks life in the pursuit of satisfaction cannot be interpreted within the horizon of life, either as self-preservation or
species preservation. The desire for recognition is qualitatively
different from the hunger and sex drives, biologically interpreted. Hegel's conclusion is that "it is solely by risking life that
freedom is obtained. Only thus is it tried and proved that the
essential thing for Self-Consciousness is not mere existence [*das
Sein*], not the immediate way in which it makes its appearance,
not its immersion in the expanse of life—but rather that for
Self-Consciousness nothing is present that might not be taken
as a vanishing moment, and that Self-Consciousness is nothing
but pure being for itself. The individual who has not staked his
life may, no doubt, be recognized as a person. But he has not
achieved the truth of this recognition as an independent
Self-Consciousness."[45] In other words, "Give me liberty or give
me death" belongs to the essence of human desire. Since love
and freedom are here identified, we can say that the unloved
life is not worth living.

A further aspect of the Lordship and Bondage discussion
needs to be considered if Hegel's concept of Spirit is to be fully
understood, especially in its relation to Marxian materialism. It
is the notion of labor, of which Marx writes in the 1844 manuscripts, "The greatness of the Hegelian *Phenomenology* and its
final result . . . is thus . . . that Hegel grasps the essence of labor
and conceives of objective man, true man because actual man,
as the result of his own labor . . . Hegel occupies the standpoint
of modern national economy. He grasps labor as the essence of
man which proves itself indeed to be such."[46]

It is true that Hegel finds in labor a distinctively human
form of desire. "Desire has reserved to itself the pure negating
of the object and thereby unalloyed feeling of self. This satisfaction, however, just for that reason is itself only something that
vanishes, for it lacks the aspect of objectivity or endurance.
Labor, on the other hand, is restrained desire, delayed vanishing. In other words, it forms the object. The negative relation to
the object becomes the form of the object, something that remains, because it is precisely for the laborer that the object has
independence." Clearly the human significance of labor is not
to be found in consumption. Labor surpasses simple desire in
that a more satisfactory form of Self-Consciousness is thereby
achieved. Hegel continues, "In forming the thing being for self

comes to be taken by the laborer as his own, and he becomes conscious that he is in and for himself."[47]

But while it is true that for Hegel labor involves creation and not just consumption, Self-Consciousness and not just self-preservation, it is just as clear that the object of labor cannot mediate as complete a mode of Self-Consciousness as another self can. The definitive characteristic of human desire is not labor any more than it is life. It is love. The essential thing is not the postponement of satisfaction but the nature of the satisfaction which recognition involves. Hegel would find Marx's account of his accomplishment one-sided and incomplete.[48]

In keeping with this priority of love over labor in Hegel's understanding of man as Spirit, he sees history as grounded in original sin rather than in the division of labor. While his account of original sin in the life and death struggle for recognition suggests Cain and Abel rather than Adam and Eve, it is clear that the master-slave relation is something subsequent, a superstructure whose basis is found in the directly interpersonal and non-economic domain of the quest for recognition. The relations of dominance and dependence within economic institutions are *Schein*. The desire to be loved and the hatred of the one who instead of loving me demands that I love him are *Wesen*. Correspondingly Hegel's analysis of the historical process will focus attention on the quest for love as recognition rather than on labor and the economic process, which in turn can only be understood in terms of the former.[49] This does not mean that Hegel will have to be an idealist in the sense of one who thinks the world's problems are solved when they are understood. Marx's 1844 critique of the *Phenomenology* is misdirected in this respect. To find the search for recognition as the horizon within which not only labor and the economic process but the whole of human history are to be understood is not equivalent to letting thought swallow up being. For the manifold encounters between persons desiring to be loved and thus ratified as persons are very real events and not merely thought processes in the mind of some philosopher.

Despite these important differences, Hegel stands with Marx over against the transcendental tradition and Kant. One might even borrow Adorno's formula to express this: "Since the author has trusted his own spiritual impulses, he has found it to be his task to break through the deceit of transcendental subjectivity with the power of the subject."[50] This would not adequately express the tension in Hegel's position, however, which seeks not so much to deny transcendental subjectivity as to discover the conditions of its possibility and thereby its conditionedness. The formula borrowed earlier from Habermas comes closer to expressing this: "The achievements of the transcendental subject have their basis in the natural history of the human species."[51] It should now be clear both why this formula is appropriate and why Hegel, too, would have to add a qualification like that of Habermas: "Taken by itself this thesis could lead to the misunderstanding that reason is an organ of adaptation for men just as claws and teeth are for animals. True, it does serve this function. But the human interests that have emerged in man's natural history . . . derive both from nature and from the cultural break with nature." In Hegel's terms, human desire is not just animal desire but the desire which restrains itself in labor and re-directs itself in the quest for recognition. It is in such desires that the achievements of the transcendental subject have their basis.

Once again we are brought to the crucial Hegelian question—Who is the transcendental subject? The question itself is directed against Kant's kind of transcendental philosophy, for it presupposes that the transcendental subject is concrete, not an abstract network of timeless, perhaps even bloodless categories. That man in the concrete, thus man as desire, is the transcendental subject means that for Hegel as well as for Marx, "It is not consciousness that determines life but rather life that determines consciousness." From this point of view "one begins with the actual living individual himself and considers consciousness only as *his* consciousness."[52]

The point of these formulas from Adorno, Habermas, and Marx is not to show that Hegel is someone other than himself but simply to indicate the implications of his concept of Spirit. His own formula, if one must be found, comes at the beginning of the 1805-06 lectures on the philosophy of Spirit where he characterizes the ego as only formally universal, Spirit as truly universal.[53] This carries with it the clear implication that a philosophy oriented to the ego is abstract and incomplete until it becomes a philosophy of Spirit, that transcendental philosophy in the Cartesian and Kantian sense finds its own foundation beyond itself.

5C. Spirit and Ethical Life.

Beginning with the epistemological issues discussed in the Introduction Hegel has developed them or watched them develop to the point where transcendental philosophy is forced to become philosophy of Spirit. If the concept of Spirit which emerges in this context is to have relevance to the issues raised in the Preface, it will have to be shown that it stands in an intelligible relation to the issues of "substantial life" and "sense of the divine."[54] After introducing the concept of Spirit in Chapter Four and before tracing its historical career in Chapter Six Hegel develops the concept further in two brief but crucial passages which fulfill this expectation.[55]

The first of these passages serves as the introduction to Sections B. and C. of Chapter Five on the practical dimensions of Reason. Hegel takes up where he left off in Chapter Four, with the concept of Self-Consciousness. "The object, therefore, to which Self-Consciousness positively relates itself, is a Self-Consciousness. This object has the form of thinghood, i.e., it is independent. But Self-Consciousness has the certainty that this independent object is nothing foreign to it. It knows itself herewith to be in itself recognized by the other Self-Consciousness. Self-Consciousness is Spirit which has the certainty of having its unity with itself in the duplication of its Self-Consciousness and in the independence of both selves."[56]

A rather dramatic change has taken place while the reader was away reading Section A of Chapter Five on Observing Reason. When he left Self-Consciousness at the end of Chapter Four recognition was only a utopian dream, a mere concept without reality in a society of masters and slaves. How different it all sounds in the passage just cited. To be sure it is only the certainty of being recognized which Self-Consciousness has, and Hegel regularly contrasts certainty as claim from truth as fulfillment. Further, Self-Consciousness knows itself to be recognized, but only "in itself." This is one of the few places where

Hegel's *an sich* requires translation as "implicitly" or "potentially." Nevertheless, the atmosphere has changed. This confidence on the part of Self-Consciousness can hardly stem from an experience which knows nothing but the futile desire of Chapter Four.

Even so, we are not quite prepared for the boldness of the question Hegel asks: Where does this concept of recognition have its "complete reality," where does it come to light as "an existing, flourishing substance"? Answer: "in the life of a people [*Volk*]," in "the realm of Ethical Life [*Sittlichkeit*]."[57] The concept of recognized Self-Consciousness opens up this realm for us "because Ethical Life is nothing other than the *absolute* spiritual unity of the being of individuals in their independent reality. It is an in itself *universal* Self-Consciousness which is so fully itself in another consciousness that this latter has complete independence for it, is looked on as a thing, and the universal Self-Consciousness is aware precisely therein of its unity with the other, and is only then Self-Consciousness when in such unity with this objective being. This ethical [*sittliche*] *substance*, taken in its abstract universality is only law as posited [*das gedachte Gesetz*], but just as much it is immediately actual Self-Consciousness, i.e., custom. Conversely, the individual consciousness is this existing unit only by being conscious in his individuality of the universal consciousness as his being, only by acting and existing in accord with universal custom."[58]

This crucial passage calls for careful comment, especially in light of the fact that as early as 1803 Hegel had identified absolute Spirit with Ethical Life in its perfection.[59]

In the first place Ethical Life involves the concept of universal Self-Consciousness. While Hegel sometimes uses the term universal to signify an abstract concept, his normal usage describes as universal only what is in some sense a concrete totality and in this sense particular. Thus he speaks, with Kant in mind, of space and time as universals, of the thing with its properties as universal, of the organism, and then again of the species as universal. In the present context where the particular is the self-conscious individual, it is well to remember that Spirit is not the unity of I with I-ness, but of I and We. That which can be described as We is the concrete totality which is universal, "the absolute spiritual unity of the being of individuals in their independent reality." Independent individuals, without ceasing to be such, form a unity which Hegel calls absolute and spiritual. Since this unity, concretely speaking a people, has its own form of self-awareness, Hegel calls it universal Self-Consciousness. It is not the abstraction which Kant called pure reason, but rather "the real substance, into which the preceding forms of consciousness return and in which they find their ground."[60]

This is the second point: Ethical Life is substance. The analysis of the thing and its properties has indicated that to speak of qualities or properties is to speak of parts or aspects in isolation from the whole to which they belong, while to speak of a thing or substance is to speak of the togetherness of the parts or aspects, and thus of something concrete. The concreteness of Ethical Life as a universal consciousness which must be described as substance can be expressed in terms of language. " . . . this universal substance speaks its universal language in the customs and laws of its people. But this existing unchangeable being is nothing else than the expression of the individuality which seems opposed to it. The laws give expression to what each individual is and does."[61] Ethical Life is thus the substantial life of a people as it is expressed in their customs and laws.

If the concept of a people as substantial subject defines the scope of Ethical Life, Hegel's refusal to separate customs from laws indicates its form, the third element of this concept. The separation of customs and laws would signify the separation of morality from legality, of private from public person, in short, of man from citizen. Ethical Life is the life of a people in so far as these distinctions do not arise.[62]

Finally, this means that the concept of individuality in the context of Ethical Life is not that "modern" concept, already present at the dissolution of the Greek *polis*, which presupposes these distinctions as ultimate.[63] In Ethical Life the individual stands in a relation of immediate unity with the social whole. He is I only as he is We. He knows himself only in the customs and laws of his people; and he knows only himself in them.

Since this dialectic of individual and society, which Hegel here introduces into the concept of Spirit, occupies more space than any other single topic in the *Phenomenology*, it is important to see that their relation is not that of simple otherness. It has already been suggested that the universal is primarily a concrete totality. Correspondingly, to be an individual is to be a part of a whole.[64] Since a totality is not merely an aggregate, being part of a whole means more than being one of a bunch. In the life of a people reason appears "as the fluid universal substance, as the unchangeable, simple thinghood which, just as light bursts asunder into stars as innumerable self-illuminating points, likewise breaks up into many entirely independent beings which in their absolute being-for-self are dissolved in the simple independent substance, not only in themselves but also for themselves. They are conscious of themselves as being these individual independent beings through the fact that they sacrifice their individuality and that this universal substance is their soul and essence, just as this universal is, on the other hand, their deed as individuals, the work which they have produced."[65]

Once again the question is inescapable—Where is this beautiful concept actualized? It comes as no surprise that our attention is directed toward antiquity. "Among a free people, therefore, reason is in truth realized. They are Spirit, living and present, where the individual . . . finds his destiny, i.e., his universal and particular nature . . . The wisest men of antiquity for that reason declared that wisdom and virtue consist in living in accordance with the customs of one's people."[66]

In Chapter Six Hegel will describe in detail the Greek experience of Ethical Life. But he knows that he is dealing with a concept which is not universally realized, even in antiquity. There are forms of interaction between individual and society which can be looked at as either not yet having achieved this harmony or as having lost it. The latter view is especially significant, for it indicates that Ethical Life is an inherently unstable harmony, limited both in scope and form. In terms of its scope it is limited to one people among many. As the life of a free people "this universal Spirit is also itself an individual. It is the totality of customs and laws of a determinate ethical substance, which casts off this limitation only when it reaches the higher moment, namely when it becomes conscious regarding its own nature. Only in this knowledge does it have its absolute truth, not immediately in its being."[67]

The limitation of Ethical Life in terms of its form is equally serious. The unity of individual and society is an immediate confidence which is easily and necessarily broken by reflection, in which the individual and not the universal Spirit becomes the essential moment. Then "the individual has set himself over against the laws and customs. They are only a thought without absolutely essential significance, an abstract theory without reality. The individual, however, as this ego, is in his own view the living truth."[68]

The forms of consciousness which pass in review through Sections B. and C. of Chapter Five are but variations on this theme. They portray a variety of ways in which perversely abstract individualism destroys any hope of a satisfactory relation to the social environment (unorganic nature) by being unwilling or unable to be part of a whole. While they indirectly illuminate the concept of Spirit, their role in Hegel's overall argument is peripheral.

More important is the question—What has the concept of Ethical Life added to our understanding of Spirit? It clearly represents an expanded conception of the We of the original definition. This is of double significance. First, while Spirit is defined as substance in its first appearance, it is not entirely clear why this should be. Two individuals appear seemingly ready made out of nowhere to struggle for recognition. We cannot be sure Hegel has avoided the state of nature *cum* social contract type thinking he otherwise repudiates.[69] Such thinking forgets that to speak of individuals apart from their social milieu is to speak of the barest abstractions. Consequently it loses half of the dialectic of individual and society. It notices that society is produced by the individual, but not that the producing individuals are first produced by society.[70] The link between Spirit and Ethical Life corrects this impression with the reminder that the struggle for recognition takes place in a social context. It is not just the relation of one individual to another, but more fundamentally of their relation to society, for all their inter-relations take place in the context of customs and laws. This is true even of the extreme case suggested by the original struggle for recognition—war.

Second, by making it clear that recognition is not to be understood in terms of social contract but of society as substance, the concept of Ethical Life links the concept of Spirit to the cultural crisis of Hegel's present with its concern for the substantial life which has been lost. Ethical Life is Spirit in its immediacy. As such its loss is inevitable and irrevocable. But at the same time it gives content to the concept of Spirit in such a way as to make clear what must be regained in a mediated way if romantic yearning and rigoristic imperatives are to give place to the enjoyment of the ideal as present.[71]

The Preface, however, speaks not only of the loss of "substantial life" but also of the desire for a renewed "sense of the divine." So far the concept of Spirit has been related to the former, since it is presented as a thoroughly historical and human reality, the life of a free people. But what of the divine? In his essay on natural right (1802-03) Hegel writes that Ethical Life comes to self-knowledge through a twofold self-representation. In the form of universality it expresses itself as the system of laws. In the form of particularity it is to be seen in the God of a people. This indicates the closest of connections between Ethical Life and the divine.[72] Only hints of such a link are found in the passage just considered, where the universal substance which is a people is twice characterized as the unchangeable substance.[73] This is the primary designation for God in the earlier analysis of the Unhappy Consciousness.

It is only when we turn to the second of the passages mentioned at the beginning of this section that we find the religious aspect more fully expressed. Just before launching into the description of Spirit's historical career, Hegel pauses to reflect on the concept of Spirit as Ethical Life. "The self-contained and self-sufficient being, however, which is aware of being actual in the form of consciousness and at the same time presents itself to itself is Spirit. Its spiritual essence has already been designated as the ethical [*sittliche*] substance. But Spirit is the ethical actuality. Spirit is the self of actual consciousness, to which Spirit stands opposed, or rather, which appears over against itself as an objective actual world, which likewise, however, has lost all sense of having a dependent or independent existence by itself, cut off and separated from that world. Being substance ... Spirit is the immoveable and irreducible ground and starting point for the action of everyone. As the essence of all Self-Consciousnesses for thought, Spirit is their purpose and goal."[74]

Spirit is here described with four characteristics of the divine. 1) It is *causa sui,* self-sufficient, self-contained, self-supporting. 2) It is transcendent, a substantial self which stands over against the individual self as an other. 3) It is the ground of the individual's action. 4) It is also the goal and purpose of that action.

The manner in which the social whole may be said to be the ground and goal of human activity is relatively unproblematic. It is illustrated by the way in which a team is the ground and goal of an athlete's activity. The team is the ground of his activity as that without which he could not perform. You can't pitch without a catcher. And the team is the goal of the athlete's activity in that it is the team's success that finally matters most. Being voted Most Valuable Player is never a satisfactory substitute for the team's winning its way to the World Series or Super Bowl. What Hegel has in mind as Ethical Life is a mode of social experience in which individuals relate to their society in the same way a real team player relates to his team. His language serves to transfer to society in this relation a function traditionally thought of as God's. For theologically speaking it is God who is the ultimate ground without which the individual cannot even be, much less act, and it is for his glory that life is to be lived.

The other two characteristics of Spirit, transcendence and aseity, must be treated with special care, least they be confused with the very different doctrines of classical theism which involve the same kind of language. The manner in which Spirit is immanent to human experience is sufficient to distinguish its transcendence from that of the theistic view. In terms of Spirit as here conceived, what stands over against the individual as a transcendent spiritual self or world is nothing other than himself. This is true for two reasons. "The substance is likewise the universal product, wrought by the action of all and each as their unity and identity." That is, Spirit is as much the individual's creation as his creator. In addition, Spirit's subjectivity is actual only in its constituent individuals. " . . . as being-for-itself the continuity of this substance is resolved into discrete elements; it is the self-sacrificing goodness in which each fulfills his own work, tears the universal being apart and takes his own share of it. This resolution of the whole into parts [*diese Auflösung und Vereinzelung des Wesens*] is precisely the moment of the action and selfhood of all the parts . . . Just because this substance is a being resolved into selfhood, it is not a lifeless essence, but actual and alive."[75] In this respect Hegel can say of the ethical substance that "it is Spirit which is for itself by maintaining itself in the reflection [*Gegenschein*] of the individuals of the community. It is in itself or substance by preserving them within itself. As actual substance Spirit is a people. As actual consciousness it is the citizens of a nation."[76] Findlay has good reason to describe Spirit as "a self-consciousness which is dispersed among a number of distinct centers."[77]

The individual participates in Spirit both as its creator and as the sole locus of its consciousness. That is to say that the transcendence of Spirit is simply that of society to the individual. Yet we have seen that Hegel is not hesitant in this very context to speak of Spirit as absolute. The theological language is important, for it serves to identify Hegel's ultimate concern. But it is also misleading, for the divine is neither God in any traditional Judeo-Christian sense, nor the metaphysical absolute of the later so-called Hegelians (including, perhaps, Hegel himself). As social substance with collective self-consciousness Spirit is more akin (to follow up the previous analogy) to team spirit than to the Holy Spirit of Christian theology or the Brahman of Hindu mysticism.

Finally, to speak of Spirit as self-contained, self-sufficient, and self-supporting is not to designate a being prior to and independent of the world of finite reality. Rather, it is to say that societies create themselves and that, unlike their constituent elements they are not abstractions in the sense of being essentially parts of a larger whole. (It is not a contradiction to speak of a universal society.)

It is instructive at this point to compare two three-point summaries of Hegelian idealism, each of which is followed by a highly significant comment. Sidney Hook writes that for Hegel 1) Reality is spiritual, 2) Reality is systematic, and 3) Reality is rational, adding that the idea of a corporate social consciousness is a deduction from these theses.[78] Jean Hyppolite's Hegel holds that 1) Spirit is a *nous* (French, not Greek), 2) Spirit is history, and 3) Spirit is knowledge of itself in its history. He adds the comment that this latter point tends to lead Hegel beyond strictly phenomenological concerns to an ontologizing of

Spirit.[79] Both Hook and Hyppolite distinguish the socio-historical elements (Spirit as *nous,* French) from the speculative or metaphysical elements (Reality as *nous,* Greek). But for Hook the former are deductions from an a priori metaphysical construction of Reality, whereas for Hyppolite Hegel's thought is first and foremost concerned with Spirit, even if at times he gets carried beyond the historical and cultural world of Spirit as phenomenon. Between the first Hegel, a Platonist who deduces things from thought, for whom time is unreal and the sensible world a mere appearance,[80] and the second, for whom time is a fundamental category and concrete social experience the starting point for philosophy, there is scarcely a family resemblance. Nor is it hard to identify the more faithful portrait so far as the *Phenomenology* is concerned.

NOTES

1. PhG, 98-99/128/211-12.
2. PhG, 34-35/87/158-59. cf. Ch. 3, n. 29. What here follows can be read as Hegel's developed reply (in advance) to Feuerbach's critique of his treatment of Sense Certainty, especially as the challenge to mediate between philosophy and what is not philosophy. See *Vorläufige Thesen zur Reform der Philosophie*, KS, 135, and *Kritik*, KS, 99-100.
3. This is just what one would expect from the *Realphilosophie*.
4. This is the leitmotif of the earliest Jena writings, *Differenz* and *Glauben*.
5. This linkage of knowledge and interest links Hegel not only to the American pragmatists but also to Heidegger's analysis of Being-in-the-world as Care, though the language in both cases is very different.
6. PhG, 34-35/87/158-59. cf. *Realphilosophie*, II, 120, "Eating and drinking make unorganic things into what they are in themselves, in truth. They are the unconscious comprehending of these things." And II, 160, "Animal desire is the idealism of objectivity, the certainty that objects are nothing foreign . . . It is the self-feeling that what is lacking to it is itself . . ."
7. PhG, 101/134/218.
8. Cf. *Realphilosophie*, I, 197, where the theoretical process is described as the ideal and the practical process as the real mastery of nature.
9. PhG, 102/134/218-19.
10. This same charge of forgetfulness is central to the critique of Idealism at the beginning of Chapter Five. Due to this forgetfulness Observing Reason is not significantly different from the Understanding of Chapter Three. See especially PhG, 164-66/176-78/273-76.
11. PhG, 103-04/134-35/219-20, Hegel's italics.
12. Cf. Hegel's early formulas in this respect from the so-called Frankfurt "System Fragment" and *Differenz* respectively: "*die Verbindung der Verbindung und der Nichtverbindung,*" *Werke*, I, 422, English translation in *Early Theological Writings*, p. 312, and "*die Identität der Identität und der Nichtidentität,*" GW, 4:64. These phrases serve as predicates, in the first instance of Life, in the second of the Absolute.
13. Dieter Henrich, "The Proof-Structure of Kant's Transcendental Deduction," *The Review of Metaphysics*, June, 1969, p. 657, his italics.

14. In Husserlian language Hegel is dealing with the relation of intending consciousness to intentional object. Something like the *epoche* of the natural standpoint is involved in reflecting on the objects of perception simply *qua* present to consciousness. Such objects have no independence for they are only the wholly immanent correlate of the intentional act which constitutes them.

15. PhG, 103/134/219.

16. PhG, 102-05/134-35/219-21.

17. PhG, 110-11/139/225. I have translated *das Aufheben* as "dominating" partly as a signal that the basic structure of the master-slave relationship is presented in the immediately following paragraph. *Re* Feuerbach, see Ch. 3, n. 27 and *Grundsätze*, #25 and #37, KS, 182 f. and 199 f.

18. PhG, 105/135/221.

19. PhG, 126/148-49/238. cf. 108/137/223.

20. PhG, 111/139/225-26.

21. PhG, 112/140/226-27. This analysis of animal desire merits comparison not only with Plato's critique of hedonism in the *Gorgias,* but also Kierkegaard's critique of aesthetic existence in the first volume of *Either/Or.*

22. Where Kant tried to show that it was logically self-defeating to treat others simply as means to our own happiness, Hegel tries to show that it is practically or existentially self-defeating.

23. See note 9 above.

24. PhG, 113/140/227.

25. See the discussion of language in section 3D. above.

26. Josiah Royce, *Lectures on Modern Idealism,* New Haven, 1919, p. 174.

27. In his lectures published in 1859 as *Philosophie der Kunst* but given in 1802-03 at Jena and in 1804-05 at Würzburg, Schelling writes, "Mythology can be the work neither of an individual person nor of a race [*Geschlecht*] or species (in so far as these are only a collection of individuals) but only of a race so far as it is itself individual and the same as an individual person . . . It requires, thus, as a necessary condition of its possibility, a race that is an individual like a person. The incomprehensibility which this idea may have for our time cannot deny it its truth. It is the highest idea for all of history in general." *Sämmtliche Werke, 1859, I. Abt., 5. Bd., 414-15.* In comparison with Hegel's concept of Spirit this formulation lacks explicit reference to the independence of the parts which make up the whole and to the need of the whole to become self-conscious if it is to be subject and not merely substance..

28. Dieter Henrich, "Hegel und Hölderlin," in *Hegel im Kontext,* Frankfurt, 1971, p. 27. cf. "Historische Voraussetzungen von Hegels System," *op. cit.,* p. 67.

29. *Werke,* I, 242, my italics.

30. *Ibid.,* p. 248. This is from another Frankfurt fragment, one included in the *Early Theological Writings.* See p. 307.

31. *Ibid.,* p. 244.

32. "System Fragment," (see note 12 above), *ibid.,* 422/312.

33. In *Early Theological Writings,* p. 309, note 2.

34. "System Fragment," *Werke,* I, 419-20/310.

35. *Ibid.,* 421/311.

36. PhG, 106/136/222. The first of these paragraphs is the one beginning *"Die Bestimmung des Lebens . . ."* Baillie has divided this passage into five paragraphs, the first of which begins "The determination of the principle . . ."

37. Hegel makes this clear just before his extended discussion of the structure of infinite life (see previous note), PhG, 105/135/221. This corresponds to the relation between philosophy of nature and philosophy of Spirit as expressed in the Jena *Philosophy of Nature* (1804-05). "The Spirit of nature is a hidden Spirit. It does not come forth in the form of Spirit. It is Spirit only for knowing Spirit, in other words, it is Spirit in itself but not for itself . . . It is Spirit as the other of itself." GW, 7:185.

38. The category of recognition first appears briefly in *Sittlichkeit,* pp. 32 ff. and 89 ff., but achieves a central place only in the *Realphilosophie,* both volumes. Its link with love is explicit in such passages as II, 204, "Love is that spiritual recognition itself which knows itself." Such a relation, Hegel adds on the margin, is the "actuality of love."

39. PhG, 114/141/229, my italics.

40. In his *Grundlage des Naturrechts* Fichte had introduced the concept of recognition in a thoroughly Kantian manner. At one point of his argument he presents the following three propositions: "I. I can expect a particular rational being to recognize me as a rational being only in so far as I treat him as such . . . II. But I must expect all rational beings outside of me in every possible instance to recognize me as a rational being . . . III. The conclusion is clear.—I must recognize the free being outside of me in every case as a free being, i.e., I must limit my freedom through the concept of the possibility of his freedom." *Werke,* III, 44-52. Later the concept of reciprocal recognition is introduced in response to the question, "How is a community of free beings as such possible?" III, 85 ff.

41. Cf. *Realphilosophie,* II, 205, where Hegel explicitly distinguishes between the mere concept of recognition as love and the task of realizing this concept.

42. See note 20 above. cf. *Realphilosophie,* II, 201-02, "Precisely by knowing himself in the other, each one has renounced himself [*auf sich selbst Verzicht getan*]: Love." This knowing of self in the other takes place when each one "*sich aufhebt,* gives up his independence as existing for himself and in distinction from the other." A similar passage is found at I, 230. In the Jena *Metaphysics,* where Leibniz's *Monadology* is the model for developing the concept of Spirit, it is this same *sich aufheben* which is the key to the harmony in which the parts retain their individuality while relating to the whole. GW, 7:169-73.

43. That desire indicates an ontological lack is suggested by *Realphilosophie,* II, 195-96.

44. I John 4:18, RSV.

45. PhG, 119/144/233.

46. *Die Frühschriften,* ed. Landshut, Stuttgart, 1968, p. 269. English translation in *Karl Marx: Early Writings,* Bottomore, trans., New York, 1964, p. 202. Marx had no way of knowing how extensive Hegel's study of modern political economy had been by the time he wrote the *Phenomenology.*

47. PhG, 126/148-49/238.

48. That human desire is distinguished from animal desire both in terms of labor and love, and that the latter of these has primacy over the former is already Hegel's view in the *Realphilosophie.* See I, 220-21 and II, 196-202.

49. This expresses a connection not only with the Augustinian tradition but also with the Aristotelian, for which *praxis* has priority over *techne.*

50. Theodor Adorno, *Negative Dialektik,* Frankfurt, 1966, p. 8. cf. pp. 20-22.

51. See Ch. 3, n. 9.

52. *op. cit.,* p. 349, Marx's italics, from *The German Ideology.* In this sense Hegel's philosophy has the same presuppositions as Marx's, men in their concrete individuality. cf. pp. 346-47. For both of them concrete individuality is socially conditioned.

53. *Realphilosophie,* II, 179. Now it is clearer why Hegel could also say on p. 183 that "language is then the true being of Spirit as Spirit in general. It is there as the unity of two free selves . . ." That is, even language involves reciprocal recognition. That it is nevertheless not

possible to comprehend Spirit adequately within the limits of the theoretical, which is the point of the cited contrast between ego and Spirit, is also expressed in the Jena *Metaphysic*, GW, 7:165, 171.

54. See section 2A. above.

55. PhG, 287-97/255-61/374-82, and 376-83/313-18/457-63.

56. PhG, 287/255/374. There follow two other formulations of this concept: "Recognized Self-Consciousness, which has the certainty of itself in the other free Self-Consciousness and finds its truth precisely in this relation . . ." What is required is "intuiting complete unity with the other in his independence, or of having the given, free thinghood of the other, which is the negative of myself, for my object as my own being-for-myself." 289-90/256-57/375-76.

57. This question and answer appear in connection with the two formulations of recognized Self-Consciousness cited in the previous note.

58. PhG, 289/256/375-76, my italics. This is a good example of Hegel's somewhat promiscuous use of the term 'absolute'. But we must take him seriously. If he calls the knowledge which a "determinate" society gains of itself "absolute" we must not assume that he must have meant something else, since *we* do not use the term in that way. See note 67 below, especially *Naturrecht*, p. 479. Speaking there of the plurality and conditioned nature of Ethical Life he says that "the World Spirit in each of its forms has its duller or more developed but nevertheless absolute self-feeling. Among every nation and within each totality of customs and laws it has its essence and its enjoyment of itself."

59. *Naturrecht*, GW, 4:484.

60. PhG, 288/256/375. This characterization of pure consciousness as the a priori We expresses succinctly Hegel's critique of the transcendental tradition.

61. PhG, 291/258/377.

62. In *Naturrecht*, where these distinctions are the subject of a sustained critique, Hegel's explicit orientation is to the political thought of Plato, Aristotle, and Montesquieu. He calls any incongruity between customs and laws a "barbarity". GW, 4:470.

63. Cf. *The German Constitution*, *Werke*, I, 516-17/189-90.

64. See note 42 above. In the *Monadology* to be an individual is to have a unique perspective on the world.

65. PhG, 290/257/376. cf. the discussion of life, note 34 above, and the discussion of man's unorganic nature, Ch. 3, n. 50. In the next

paragraph of the PhG, this structure is developed in terms of abstract labor. cf. *Realphilosophie*, II, 213 ff.

66. When Hegel speaks of this wisdom of antiquity in *Naturrecht* he also mentions the Pythagorean notion that the best education for a young man is to become the citizen of a nation with good institutions. GW, 4:469.

67. PhG, 292-93/258-59/378. On the determinate particularity of Ethical Life and the relation of this to the issue of war see *Naturrecht*, GW, 4:449-50, 479-81.

68. PhG, 293-94/259/379. For Hegel's discussion of this phenomenon in connection with attitudes toward war see PCR I, HTJ, 222-24/155-58 and 229-30/164-65.

69. For example, see *Naturrecht*, GW, 4:424-27.

70. Just in those passages where Hegel describes the social substance as unchangeable he emphasizes this reciprocity. See notes 61 and 65 above.

71. That *Sehnsucht* and *Sollen* express an imperfect relation of the self to the social whole is emphasized in the Jena *Metaphysics*, GW, 7:170.

72. *Naturrecht*, GW, 4:470.

73. See notes 61, 65, and 70 above.

74. PhG, 377/314/458. The rendering of *das an-und-fürsichseiende Wesen* as "the self-contained and self-sufficient being" is supported by Hegel's characterization of Spirit as *das sich selbst tragende absolute reale Wesen* and as *der die Existenz ist.* 378/314/459.

75. PhG, 377-78/314/458-59. See note 70 above.

76. PhG, 385/319/467.

77. J. N. Findlay, *Hegel: A Re-Examination,* New York, 1962, p. 95.

78. Sidney Hook, *From Hegel to Marx,* Ann Arbor, 1962, p. 41.

79. Jean Hyppolite, *Genèse et Structure de la Phénoménologie de L'Esprit de Hegel,* Paris, 1946, II, 312-14. He adds, "Spirit is precisely the We in so far as it simultaneously actualizes the unity and the separation of the I's."

80. Hook, *op. cit.,* pp. 18, 30-35, 54, 62.

CHAPTER SIX: The Career of Spirit

6A. The Legal Self as the Destiny of the Ancient World

The concept of Spirit is the linchpin which holds the *Phenomenology* together. It has been developed out of epistemological reflection through a deepened questioning into the "I think" of Descartes and Kant, the self-consciousness which is presupposed in every consciousness. Hegel's conclusion is that this self-consciousness is concrete and that it is rooted in the social interaction of persons seeking recognition. This inseparability of the I from the We is what brings the concept of Spirit into vital contact with the other problem area to which Hegel has addressed himself, the present spiritual crisis. This crisis is so plainly an historical event that Hegel's description of it will have to be a kind of narrative. It is none other than the concept of Spirit which permits Hegel at this point to take up the historical perspective. We must see how this is possible.

The transition to Spirit is qualitatively different from earlier advances, for Spirit, understood in terms of Ethical Life, is "the real substance, into which the preceding forms of consciousness return and in which they find their ground."[1] More specifically, "Spirit is thus the self-supporting, absolute, real being. *All the previous forms of consciousness are abstractions from it.* They are constituted by the fact that Spirit analyses itself, distinguishes its moments, and dwells on each of these. The isolating of such moments presupposes Spirit itself for its own reality. In other words, this isolation of the moments exists only in Spirit, which is existence."[2] Like Consciousness, Self-Consciousness, and Reason, Spirit represents a dimension of human experience within which a movement from immediacy and mere certainty to mediation and truth must take place. But whereas the first three dimensions are abstract, Spirit is concrete. This means that the forms through which Spirit passes on its way from immediacy to self-knowledge "distinguish themselves from the preceding forms in being real spiritual totalities [*Geister*], authentic actualities. They are forms of a world, not merely forms of consciousness."[3]

153

The most important consequence of this is that while the *Phenomenology* up to this point has called increasingly explicit attention to the historicity of man in developing the concept of Spirit, it turns in Chapter Six for the first time to the question of human history as such. The movement from Consciousness to Self-Consciousness to Reason to Spirit is not a temporal progression. Nor is the movement within each of the first three dimensions to be understood in that way. "It is only Spirit in its entirety that is in time, and the forms of the totality of Spirit as such present themselves in a temporal succession. For it is only the whole which has authentic actuality and hence the form of pure freedom relative to anything else, the form which expresses itself as time."[4]

We know that Hegel wants to concentrate his historical account of Spirit on the transition from the old modernity to the new modernity, the revolution he believes to be occurring as he writes. This will involve a structural analysis of the old modernity as well as an account of both its demise and the new forms that seem to be replacing it. The structural analysis will function as the socioanalysis of critical finitism, for it is by understanding this world that we will understand the philosophical dogmatism which denies that we can know the Absolute. But this will not be the "refutation" of that anti-philosophical philosophy. That can come only in the account of the demise of the old modernity and the birth of the new, for it is Spirit and not Hegel who refutes that tradition. To broaden our understanding of the old modernity Hegel will first take us back in time beyond it to the world from which he believes it arose and which provides striking typological contrasts with it.

There will therefore be three stages to Hegel's narration of the historical career of Spirit in Chapter Six: Ethical Life—True Spirit, Culture—Self-Estranged Spirit, and Morality—Self-Certain Spirit. These represent three historical epochs which culminate in three types of selfhood or three kinds of social self-knowledge: the legal self, the revolutionary self, and the conscientious self.[5] Each epoch represents a determinate form of "the essential opposition between individual and universal."[6] Each form of selfhood represents that relation as it structures individual consciousness. The legal self is the culmination of Greco-Roman paganism, the process that leads from

Ethical Life to empire. The revolutionary self marks the end of the development of medieval and early modern Christian Europe. Hegel's analysis, under the rubric 'Culture', concentrates on France. The conscientious self is Hegel's attempt to understand the world-historical significance of the new world whose birth pains were the French Revolution. The orientation here is to German Idealism and Romanticism.[7]

At the beginning of this longest chapter of the *Phenomenology* we are told that the goal and result of this historical progression is "that the actual self-consciousness of absolute Spirit will come forth."[8] That would be no minor result, for if the self-consciousness of absolute Spirit is not Absolute Knowledge, it's hard to say what would be. In this sense Hegel promises to complete his phenomenological task by the end of Chapter Six. But since he describes this with the very idea which is basic to his understanding of religion, Spirit's self-consciousness, we have a preliminary clue why the result of Chapter Six might not be fully understood apart from a further chapter on religion.

The story begins, however, not with the self-consciousness of absolute Spirit but with Spirit in its immediacy. As Ethical Life, the beautiful simplicity of social wholeness, it is not aware of itself as Spirit. Just for that reason it is not fully absolute. But the process of coming to self-consciousness destroys Ethical Life by disrupting the immediacy which defines it. "Spirit, so far as it is the immediate truth, is the ethical life of a people . . . It has to advance to the consciousness of what it immediately is, transcend the beautiful ethical life, and come to a knowledge of itself by passing through a series of forms."[9] When this has happened "the ethical substance has by this process become actual self-consciousness. In other words, the particular self has come to be in and for itself. But precisely thereby is Ethical Life ruined."[10]

In his earlier discussion of Ethical Life Hegel describes its lability in terms of a two-fold immediacy.[11] Immediacy for Hegel means relation solely to self, excluding relation to an other. Thus Sense Certainty seeks to maintain immediacy in the relation of perceiving subject to perceived object by making first the one term and then the other fully unessential, thus leaving the essential moment to determine the perceptual result entirely apart from its relation to the unessential moment.[12] The two-fold immediacy of Ethical Life, therefore, is to be understood as the failure of the whole to be grasped in terms of its relations to other similar wholes and to its parts. Ethical Life is immediate in so far as it lacks the awareness of its determinate character, that is, fails to see itself as just one society among many and takes itself to be, as it were, the center of the world.[13] It is also immediate in so far as the relation between the social whole and the personal parts is not seen to be just that, a relation, presupposing at least a relative difference and independence.

It is this second immediacy which distinguishes Ethical Life from Morality in Hegel's technical usage. The laws and customs of Ethical Life are immediately valid and immediately effective. It is not for the individual to examine and validate them. His station defines his duties. The tragedy of Antigone is thus unlike that of Hamlet. As a moral person his conflict is an inner one. He reflects on his situation and tries to bring action out of soliloquizing meditation. She, however, like her antagonist, Creon, does not reflect. Both experience the conflict between the duties of their respective stations in the family and state, but not an inner conflict of soul. Each is directly identified with the role he or she is to play. Just because the social norms do not require the individual's insight and sanction they are also immediately effective. They are not a master whom the individual might disobey. Hegel expresses this double immediacy of laws and customs by saying of them simply, "They are." Neither as the question—What is my duty?—nor as the question—Shall I do it?—does reflection separate the individual from the principle of his action. But when the laws and customs of the whole have this validity and effectiveness in the parts it is difficult to speak of a relation between parts and whole, for the difference between them has vanished. One is left with the immediacy of the whole and can speak of society, but not of the individual.[14]

For Ethical Life to pass out of its immediacy and come to self-consciousness it must become aware of its relatedness as a whole to other similar wholes and to its own constituent parts. Hegel finds this double experience exquisitely expressed in Sophocles' *Antigone*.[15] First of all the social substance "tears its moments asunder." Just as the immediacy of Sense Certainty turns out to be a part of Perception, in which the moment of universality, the one, conflicts with that of particularity, the many, so Spirit's immediacy is found to involve spheres or powers which represent these same abstract aspects, the state and the family respectively. By dividing itself in this way Ethical Life plants the seeds of its own destruction, creating an enemy within its own gates. Since each of the spheres into which the substance divides itself takes itself to be the whole, the whole becomes a living contradiction.[16]

Actually each of the parts is, in an important sense, the whole. The family as well as the state is a community [*Gemeinwesen*] in which reciprocal recognition takes place. Apart from the question of size the categories of Ethical Life apply at least as well to the family as to the state. Though family and state are reciprocally dependent, it is easy for each to see the other simply as a means to its own ends. Thus the family becomes "the rebellious principle of individuality" vis-a-vis the larger community, which in turn becomes the violator of the divine law which expresses the sanctity of the family.[17]

Antigone illustrates this nicely. She comes into conflict with the state, not in virtue of the particularity presupposed by social contract theory, but in terms of her own immediate identity with another, smaller universal, the family. Creon, too, acts as the executive of the state, not a private individual. Both agents become guilty through the one-sidedness of their action. It is not merely they who perish, however, (Creon does not survive his victory over Antigone) but Ethical Life itself.[18]

Still following Sophocles, Hegel finds war to be the catalyst of their experience. It is through war that both aspects of Spirit's immediacy are overcome. To begin with war is a counter force to the centrifugal tendencies of family and economic life. "In order not to let these get rooted and settled in this isolation and thus break up the whole into fragments allowing Spirit to evaporate, the government from time to time has to shake them to the very center through war."[19] By claiming the life and wealth of its citizens the state makes clear the tension between the whole and the parts. In this respect Ethical Life passes out of its immediacy.

But war is also the struggle for recognition between communities. Each community seeks to be for itself, as Hegel would put it, by negating the other communities and reducing them to the status of something for it. The dialectic of master and slave repeats itself at the collective level. Whether as the master or slave community the ethical totality in this way becomes aware of the other totalities and thus of its own determinate and limited character.

In these two ways war enables Ethical Life to come to self-consciousness and thus achieve its "absolute truth."[20] But in doing so it destroys the *polis* and the form of Spirit associated with it. In overcoming the first immediacy war signifies only the victory of the national spirit over the household gods. As a confrontation between peoples, however, war has deeper consequences. " . . . the living nations [*Volkgeister*] are ruined through their individuality and pass over into a universal community, whose bare universality is spiritless and dead, and whose living activity is found in the particular individual as particular. The ethical form of Spirit disappears and another takes its place." Ethical Life is overrun by empire.[21]

Hegel discusses the Roman Empire as a form of human experience which he entitles "Legal Status" [*Rechtszustand*]. Instead of the unity of law and custom we have here the primacy of law.[22] Hegel finds in the notion of a legal person the form of recognition and corresponding self-consciousness which are the destiny of the ancient world. In antithesis to the immediate unity between the individual and the social substance which characterizes Ethical Life, the two are here in total separation and opposition to each other. "The substance comes forth as a formal universal over against its component individuals and no longer dwells within them as living Spirit. Rather the simple solidarity of their individuality is dispersed into a plurality of separate points . . . The universal unity into which the living, immediate unity of individuality and substance regresses is the spiritless community which has ceased to be the un-self-conscious substance of individuals. In this community they now count in their individual being-for-self as selves and substances on their own account. The universal, split up into the atomic units of the absolute plurality of individuals, this dead Spirit, is an equality in which all count for as much as each, that is, have the significance of persons." To be a legal person is to be an instance of a kind, not the part of a whole.[23]

It is true that as a legal person the individual is recognized. But Hegel finds this to be an abstract recognition since it is only as the bearer of legal rights and thus for all practical purposes as the owner of property that the individual is recognized, "only as this brittle or obstinate [*spröde*] self, not the self dissolved in the substance . . . as the bare, empty unit of the person."[24] Whatever the individual may be beyond his property, that is, his personhood in the non-legal sense, is not recognized. Only the Emperor is more fully recognized. Since he is recognized without having to recognize his citizens except as legal persons, he is rightly called the Master of the World, suggesting that legal persons, in spite of their rights as slave owners, are themselves little more than slaves.

But this is no ordinary master. "This Master of the World takes himself in this way to be the absolute person, comprising at the same time all existence within himself, for whom there exists no higher Spirit." The overtones of divinity here are not accidental. "Knowing himself in this way to be the sum and substance of all actual powers, this Master of the World is the numinous [*ungeheuer*] self-consciousness which knows itself to be the actual God." He is not, however, the God of love. It is only a "destructive power which he exercises against the selfhood of the subjects over against him. For his power is not the harmony of Spirit in which each person would perceive his own self-consciousness . . ." Rather the individuals relate as externally to him as to each other. He is a "foreign content" and a "hostile being" in relation to them. Individuality, defined in economic-legal terms, finds the state to be substantial and divine, but at the same time an alien and hostile power in which it has no share.[25]

The form of recognition realized in legal personality is thus an intense form of the alienation Hegel seeks to overcome, by no means its solution.[26] Yet this is presented as "the truth of the ethical world."[27] Antiquity founders on the problem of the individual and society. Their relation swings violently from the extreme of immediacy to the extreme of reflection, from identity to difference, without being able to find the classical ideal, expressed by Aristotle as the mean, more profoundly by Hegel as the identity of identity and difference, of immediacy and reflection.

Whereas at first one can hardly speak of individuals at all, Antigone and Creon being merely the executives of family and state, the classical world ends in such an extreme and alienated form of individualism that Hegel can describe the larger process he is tracing as the movement from independence to freedom.[28] Because the world of legal persons is structured by a "spiritless independence" which is not freedom but slavery, Hegel finds it to be the fulfillment of the "slave ideologies" (Kojeve) presented in conjunction with the Lordship and Bondage section of Chapter Four, namely Stoicism and Scepticism. Just as these develop into Unhappy Consciousness, "so here the actual truth of that view has made its appearance. This truth consists in the fact that the universal worth of self-consciousness is reality estranged from self-consciousness . . . The actuality of selfhood which was not found in the ethical world has been gained by this world's regression into the world of the legal person. What was harmonious in the former now comes on the scene as developed but self-estranged."[29] With this we have entered a new world, that of Self-Estranged Spirit. This world is the truth of Unhappy Consciousness, or, put the other way around, Unhappy Consciousness tells us the truth about this world. The transition from Stoicism and Scepticism to Unhappy Consciousness only mirrors at the ideological level the way in which Roman civilization is transformed into Christendom. This is the background of the old modernity.

6B. The Revolutionary Self as the Destiny of Christendom

In *Differenz* (1801) Hegel writes, "Estrangement [*Entzweiung*] is the source of the need of philosophy, and as the culture [*Bildung*] of the age, the unfree, given aspect of philosophy's form. In culture the appearance of the Absolute isolates itself from the Absolute and fixes itself as something independent."[30] This definition of culture in terms of estrangement guides Hegel's interpretation of the modern national Christian state in France from its feudal origins through the Revolution. It appears in the title of Chapter Six's second section: Self-Estranged Spirit—Culture.

There seems to be something of a gap in the historical narrative here, for Hegel does not narrate the transition from the Roman Empire to the feudal world to which he now turns. But the world he calls Culture spans the entire career of the Holy Roman Empire and is in essence the world of that peculiar political entity, though not in any geographically exclusive sense. Since the Holy Roman Empire took itself to be not merely the successor to the Roman Empire but in large measure its continuation, Hegel's jump is less abrupt substantially than it is chronologically.

Hegel takes seriously his own suggestion that Unhappy Consciousness is the model for the estrangement which defines the world of Culture. This means that the individual takes what is essential [*das Wesen*], the substantial and divine, to be external and negative to him, excluding his participation. Yet he knows the essential to be Spirit and thus essentially to be "the interpenetration of being and individuality. This its existence is the work of self-consciousness, but likewise an immediately given actuality, foreign to self-consciousness, with a being of its own in which self-consciousness does not recognize itself." The essential world is the "work" of self-consciousness because this world "acquires existence by self-consciousness of its own accord alienating itself [*Entäusserung*] and giving up its own essentiality [*Entwesung*] . . ." The substance becomes actual through "the estrangement of selfhood, for the immediate self, that is, the self whose validity is in and for itself apart from estrangement, is without substance . . . Its substance is thus just its alienation, and the alienation is the substance, that is, the spiritual powers forming themselves into a coherent world and thereby maintaining themselves."[31]

Because the production [*Erzeugung*] of the actual world comes about through the renunciation [*Entsagung*] by self-consciousness of its being-for-itself, this world has an objectivity over against its maker, who therefore "treats it as something foreign of which it must take possession [*sich bemächtigen*]." Culture is this taking possession. It becomes the basis of recognition. Since the self is actual only through self-estrangement, its recognition is based, not on its mere being, but on the further self-estrangement in which it overcomes its natural self by conforming itself to the universal, the world it has already helped to produce. "This individuality forms itself [*bildet sich*] to that which it is in itself." It takes possession of its world by taking as its essence or second nature that by which it has made the world the essential reality in giving up its own essentiality. Socialization creates both the individual and society, "for the power of the individual consists in conforming himself to the substance."[32]

For Culture this process of repossession remains essentially incomplete, just as with Unhappy Consciousness the essential remains irreducibly other. Culture is thus the world of dualism. In the ethical world all reality belonged to the present and nothing was understood to be radically transcendent. But for Culture the world divides into the world which is present here and now and the world beyond, the actual world and the world of pure consciousness or thought, the real world and the ideal world, the profane world and the sacred world. Over against the present, actual, real, profane world there arises a transcendent world, the distant world where the harmony so conspicuously missing here and now is restored. These two worlds, out of harmony with each other, are also out of harmony with themselves. By dividing itself into conflicting forces each is estranged from itself. The actual world becomes the struggle between State Power and Wealth, while the ideological world becomes the struggle between Faith and Enlightened Insight.[33]

The description of Culture thus divides into three subsections. The inner tensions of the actual world are presented in terms of the rise of absolute monarchy and capitalism. The revolutionary potential of these developments is noticed, but not seen as leading directly to revolution. The immediate result, the second moment, is the intellectual revolution known as Enlightenment. Out of it arises the third moment, the revolutionary self as the destiny of the estranged world of Culture. Since the immediate ground of the Revolution is found in the Enlightment, one must say that for Hegel ideas change the world. But these ideas themselves have their basis in the world that is to be changed. Ideology is not impotent. The world of the old modernity gives rise to ideas which are the vehicles of the historical change which ushers in the new modernity. Among these ideas are those which Hegel wishes to repudiate. Instead of seeking to refute them directly, he traces the path by which they undercut their own worldly basis.

The division of the actual world into spheres or estates is not peculiar to Culture. It is as natural as the division of nature into earth, air, fire, and water,[34] and was already present in the ethical world as the distinction of family from state. Nor is the fact that it is now the economic domain rather than the family which stands in conflict with the state what distinguishes the world of Culture. It is rather the non-immediate relation of the individual to these conflicting spheres of interest. Antigone was born to her role. The medieval nobility, original bearers of the world of Culture, must choose whether they shall serve State Power or Wealth.[35]

The former choice is "the heroism of service, the virtue which sacrifices the being of the individual to the universal and thereby brings the universal into being . . . Through this alienation the existing consciousness makes itself [*bildet sich*] something essential . . . Through this culture it acquires self-respect and respect from others."[36] State Power is at first this collective undertaking, and the proud vassal finds no conflict between serving the common good and his own interests, even where this service costs him his life in feudal warfare.

But State Power in the full sense involves the concept of particular will, and only with the emergence of unlimited monarchy is it fully *begeistet,* fully in possession of the union of universal and particular which typifies Spirit. Hegel stresses the linguistic character of royal authority and introduces the monarch as the linguistic creation of the nobility. He is the king because he is called the king, because they pledge him their allegiance. "Through the name the universal power is the monarch." Of course the king is not the alienated independence of just anyone. Only the speech of those with the power to confer kingship can make a king. That power resides in the wealth of the nobility. It is the ultimate source of State Power.[37]

When the nobility is seen to be wealth pursuing its own interest its nobility is somewhat tarnished. While it poses as in service to the common good, "its true nature lies rather in retaining its own being-for-itself through its service. Its spontaneous renunciation of its selfhood is actually the breaking up and tearing asunder of the universal substance. Its spirit is the attitude of thoroughgoing discordance."[38] As this comes to consciousness the distinction on which medieval society was based, between noble and base, is undercut, and the modern world takes shape in the tension between State Power and Wealth, absolute monarchy and the bourgeoisie.

The bearers of the world of Culture are now caught in an acute predicament. They have created not one but two powers which now confront them as independent and indifferent to their purposes. Not only the political power of the monarch but also the economic power of the market have this character. The wealth which began as the very principle of self-esteem has become something foreign. In both the economic and political realm bourgeois consciousness "sees itself in the power of an alien will on which it depends, which may or may not transmit being-for-itself to consciousness." Because selfhood and recognition have become so identified with political and economic power, the bourgeoisie "sees its selfhood as such dependent on the contingent individuality of an other, on the accident of the moment, of an arbitrary choice, or some other utterly indifferent circumstance."[39]

At the stage of Legal Status the self was at least recognized, imperfect as this recognition may have been. "But here the self sees its self-certainty as such to be the most unessential thing, its selfhood to be the absolute lack of selfhood. It is grateful [for its wealth] in the spirit of one who feels the deepest reprobation as well as the deepest rebellion. In this inner strife in which the pure ego sees itself outside itself and torn asunder, everything which has continuity and universality, all that bears the name of law, of good, and of right, is at the same time dispersed and destroyed . . . The pure ego itself is absolutely disintegrated."[40]

There is an important difference between the spirit of beneficent Wealth and the spirit of those who receive its benefits. Hegel has in mind the distinction from classical political economy between the capitalist whose wealth is seen as producing goods and employment for the community at large and the wage laborer in his dependence on the entrepreneur.[41] But the difference is not what it might appear to be. "Wealth thus shares reprobation with its clientele, but in the place of rebellion appears arrogance. For, on the one hand, it knows as well as the self it benefits that its being-for-itself has the character of contingent thinghood. On the other hand, it is itself this contingency in whose power selfhood is placed. In this arrogance, which thinks it has sustained an alien self through a meal and thus obtained the submission of this self in its innermost being, Wealth overlooks the inner rebellion of the other . . . It stands directly in front of this innermost abyss, this bottomless pit in which all stability and substance have vanished. It sees in this pit nothing but a common thing, a plaything for its whims, a chance result of its own caprice."[42]

Over against this arrogance is the rebellion of alienated labor. Its language is "the linguistic epitome of this whole world of Culture, the spirit of this world in its truth and objective reality." If you want to know what the world of Culture is all about, listen to the proletariat. The revolutionary attitude of this group is to be understood in terms of its experience of selfhood. "This self-consciousness, the rebellion which reprobates its reprobation, is immediately absolute self-identity in absolute dismemberment, the pure mediation of pure self-consciousness with itself." That is to say that it has been reflected out of its social substance. Social rules no longer have any value for it, and it can no longer find recognition or fulfillment through participation in the economic, political, or family life of its people.[43]

While Hegel finds proletarian consciousness to be the revolutionary truth of the world of Culture, he does not proceed directly to a description of the revolutionary self. He knows that the French Revolution was not a proletarian revolution. It is clear from this passage as well as from the earlier analysis of the master-slave relationship that Hegel understands the character of alienated labor. But though he brings this phenomenon to our attention on two separate occasions, he does not find it to be the vehicle of historical change. It is clear that on his analysis there can be no "happy consciousness" as long as alienated labor remains. But he does not see the laborer as an effective revolutionary. The world of Culture is not revolutionized directly through itself, but indirectly through that other world which reflects it, the world of pure but by no means proletarian consciousness.

The house of Culture is, as we have already seen, divided against itself. Hegel now directs our attention to the ideological world which lies beyond the world of State Power and Wealth he has just been describing. "The first world is the actual world where Spirit's estrangement is realized. The other is that which

Spirit constructs for itself in the ether of pure consciousness, raising itself above the first. Set in opposition to that estrangement, this second world is just for that reason not free from it, but rather only the other form of that very estrangement, which consists precisely in having one's consciousness divided between two worlds. Thus both worlds are included in this second world. It is therefore not the self-consciousness of absolute being as it is in and for itself, that is, not Religion which is considered here, but Faith, in so far as it is a flight from the actual world and thus not something in and for itself. This flight out of the realm of the present is therefore immediately divided against itself. Pure consciousness is the element into which Spirit raises itself, but it is not only the element of Faith but just as much of the concept. Consequently both appear on the scene together at the same time, and the former comes before us only in opposition to the latter," i.e., Faith in opposition to Enlightened Insight, religion in conflict with philosophy.[44]

This pivotal paragraph introduces the second stage of Hegel's account of Culture with three important points. First, Hegel is dealing here, as in the case of Unhappy Consciousness, with a form of religion which does not fulfill its own aspirations. The faithful desire to experience the presence of the divine, but find their present devoid of divinity. The use of the term 'Faith' to describe this experience is introduced in Hegel's earlier discussion of Ethical Life under the heading, Reason as Testing Laws. Ethical consciousness does not believe in the laws it obeys, "for faith, while it surely intuits the divine [*das Wesen*], sees it as something alien. The ethical self-consciousness is immediately one with the essential [*das Wesen*] in virtue of the universality of its own self. Faith, on the other hand, begins with the individual consciousness. It is the process in which this consciousness is always approaching this unity without ever entering the presence of its own essence."[45] For Faith, then, the divine has the character of positivity which was the subject of Hegel's earliest theological critiques.[46]

Second, faith is presented as ideology. As a reflection out of the world of Culture it is at the same time a reflection of that world. Thus its worship can be described as the "obedience of service and of praise," precisely the language used to describe the earthly role of the feudal nobility.[47] But ideologies are never exact mirrorings of the real world. The object of faith is, "according to the concept of Faith, nothing else than the real world lifted into the universality of pure consciousness. The structure of the real world, therefore, also constitutes the organization of the object of faith, except that in this case the parts have the character of Spirit without being estranged from each other."[48] The world beyond is simply this world purified of its flaws. Much of Enlightment's critique of Faith revolves around this point. Anticipating Feuerbach and Freud, it seeks to discredit Faith by interpreting it as a wish-fulfilling projection of its own self-image. God is but the fictitious product of its own undisciplined imagination.

Hegel describes this familiar Enlightenment critique, but he finds Enlightenment to be every bit as ideological as Faith. This is the third and perhaps crucial element of his account of self-estranged Spirit as pure consciousness. If Enlightenment wins out in the struggle with Faith it is not because it is any less a reflection of the world of Culture than its opponent. Hegel does not overlook the real differences between the two, which he seeks to express in formulations like these: Faith has the content without insight, while Enlightenment has insight without content, or, Faith is consciousness without self-consciousness, Enlightenment the reverse. But having a common origin, the two views end up looking more similar than different to Hegel. "Insight therefore is victorious over Faith, because in relation to Faith it validates what is necessary to and contained in Faith."[49] As reflections out of the world of Culture both find the world here and now to be unacceptable. Both point beyond it to a world in which estrangement is overcome. The beyond of Enlightenment is that of the "not yet," while that of Faith, in the form presented here, is the beyond of "once upon a time" and of "somewhere else, not here." Even here Hegel finds identity, for he suggests that the "here, but not yet" hope of Enlightenment is not really alien to a Faith which prays, "Thy will be done in earth as it is in heaven."

Enlightenment's commitment is to a secularized form of the Kingdom of God. "Both worlds are reconciled and heaven is transplanted to the earth below."[50] It is a secularized version of this dream because man alone is to do the transplanting. Yet Hegel sees Enlightenment as reminding Faith of its own claim that "God sent his son into the world, not to condemn the world, but that the world might be saved through him."[51] A religion with Incarnation at its core cannot be entirely otherworldly. Enlightenment's arguments against Faith are always *ad hominem*, though neither party to the quarrel realizes this.

The this-worldly *Weltanschauung* of Enlightenment, the immediate source of the revolution, is presented in its metaphysical, epistemological, and ethical dimensions. As metaphysics it is either deism or materialism. Hegel finds it hard to distinguish between the two, since on both views "the absolute Being turns out to be a mere vacuum, to which no characteristics or predicates can be attributed." Enlightened insight into the absolute Being is that "which sees nothing in it but just absolute Being, the être suprême, the great void."[52] This is in keeping with Enlightenment's "Feuerbachian" view that the wealth ascribed to the divine world belongs to the human world by nature. It is as if deism and materialism signify the emptiness of a transcendent absolute after man reclaims for himself what was, according to Enlightenment, orginally his.

Enlightenment's empiricism is equally motivated by its this-worldliness. Hegel describes it as a return to Sense Certainty, which we have come to recognize as an attempt to validate the knowledge of Perception and Understanding, the knowledge of this world. This empiricism goes hand in glove with deism or materialism. Just because Enlightenment "conceives all determination in general, that is, every content and filling, to be a finite, human representation,"[53] it accuses Faith of anthropomorphism in its concept of God and in turn refuses to predicate anything of the absolute Being.

Enlightenment's this-worldliness, however, comes to its fullest expression in an ethics oriented to utility. The world is to be a Garden of Eden for man. "As he is immediately, as natural consciousness in itself, man is good. As individual he is absolute, and everything else exists for him . . . everything is for his pleasure and delight. As he comes from the hand of God, he walks in the world as in a garden planted for him. He is bound also to have plucked the fruit of the tree of the knowledge of good and evil. He has a use for this knowledge . . . his individuality has its limits and can overreach itself and destroy itself. Reason is a useful means against this possibility . . ."[54] The usefulness of reason is by no means restricted to the knowledge of good and evil. For Enlightenment this is the important thing about the whole range of empirical knowledge.

We are suddenly brought back to the apparently forgotten link between epistemology and the history of Spirit. Having developed the concept of Spirit as the necessary framework within which transcendental philosophy must be placed, Hegel does not pause in his analysis of the Greco-Roman period to comment on the modes of knowledge made possible by its forms of social experience. Here the situation is necessarily different, for the Introduction makes it clear that Hegel wants to understand critical finitism in terms of the world in which it thrives. That world is now before us as Culture, a world of political, economic, and religious alienation. Culture is the attempt to take possession [*sich bemächtigen*] of this world which has gotten out of hand. This is just the language used in the Introduction to describe that instrumental reason which is by definition unable to comprehend the Absolute.[55] In an epoch when the spiritual or social world has gotten so out of man's control that he finds his own products hostile to him, the knowledge which is power inevitably has a special attraction.[56] If man must be the slave of his own institutions and ideas, perhaps he can at least be master of nature. While spiritual estrangement may not account for the rise of the natural sciences as useful knowledge, it does throw light on the apotheosis of instrumental reason, which is Hegel's starting point in the Introduction.

The sense of impotence which defines the world of Culture not only makes instrumental reason attractive, but also tends to confirm the sense of finitude which knows it cannot know the Absolute. This is not the standpoint of Faith, but as it succumbs to the assaults of Enlightenment it turns into that "pure yearning" whose truth is an "empty beyond," that is, the new "religious" opponent of Enlightenment is Romanticism. But again identity is stronger than difference. "In this way Faith has in fact become the same as Enlightenment, namely the consciousness of the relation of an isolated [*an sich*] finitude to the unknown and unknowable Absolute without predicates." The prevailing conception acknowledges the essential "only in the form of an objective realm beyond and it acknowledges consciousness, distinguished from this realm and thus having

the in itself outside itself, as finite consciousness."[57] It is clear
that only through overcoming the estrangement of Culture will
knowledge of the Absolute be possible. A different philosophy
will be possible only in a different world.

Though Hegel interprets Romanticism as Faith capitulat-
ing to Enlightenment, it appears at first as if there is a significant difference between them. For the Enlightenment seems to
be satisfied finitude, Romanticism unsatisfied finitude. But
Hegel reminds us that utility is the truth of Enlightenment. As
long as only nature but not Spirit has been brought under control, as long as the social world resembles hell more nearly than
the Garden of Eden, Enlightenment cannot remain satisfied.
Through its critique of Faith Enlightenment has created a
thoroughly secular consciousness, one which has repudiated
the longing for transcendence characteristic of both Faith and
Romanticism. But it has a longing of its own. It wants to trans-
plant heaven on earth, but this has not yet happened. The result is that God is nowhere to be found, neither in heaven nor
on earth. Since nothing is holy there is no basis for affirmation.
Enlightenment turns from the battle with Faith to its real
enemy, the actual world which stubbornly refuses to be the
Kingdom of God. It does so as an entirely negative and destructive force. The revolutionary self is before us. "Out of this inner
revolution emerges the actual revolution of the actual world,
the new form of consciousness, Absolute Freedom." This freedom is absolute because for it there is "nothing on hand
separating self-consciousness from its inheritance other than
the empty semblance of objectivity."[58]

The new self whose possession the world is to be is not the
individual but the universal, collective subject "which knows its
self-certainty to be the essence of all spiritual spheres, both of
the real and of the supersensible world . . ." This Absolute
Freedom is the general will of Rousseau. As it takes charge of
the world "the whole system of spiritual domains or powers,
which organizes and maintains itself through the division into
separate spheres, collapses . . ." Through this collapse "each individual consciousness raises itself out of the sphere to which it
was assigned and no longer finds its essence and its role [*Werk*]
in this separate sphere. It rather grasps itself as the concept of
will and all spheres as the essential expression of this will. Con-

sequently it can realize itself only in that work which is a work of the whole. In this Absolute Freedom all social ranks or classes [*Stände*] . . . are abolished." This abolition is simultaneously the "cancelling of the distinct spiritual spheres and of the restricted life of the individual."[59]

Hegel here stresses the sociological aspects of the Revolution over the political. It is not so much that Absolute Freedom as the general will wants to replace the king with itself on the throne of national sovereignty, for it is not simply power but participation which is demanded. The social structure of society cuts off participation not only in the palace but in many other domains of human endeavor. Whereas the individual had been assigned his own special nook and cranny of human possibility, he now demands to be free to share in the whole gamut of man's life together. This means that the limitations imposed by every form of social hierarchy must be eliminated.

This abolition cannot at first be described as a restructuring of the social whole for two reasons. First, the call is not for a different social structure but for freedom from the limitations of social hierarchy as such. Second, there is for this mode of consciousness nothing objective to be reshaped, only the "empty semblance of objectivity." Presumably it could constitute itself as something objective and enduring. That would involve once again dividing the social substance into such spheres as government on the one hand, sub-divided in turn into legislative, judicial, and executive branches, and on the other hand the various spheres of labor, the different estates. Individuals would once again belong immediately not to the whole but to one of the parts. "They would find their activity and being, however, by this process confined to a branch of the whole, to one kind of action and existence. Placed in the element of being, they would have the significance of something determinate. They would cease to be universal self-consciousness." For the first reason given above Absolute Freedom cannot be persuaded to accept this. The idea that the assignment to various roles is the result of self-imposed legislation or at least of legislation in which it has had a share through representation is regarded by Absolute Freedom as an attempt to steal its birthright by fraud.[60]

This is the attitude which expresses itself in the Terror.

"Universal Freedom can thus produce neither a positive achievement nor a positive deed. There is left for it only negative action. It is merely the fury of disappearing."[61] But the Terror is self-contradictory. Its reality does not correspond to its concept, for while its action is supposed to stem from the general will, it finds that action presupposes individual will, and it turns out to be government by faction. The built-in instability of such a "system" is dramatically illustrated by the guillotine. ". . . thus the organization of spiritual spheres to which the plurality of conscious individuals is assigned, takes shape once more. These individuals, who have felt the fear of the absolute master, death, submit to negation and distinction once more, distribute themselves among the spheres, and return to a restricted and assigned role, but thereby to their substantial actuality."[62]

But restoration is not the truth of revolution. If this were the case one would have to say that Spirit has been thrown back to its starting point, the worlds of Ethical Life and Culture, and that this revolutionary interpenetration of substance and self-consciousness was a process ever in need of repetition in order that Spirit might be "refreshed" and "rejuvenated" by the fear of the Lord and better able to "endure" the objectivity of the world from which its individuality is excluded. But this is not the meaning of the Terror's inability to sustain itself. "All the determinations of the world of culture disappear in the disaster which the self experiences as Absolute Freedom."[63]

Strictly speaking, of course, this disappearance does not take place. There are social structures that survive the Revolution, and one might even find some left-over nobility around afterwards. The point is that Spirit's destiny is not found in whatever may have survived from the world of Culture but rather in a new experience, born in the revolution, in which the general will finds a new and less frenzied career. The demand of consciousness to be immediately identical with the universal will is given up. What is sacrificed "is the abstract being or immediacy of insubstantial individuality, and this vanished immediacy is the general will itself, which consciousness now knows itself to be, in so far as it is transcended immediacy, in so far as it is pure knowledge or pure will. By this means it knows that will to be itself, and it knows itself to be what is essential;

but not as an immediately existing being, nor as will in the form of revolutionary government, nor as anarchy struggling to establish an anarchical constitution."[64]

The one thing that is clear from this passage is that the individual's participation in the general will is not immediate. It is not his empirical preferences at any given moment which share the dignity of the general will, but only his "pure" knowledge and will. Here we are only told what this general will as vanished immediacy is not. The positive account of what it is belongs to the third and final section of Chapter Six, Self-Certain Spirit—Morality. "Just as the realm of the actual world passes over into that of Faith and Insight, Absolute Freedom leaves its self-destroying sphere of reality and passes over into another land of self-conscious Spirit, where in this unreality it is acknowledged to be the truth."[65] We need not panic at this reference to the truth in its unreality. Just as the unreal world of thought defined by Faith and Enlightened Insight mediated between two actual worlds, that of Culture and that of the Revolution, we can expect Morality to mediate between the actual world created (or better, destroyed) by Absolute Freedom and a new world of actuality in which, according to Hegel's promise, absolute Spirit will appear.

6C. The Conscientious Self as the Destiny of the Post-revolutionary World

The new land to which Absolute Freedom migrates is Germany. In its unreality it is, in the first instance, the autonomy of pure practical reason as developed by Kant and Fichte. This form of Morality can be seen as akin to Absolute Freedom in that it involves a dignity and recognition for the individual based on personhood as such, wholly independent of class and social status. By speaking of this practical reason as "knowing will" Hegel makes it clear that his reference is not just to a theory of right action but to an entire outlook on the world, the moral *Weltanschauung*.

Over against the knowing will of Morality there no longer stands a world of objectivity. This has been withdrawn into that knowing will. That is to say that Morality finds duty to be the essential and substantial thing, but that as autonomous, self-legislating practical reason it finds duty to belong to its own pure consciousness and to be nothing foreign or alien to it. The object of its knowledge is its own self-certainty as rational will, and we therefore "seem" to be dealing with a form of knowledge which is adequate to its truth, with a subjectivity which is its own object and its only object in total transparency.

As in the transition to Self-Consciousness the moment of Consciousness is at first missing to this moral freedom which takes itself to be absolute. Of course the world of nature is still there. But Morality has its own purpose and creates its own object. It finds the world entirely unessential and meaningless and takes the attitude of complete freedom and indifference toward nature. Its virtue is as independent of happiness as its duty is from inclination. There is something Stoic about Morality. It wins its freedom by withdrawing into the inwardness of its own intentions and treats the world of consequences as unessential.[66]

But Morality is not Stoicism, and it cannot so easily let the world go its own way. Happiness as well as virtue belongs to its full conception of the highest good. Further, if the self-estrangement of Culture is to be overcome, Morality cannot endure the essential separation of duty and inclination, pure and empirical self, intention and consequence. So reason demands that nature conform itself to Morality, and it postulates the harmony of happiness and virtue, of inclination and duty. It takes their identity to be ultimately certain, even if not yet actual. As a kind of guarantee for these first two postulates, Morality makes a third. It affirms the reality of a God independent of moral consciousness, whose function is not only to validate the specific laws, which cannot be derived from pure reason, but also to bring about the harmony of reason and nature.[67]

With this new "Lord and Master of the world" the previously missing moment of Consciousness or outward objectivity is re-established. But Morality falls in this way into contradiction with itself. On the one hand it claims to have overcome estrangement, while on the other it finds the essential to be fully beyond it both as the "not yet" of freedom and nature's unity and as the transcendence of the God from whom it receives this reward for its virtue as a form of grace. The self-confessed reality of Morality does not correspond to its concept. "The object of its actual consciousness is not yet transparent to it; it is not the absolute concept, *which alone grasps otherness as such, its absolute opposite as its very self.*" Both God and nature become essential but remain fully independent of Morality.[68]

Because of this inner contradiction Morality is given over to a vacillation which Hegel calls dissemblance. Rather uncharitably he interprets its confusion as a lack of seriousness. It is in reaction to the perceived inadequacies of this form of consciousness that a new one arises. "It is pure Conscience, which scorns such a moral world-view. It is in itself the simple, self-certain Spirit which, without the mediation of those ideas, acts in immediate conscientiousness, and has its truth in this immediacy."[69] To understand Conscience as the form in which absolute Spirit makes its appearance we have to understand both the meaning of this immediacy and the nature of the new mediation in which it necessarily disappears. The necessity of its disappearance has already been indicated in Hegel's account of the general will as vanished immediacy.[70] It belongs to the nature of Spirit to be intersubjective and actual. But when moral autonomy in its immediacy seeks to form an actual community of persons, it creates only the destruction of the Terror. If Morality is to get beyond its "unreality" to an actual human community, the immediacy with which Conscience first appears will have to be transcended.

This immediacy of Conscience is its fundamentally anarchistic nature. Its self-mediation can only be the process by which community arises out of anarchy. We have now to understand both dimensions of Conscience. In its so-called "Oldest System Program" German Idealism had begun in praise of anarchy. The idea of beauty and the hope for a re-union of mythology and philosophy are directed against the state. The author of this fragment, whether he be Schelling or Hegel, wants to show "that there is no Idea of the state, because the state is something mechanical, just as little as there is an Idea of a machine. Only the object of freedom is called Idea. We must therefore go beyond the state!—For every state must treat free men as mechanical cogs, and it should not do so; therefore it should cease."[71]

When Hegel wrote the *Phenomenology* he had moved a long way from the uncompromising atmosphere in which this was written. This is surely one of the reasons why it is so hard to see and to take seriously the fact that it is in a setting which can only be described as anarchy that absolute Spirit comes on the scene in the *Phenomenology*. No doubt it sounds strange to characterize in this way so crucial a passage in so important a work of the author of *The German Constitution* and *The Philosophy of Right*. But the structure of Chapter Six gives a three-fold justification for such an interpretation.

First, while the state plays an important role in the discussions of Ethical Life and Culture it has fully disappeared in the analysis of Conscience. Yet it is as Conscience that Morality, the third and last moment of Hegel's phenomenological philosophy of history, achieves its truth.[72] In this connection it should be noted that Hegel sees the world of Ethical Life and its truth, Legal Status, as a fulfillment of Stoicism and Scepticism, just as he finds the world of Culture to realize Unhappy Consciousness.[73] But no slave-ideology stands in such a relation to Conscience. One can say that in the *Phenomenology* slavery and the state are only overcome together. This is not to deny that, as Hegel writes in *Differenz*, "the highest community is the highest freedom."[74] It is just that in the *Phenomenology* Hegel does not find the state to be the only or highest community, nor, consequently, the only or the highest freedom.

Second, it is not only a matter of the state. The community in which absolute Spirit appears is also sociologically anarchic. This is because it is the positive result of the French Revolution. The concluding paragraphs of the preceding section[75] have shown how revolutionary freedom takes the objectivity of the world to be "nothing more than empty pretense [*Schein*]," and how this means that for it the role of social roles is past. Hegel knows that they have not simply disappeared, but he claims that for the new experience he is seeking to describe as Conscience they play no essential role. They cannot be the basis of post-revolutionary community.

Third, Conscience is ethically anarchic as well as politically and sociologically. It acknowledges no obligation to any rule or law whatever, inner or outer. The freedom of Conscience is not that of Luther, which is free from all human authority in order to be subject to the authority of God, nor that of Kant, which is free from all external authority, human and divine, but subject to the inner authority of pure practical reason. For Conscience this is not freedom but bondage.[76] For this reason "Conscience is free from every possible content. It absolves itself from every specific duty which is supposed to be binding as law. In the strength of its self-certainty it has the majesty of absolute autarchy, to bind or to loose."[77] When this autarchy acts "the agent's own immediate individuality constitutes the content of moral action, and the form of moral action is just this very self as pure process, namely as knowing in the sense of personal conviction. It is because "this pure conviction is as such just as empty as pure duty" that the content must come from the immediate individuality of the agent. This natural individuality giving content to the emptiness of conviction is the instincts and inclinations of man's sensible nature and his arbitrary choices. One is reminded of the Old Testament, where we read, "In those days there was no king in Israel; every man did what was right in his own eyes."[78]

It looks as if Conscience has left the realm of Spirit altogether. For Spirit means mediation and Spirit means community.[79] But we have been told that the truth of Conscience is its immediacy, and we have seen that this immediacy is a threefold anarchy which seems to exclude any possibility of community. If absolute Spirit is to emerge a mediation is called for which would simultaneously preserve the truth of Conscience's immediacy and make possible a community of the conscientious. This new mediation was anticipated in the discussion of Absolute Freedom as the means by which its pure negativity could be transformed into something positive.[80] Its concrete form and its emergence out of the anarchic immediacy of Conscience must now be shown.

It is important to remember what the new community cannot be, according to the preceding analysis. In his famous essay, "Hegel and the French Revolution," Joachim Ritter suggests that two ideas from the Revolution are built into Hegel's idea of freedom, "the grounding of political freedom as right in the substantial freedom of being oneself [*Selbstsein*] and the consequent determination of the content of political regulations for the purpose of making possible the realization of human existence in its freedom . . . The problem which the Revolution's demand for political freedom has raised is to find the legal form [*Rechtsform*] of freedom, that is, to construct a legal order which is suited to the freedom of being oneself." For Ritter's Hegel "subjectivity is only able to be actualized when the political and social institutions are the actuality of its action in accord with its being itself . . . the freedom of being oneself, of intention, of conscience, and thus the ethical life of free men is only able to have enduring reality when political and social institutions are in accord with these freedoms."[81] Ritter is speaking primarily about the *Philosophy of Right,* and it is tempting to see that treatise as a kind of completion of the *Phenomenology's* sixth chapter, working out in detail what is only stated in principle in the earlier work. This is simply not possible. In the *Phenomenology* the condition of Legal Status is presented as an independence lacking true freedom, and instead of the construction of new institutions in harmony with freedom it is concerned with man's elevation above those limited identities which institutions and their accompanying roles provide. The truth of Conscience's anarchic immediacy cannot be simply abandoned. We are explicitly told that the new world is not that of "anarchy struggling to establish an anarchical constitution."[82]

The mediating process by which community arises out of anarchic individualism is not that of political reform. It is most adequately described, on Hegel's view, in religious categories, confession and forgiveness. It is in these terms that the reciprocal recognition in which Spirit is fully realized must be understood. Although the pure duty in terms of which Morality defined itself left it an empty formalism, Conscience does not simply dispense with the impetus to universality which underlies the concept of pure duty. This remains rather as essential to Conscience, which thereby realizes its need to relate to the other, to win recognition from him, and thus to be self-consciousness in community, the only freedom that is actual. Conscientious action is not merely the externalization of an inner content but also the seeking of recognition for the self revealed in that action. Only in terms of recognition can Conscience be Spirit.[83]

Language becomes essential at this point. Though it is

through action that the agent enters the public domain in which recognition is possible, it is the agent and not his act which is to be recognized. Since there is no immediate identity between the act and the agent, acts which conceal being as possible as acts which reveal, the agent must affirm his conviction, must tell the world that he is acting out of conscience. It is only through the two-fold self-expression of action and speech that the self becomes sufficiently public to be recognized.[84]

But this recognition is by no means automatic. The act which the self presents as conscientious may be taken as evil, his profession of conscientiousness as deception and hypocrisy. Having rendered itself public in action and speech, the self may find his efforts rewarded by judgment and rejection rather than recognition. There is nothing to keep the other self from withholding recognition in the name of his own conscientious conviction. There seems to be no way from anarchy to community. Nor could this war of all against all be terminated by a social contract, for this would only be the reversion to Legal Status.

Conscience, however, is already two steps beyond this impasse. In *saying* that it acts out of conviction it transcends its particularity and recognizes the necessary universality of the self, its own need for recognition. At the same time, by saying that it acts in accordance with its own private conviction and not according to what is already universally recognized it confesses that it is evil.[85] Forgiveness is now the form which recognition must take. It is no more automatic than before, but when the other recognizes itself in the first self, the hard heart is melted and forgiving recognition occurs. The self-recognition which makes possible recognition of the other is two-fold. The judging self realizes that its judgment rests on private conviction as much as the act it judges, and it realizes that it too must act and that its act, though different in content, will be identical in form to the act judged as evil, that it too will be grounded in the privacy of conscience. The community which comes into being through forgiveness is thus a community of mutual tolerance. "The word of reconciliation is the existing Spirit which intuits the pure knowledge of itself as something universal in its opposite, in the pure knowledge of itself as absolutely self-existing individuality,—a reciprocal recognition which is

absolute Spirit . . . The reconciling Yes with which both selves
desist from their existence in opposition is the existence of the I
expanded into a We [*Zweiheit*], which remains itself in that We,
and which has the certainty of itself in its complete
relinquishment and its opposite;—it is the appearing God in the
midst of those who know themselves to be pure knowledge."[86]

With this sudden appearance of absolute Spirit we are at
the end of the long journey through which we were to learn
what Spirit has become and what knowledge truly is. What remains is to unpack and clarify this result in order that its definitive character may become evident. It must be made clear that
the knowledge of which so much is said, not only in the passage
just cited but throughout the entire conclusion of Chapter Six
and which is an essential element of the community of tolerance,
is Absolute Knowledge, the resolution to the whole problem of
knowledge as a philosophical task. This is the job of Chapter
Eight.

But before proceeding to this task Hegel feels it necessary
to clarify the religious dimension into which Spirit is suddenly
cast. It is not just that reciprocal recognition is understood as
confession and forgiveness; at issue is the inherent divinity of
Conscience which makes possible the identification of the
community of tolerance with God. This identification occurs
not only in the passage just cited, but earlier as well, where
Hegel writes, "Conscience, then, in its majestic sublimity above
any specific law and every content of duty puts whatever content it pleases into its knowledge and willing. It is moral genius,
which knows the inner voice of its immediate knowledge to be a
voice divine; and since in this knowledge it knows existence just
as immediately, it is the divine creative power . . . It is just as
much itself the worship of God, for its action is the intuition of
its own divinity." Since, as we have seen, moral genius moves
toward community and reciprocal recognition, Hegel is able to
continue, "This solitary worship is at the same time essentially
the worship of a congregation." It is now the congregation or
community of tolerance which intuits its own divinity. This
makes it possible to define religion, so far as knowledge is concerned, as "the utterance of the congregation regarding its own
Spirit."[87]

The movement of Chapter Six is from community [*Gemeinwesen*][88] to congregation [*Gemeinde*], from the city of man to the city which is the self-intuition of God. It hardly needs to be argued that the divine self-knowledge is Absolute Knowledge, which is why there is little new in Chapter Eight. What needs clarification is the movement by which the human community becomes not simply a worshipping community but a congregation whose worship is God's knowledge of himself. This is the task of Chapter Seven. It supports the interpretations of Chapter Six by repeating them in the opposite direction. It moves from congregation to community, seeking to show that the tendency of the human community to be a congregation is matched by the tendency of religion to find its final horizon in the human community, in an earthly Kingdom of God. While Chapter Six portrays the deifying of society, Chapter Seven supports this with its interpretation of the humanizing of God.

NOTES

1. See Ch. 5, n. 60.
2. PhG, 378/314/459, my italics.
3. PhG, 380/315/460.
4. PhG, 630/476/689.
5. PhG, 581-84/445-46/644-45. cf. 380-81/315-16/460-61.
6. PhG, 384/318/466.
7. Earlier in *The German Constitution* Hegel had given a different sketch of world history in three stages: oriental, Roman, and Germanic. This earlier scheme is the one to which he returns in the Berlin lectures on the philosophy of history. See *Werke,* I, 533/203. cf. I, 428 ff. for still earlier reflection on the spirit of the oriental world.
8. PhG, 382/316/461.
9. PhG, 379-80/315/460.
10. PhG, 383/318/463.
11. See Ch. 5, n. 67 and n. 68.
12. See section 3B. above.
13. On the "symbolism of the center" see Mircea Eliade, *Images and Symbols,* trans. Mairet, New York, 1969.
14. PhG, 404-06/331-32/484-86. cf. 372-75/310-12/451-53. In the latter passage, "Reason as Testing Laws," it is this contrast between Ethical Life and Morality which is posed as the crucial question for a Kantian type moral theory. The question of an empty formalism is secondary. The religious aspect of this same immediacy is expressed in Wilamowitz's oft cited summary of Greek polytheism, *"Die Götter sind da."*
15. On Hegel's early enthusiasm for Greek tragedy, and especially *Antigone,* see Rosenkranz, *Georg Wilhelm Friedrich Hegels Leben,* Darmstadt, 1963, pp. 11 and 25.
16. PhG, 382-84/317-18/462-66 and 418-21/340-42/496-99. On the relation of parts and whole see 400/329/480.
17. PhG, 386-99/320-28/468-79, and 416/339/494. The elevation of the brother-sister relation over that of husband and wife is partly to be understood from the fact that while Hegel was writing the *Phenomenology* he was awaiting the birth of an illegitimate son. In the *Philosophy of Right,* written after he was happily married, the husband-wife relationship assumes priority again.
18. Compare PhG, 412-13/336/491 with the passage quoted in note 10 above. In the former it is the individual who *"ist zu Grunde gegangen"* while in the latter this is the fate of Ethical Life itself.

19. PhG, 393/324/474.
20. See Ch. 5, n. 67 and n. 68.
21. PhG, 419-21/341-42/497-98.
22. For Hegel's early views of the relation between Ethical Life and Roman law, see *Naturrecht*, GW, 4:456-57 and Werke, I, 439-40.
23. PhG, 421-22/342-43/499-501. In a fragment on love from 1797-98 Hegel notes that equality of rights can mean equality of dependence, and in SC he writes, "The Greeks were to be equal because all were free, self-subsistent; the Jews were equal because all were incapable of self-subsistence." HTJ, 378/302 and 255/198. Though Hegel's enthusiasm for Napoleon and the Napoleonic Code at the time of the *Phenomenology* are well documented, this can hardly be, as is sometimes suggested, what he means by the birth of a new era. The description of Legal Status makes it clear that the revolution he believes to be taking place is not essentially one of legal reform.
24. PhG, 422-24/343-44/502-03.
25. PhG, 426-27/345-46/504-05.
26. From his studies in modern political economy, beginning with a commentary in 1799 on Sir James Steuart's *Inquiry into the Principles of Political Economy* and continuing in his study of Adam Smith while at Jena, Hegel developed an appreciation of abstract right or legal status and its place in the modern world. But this principle was clearly in conflict with his "Greek ideal." On the basis of this part of the *Phenomenology* it would be fair to say that any tendencies toward a romantic longing for a return to Ethical Life, observable in both *Sittlichkeit* and *Naturrecht*, were checked by Hegel's understanding of the economic structure of the modern world. This is already clear in *Realphilosophie*. But it is equally clear that the *Phenomenology* does not find either bourgeois civil society or the bourgeois state to be the basis for a truly human existence. Nor (to repeat note 23 above) would a new emperor in the form of Napoleon be of any help.
27. PhG, 582/445/645. This is in sharp contrast to the idealizing of everything Greek in *Naturrecht* and *Sittlichkeit*. Hegel's mature view of Greek culture is Nietzschean. Beneath the Apollinian peacefulness he sees the Dionysian conflict and tragedy. He sees that "despite its calm there is a conflict in pagan society, tragic conflict which results in the destruction of the individual and of society itself." Alexandre Kojeve, *Introduction a la Lecture de Hegel*, Paris, 1947, p. 102.
28. PhG, 288/255-56/375. cf. *Differenz*, GW, 4:54. The contrast between independence and freedom is also basic to Hegel's critique in *The German Constitution*.

29. PhG, 428/346/506. cf. 423-25/343-44/502-03.

30. GW, 4:12.

31. PhG, 429-30/347-48/509-10. *Entäusserung* is a crucial term in the *Phenomenology*. It has connotations of externalizing what is inner and Baillie quite properly translates it as kenosis when Hegel applies it to the incarnation, alluding to Philippians 2:6-7, which says that Christ, though in the form of God "did not count equality with God a thing to be grasped, but emptied himself, taking the form of a servant, being born in the likeness of men." (RSV)

32. PhG, 435-38/351-53/514-17. cf. XXXII-XXXVI/26-28/88-91. Both these passages are illuminated by Peter Berger's account of society in terms of externalization, objectification, and internalization. See *The Sacred Canopy*, Garden City, 1967, Chapter One.

33. PhG, 430-33/348-49/510-12. cf. *Differenz*, GW, 4:14, 79-80.

34. PhG, 439-40/353-54/517-19.

35. PhG, 443/355-56/521.

36. PhG, 449-50/360/527.

37. PhG, 450-59/360-66/527-35.

38. *Idem.*

39. PhG, 461-62/367-68/537-38.

40. *Idem. Verworfenheit* means both depravity and reprobation. The related verb, *verwerfen* is used to speak of quashing a verdict.

41. See note 26 above.

42. PhG, 463-64/369/539.

43. PhG, 465-66/370/540-41.

44. PhG, 434/350/513. For a longer version see 474-81/376-80/549-54.

45. PhG, 372/310-11/451-52.

46. PhG, 478-79/378-79/552. This passage brings together the concept of positivity with the two concepts crucial for the analysis of religion in Chapter Seven, *Vorstellung* and *Gegenständlichkeit*.

47. Compare PhG 482/381/556 with 447-58/359-65/525-34. Here as in PCR I, Christianity is seen less as the cause than the effect or evidence of underlying social alienation.

48. PhG, 480/480/554. Hegel here employs the Trinity as a model of reciprocal recognition.

49. PhG, 515/402/583. cf. 520/405/587.

50. PhG, 532/413/598.

51. John 3:17 (RSV).

52. PhG, 507/397/576 and 511/400/580.

53. See reference in previous note.

54. PhG, 510/399/579.

55. See note 32 above. For the relation of this passage to the Introduction see section 1A. above.

56. The place of honor given to Francis Bacon in d'Alembert's Preliminary Discourse to the French *Encyclopedia* is most instructive here. To begin with, the *Encyclopedia* borrows its system of organization from Bacon. Then comes a brief Enlightenment hagiography, describing "the principle geniuses that the human mind must regard as its masters and for whom the Greeks would have erected statues." Before a longer list, the four greatest heros, including Descartes, Newton, and Locke is given. "At the head of these illustrious personages must be placed the immortal Chancellor of England, Francis Bacon." Denis Diderot, *The Encyclopedia: Selections,* ed. and trans. by Stephen J. Gendzier, New York, 1967, pp. 10, 26, and 19.

57. PhG, 521-24/406-08/588-91. In *Differenz* Hegel develops the intimate relation between *Bildung* and *Verstand,* the finite understanding. GW, 4:12-13, 15.

58. PhG, 533/414/599. On objectivity [*Gegenständlichkeit*] see note 46 above.

59. PhG, 535-37/415-16/600-02.

60. PhG, 538-39/417/603-04.

61. PhG, 539/418/604. cf. the section in Chapter Five on the Law of the Heart.

62. PhG, 539-43/418-20/604-07.

63. PhG, 543-45/420-21/607-08.

64. PhG, 545-46/422/609.

65. PhG, 546-47/422/610. On this migration of Spirit to a new land, see 433/350/512.

66. PhG, 548-51/423-25/613-16.

67. PhG, 551-59/429-30/616-20.

68. PhG, 559-64/430-33/622-26, my italics. On the question of grace see 573/440/635 and Kant's *Critique of Practical Reason,* pp. 122 ff. (Academy edition pages), especially the note on p. 127. The italicized phrase from Hegel indicates why grace is not the solution which Hegel finds acceptable, why Boehme rather than Luther is his first German hero.

69. PhG, 580/444/641.

70. See next to last paragraph of previous section, 6B.

71. Hegel, *Werke,* I, 234-35.

72. PhG, 583/446/646. For a similar interpretation of the theme of anarchy in Chapter Six, see my essay, "Verzeihung und Anarchie," *Hegel-Jahrbuch*, 1972, pp. 105-109.

73. PhG, 423-28/343-46/502-06.

74. *Differenz*, GW, 4:54.

75. Beginning with the one which includes note 58.

76. Cf. *Differenz*, GW, 4:59.

77. PhG, 598/456/658. cf. Matthew 16:19.

78. PhG, 587/449/648-49, 592-94/452-53/653-54, 597-98/456/657. Judges 21:25 (RSV).

79. Both of these are involved in the definition of Spirit as the I that is We and the We that is I.

80. See note 64 above.

81. *Metaphysik und Politik*, Frankfurt, 1969, pp. 198-99. The second quotation is from another essay in the same volume, "Moralität und Sittlichkeit. Zu Hegels Auseinandersetzung mit der kantischen Ethik," pp. 307-08.

82. See note 64 above.

83. PhG, 589-90/450/650.

84. PhG, 601-05/458-61/660-64.

85. PhG, 612-13/465/670.

86. PhG, 621-24/471-72/677-79. Hegel calls this forgiveness the self's *Verzichtleistung auf sich*. Thus *Entäusserung* is rendered as relinquishment toward the end of the quotation rather than as alienation.

87. PhG, 605-06/460-61/663-65. The deification of the social whole is particularly strong in *Sittlichkeit*.

88. See Kant, *Religion Within the Limits of Reason Alone*, trans. Greene and Hudson, New York, 1960, pp. 85-93, where he describes the Kingdom of God on earth, in contrast to the ethical state of nature as an ethical commonwealth [*ein ethisches gemeines Wesen*].

7A. Spirit as the Object of Religious Knowledge

The abiding goal of the *Phenomenology* is "insight into what knowing is," the discovery of that point where "knowledge is no longer compelled to go beyond itself." With the help of Kant's transcendental method of reflecting on the nature of knowledge, Spirit has been discovered as the concrete source of transcendental subjectivity, and the historical analysis of Spirit's career has illuminated the bond between the transcendental subjectivity which makes instrumental reason possible and the life of Spirit in the modern world. All this provides considerable "insight into what knowing is" but it hardly indicates the point where "knowledge is no longer compelled to go beyond itself." For instrumental reason has both the world of nature which it knows and the Absolute which it does not know beyond itself. Subject and object are distinctly other to each other. Nature is not wholly other to instrumental reason, of course, though it has become the object and not the home of consciousness, and beneath its luminous surface it remains a dark and mysterious unknown about which the prudent Newton dares not hypothesize. At the same time instrumental reason has no surer conviction than that it cannot know the Absolute, being suited only to finite objects. This is just as true of transcendental philosophy, for while it knows instrumental reason in all its finitude, it does not know the Absolute either.

While learning all this we have also learned something else. Spirit is not only the transcendental subject which grounds our knowledge of nature. Spirit knows itself. Here subject and object are not other to each other, for the knower is the known. In this sense knowledge is not compelled to go beyond itself. If Spirit is able to find the Absolute within this knowledge of itself rather than outside it, its cognitive task would not have to remain essentially unfinished. It would learn that nature is not the Absolute and that its knowledge of nature consequently cannot be Absolute Knowledge. Spirit is what is absolute, and only Spirit's knowledge of itself can be Absolute Knowledge.

Now Hegel has characterized Spirit as absolute in so far as it is the community of tolerance characterized by reciprocal recognition. This community is not just a brute fact. It is aware of itself. But the community which is thus aware of itself is absolute Spirit and thus divine. Its collective self-knowledge, being God's knowledge of himself, can only be Absolute Knowledge. Hegel finds Spirit's knowledge of itself to be at once the clue to Absolute Knowledge and the essence of Religion. This is the result of Chapter Six. Its detailed development is the task of Chapter Seven.

If Religion is Spirit's knowledge of itself as Spirit, it follows that Spirit is the object of religious knowledge. This is suggested by the description of religion as "the utterance of the congregation regarding its own Spirit."[1] It is even clearer in the definition of religious truth given in Chapter Seven. "The truth of the belief in a given determination of the religious Spirit shows itself in this, that the actual Spirit [*der wirkliche Geist*] is constituted after the same manner as the form in which this actual Spirit beholds itself in Religion. Thus, for example, the incarnation of God, which is found in Eastern religion, has no truth, because the actual Spirit of this religion [*ihr wirklicher Geist*] is without the reconciliation this principle implies."[2]

In the light of Chapter Six it is not difficult to recognize what Hegel intends by the notion of actual Spirit. It is the social reality which he calls the life of a people. Since this social reality must correspond to religious ideas if they are to be true, it must be the real object to which they refer. Incarnation entails reconciliation, but since, on Hegel's view, oriental society is not even developed enough to sense a need for reconciliation, the idea of incarnation is false in that context. It is an idea which, if true at all, is true only where the substantial life of a given society has achieved subjectivity through coming to self-consciousness without losing its substantiality in the process, since this is what Hegel means by reconciliation.

This notion that in Religion Spirit moves beyond its mere being or actuality to the knowledge of itself permeates Hegel's interpretation of Religion. For example, Hegel interprets the use of animal symbols for the divine as appropriate to the experience of Spirit's dispersal into warring tribes which "fight each other in their hatred to the death."[3] Or again, "If we ask next what the actual Spirit is which finds in the religion of art the consciousness of its absolute essence, it turns out that this is the ethical or true Spirit."[4] This last phrase takes us directly back to the first part of Chapter Six and its description of Greek social life. It is this which Greek religion, the religion of art, brings to consciousness.

Since Hegel interprets the Christian religion, upon which his attention ultimately focuses, more in its relation to Greek religion than to Judaism, it is worthwhile to look more closely at the correlation between the actual Spirit of Greek experience and its religious expression. The implication of Greek society being the object of Greek religion is developed most fully in the discussion of its highest stage, the literary. The development from epic through tragedy to comedy is one of increasing humanism, or, as Loewenberg puts it, of increasing "theoclasm" and "anthropolatry."[5] The gods of the epic pantheon are already fully humanized (in contrast to the Titans), as is fitting, inasmuch as they actually represent the variety of the Greek peoples brought to political unity for the first time in the Trojan war. To the united people [*Gesamtvolk*] corresponds a unified heaven [*Gesamthimmel*].[6]

The religion of the epic is awkward, however, since all events are attributed to both gods and men. In the language of E. R. Dodds, they are "overdetermined." This redundancy of the divine world is largely corrected in the religion of tragedy, where the gods play a much less prominent role. Tragedy involves the "depopulation of heaven."[7]

The full significance of this is grasped only by comedy. There the gods are consciously recognized to be mere clouds (Aristophanes), and it becomes clear to all that the true reality behind the masks which signify the gods is man himself (the actor). The truth of anthropomorphic paganism is the discovery of man's own divinity. On Hegel's interpretation, "the Homeric poems, the tragedies of Aeschylus and Sophocles, and the comedy of Aristophanes constitute together a dialectical movement whose general sense is the following: the return of the divine into the human."[8]

Because this result is misconceived in an individualistic manner Greek comedy is not absolute religion. This involves the isomorphism of religious and actual Spirit in Greece. The final proposition of Greek religion—"The self is absolute Being"—is a statement which belongs, "as is evident on the face of it, to the non-religious, the concrete, actual Spirit." Since "the religion of art belongs to the Spirit animating the ethical sphere," we find that the final statement of Greek religion is the same as the final statement of Greek social experience, expressed in legal personality, which also took the individual to be absolute. Both, when they realize what they are, are unhappy forms of consciousness, subjectivity without substance.[9]

Gerardus van der Leeuw has written, "If God speaks humanly, then either a miracle has occurred, or sacrilege has been committed."[10] In Greek comedy and Roman emperor worship, which is not so different from the former as it may appear to be, antiquity was unable to prevent the miracle from degenerating into sacrilege. Precisely this is the developmental task of Christianity. Its mission is to correct the individualistic error of comedy while preserving its humanistic truth. Against the background of *The Spirit of Christianity and its Fate* this assignment is not quite as unexpected as it might otherwise seem. There the view of Christianity which continues in the *Phenomenology* is derived, not from the necessity for historical development beyond classical antiquity, but from a direct (if highly problematical) interpretation of Jesus' teaching in the light of its own immediate historical context. Jesus is portrayed as opposing to the Jewish conception of subjection to an infinite Lord and Master the idea of God's relation to man as that of father to son. "Father and son are simply modifications of the same life, not opposite essences. . . Even in the expression 'a son of the stem of Koresh,' for example, which the Arabs use to denote the individual, a single member of the clan, there is the implication that the individual is not simply a part of the whole. The whole does not lie outside him. He himself is just the whole which the entire clan is. . . A tree which has three branches makes up with them one tree; but every 'son' of the tree, every branch . . . is itself a tree."[11] Whereas the Jews could see only an "impassable gulf between the being of God and the being of men," Jesus saw something entirely different in true faith. "Faith in the divine is only possible if in the believer himself there is a divine element which rediscovers itself, its own nature, in that on which it believes, even if it be unconscious that what it has found is its own nature . . . Hence faith in the divine grows out of the divinity of the believer's own nature. Only a modification of the Godhead can know the Godhead." Thus when Jesus responds to Peter's confession of faith in Matthew 16 by saying "My Father in heaven has revealed this to you," he is actually saying. "The divine in you has recognized my divinity. You have understood my essence. It has re-echoed in your own."[12]

The heart of this interpretation of Jesus' teaching is taking his statements about his relation to God as his father to be general statements about the relation of man to God. Hegel is explicit about this. "Thus specifically does Jesus declare himself against personality, against the view that his essence possessed an individuality opposed to that of those who had attained the culmination of friendship with him (against the thought of a personal God)."[13] To make it clear just why this concept of friendship is in conflict with that of a personal God, Hegel indicates that this friendship *is* God. In opposition to the overtones of "union through domination" carried by the idea of the Kingdom of God, Jesus preaches love. "*This friendship* of soul, described in the language of reflection as a being, as Spirit, is the divine Spirit, *is God* who rules the congregation. Is there an idea more beautiful than that of a nation of men related to one another by love?"[14]

The consequence of this is that "the objective aspect of God, his form, is objective only in so far as it is the presentation [*Darstellung*] of the love which unites the congregation." It was the fate of the Christian church that it did recognize its own love in the form of its risen Lord, but did not realize that what it adored was its own love. It therefore continued to find the divine to be something given, something positive, something alien.[15]

It is this same notion of the loving community (reciprocal recognition) as divine which culminates Chapter Six and leads to the chapter on Religion. When Christianity is so conceived, the task of preserving the humanism of Greek comedy while correcting its individualistic misconstrual is not an arbitrary assignment. Both appearances of Christianity in the *Phenomenology* prior to Chapter Seven prepare the reader for this interpretation of Christianity. As Hegel presents it Unhappy Consciousness is primarily if not exclusively a Christian experience. But the truth of the Christian religion is not to be found in the far off God for whom Unhappy Consciousness pines in mystical devotion. Hegel's trinitarian speculation suggests that the overcoming of the contradictions which torment Unhappy Consciousness is to be found in the church, in so far as it comes to a proper kind of self-consciousness, not in a transcendent personal deity.

Similarly in Chapter Six Hegel writes, "This action of Faith does not indeed make it appear as if absolute Being is thereby produced. But the absolute being for Faith is essentially not the abstract Being that is supposed to lie beyond the believing consciousness. It is the Spirit of the religious congregation . . The action of the congregation is an essential moment in bringing about that there should be this Spirit of the congregation. That Spirit is what it is by the productive activity of consciousness."[16] Since the truth of Faith is to be found in the religious community and not in some super-human, extra-mundane realm, Enlightenment provides an essential corrective to Faith in rejecting the beyond and focusing all interest on the here and now. "Both worlds are reconciled and heaven is transplanted to the earth below."[17]

It is against this background that Hegel develops the central categories for his philosophical interpretation of Christianity in Chapter Seven: incarnation and community. Whereas for Greek experience God's speaking humanly meant the sacrilege of comedy, for Christian experience it means the miracle of incarnation. For Hegel this miracle reveals that "the divine nature is the same as the human, and it is this oneness which is intuited" in the incarnation, the "simple content of absolute Religion."[18] But there is always the possibility (to say nothing of the historical actuality) that incarnation will be interpreted as uniquely true of Jesus rather than a universal truth about the relation of the human to the divine. This means, in Hegel's terms, that the religion of incarnation lives in perpetual danger of being a religion of consciousness, sorrow, and alienation rather than of self-consciousness, joy, and reconciliation. In other words, Hegel's hostility towards orthodox Christianity has not lessened since the days just following his seminary education. The difference is that now he sees other possibilities in the Christian tradition.

These other possibilities lie in the fact that Christianity is not only a religion of Father and Son, but also of Spirit. It teaches not only incarnation but also community. In the context of this community the immediacy and sensuous individuality in which the truth at first appears as an historical fact is replaced by the mediation and universality in which "God's individual self-consciousness [the incarnation as expressed in Jesus] is transformed into something universal, into the congregation."[19]

With this centrality of the community the individualism of Greek religious humanism is overcome. "Spirit remains the immediate self of actuality, but in the form of the universal self-consciousness of the congregation, a self-consciousness that rests in its own proper substance, just as in this self-consciousness this substance is universal subject. It is not the individual by himself, but the individual along with the consciousness of the congregation, and what he is for this congregation is the complete whole of its consciousness."[20] The content of this religion is thus "the certainty the congregation has of its own Spirit."[21]

In overcoming the individualism in which the classical world dead-ended, there is no reversion from its humanism to the theism of Unhappy Consciousness and Faith. Instead the Christian church is seen to be the universal version of the community of tolerance which appeared with such striking religious overtones as the upshot of Conscience. The Kingdom of God is indeed "a nation of men related to one another by love."[22]

Hegel knows that the religious and social communities do not automatically coalesce, that Spirit's actuality and its self-consciousness are not always perfectly congruent. "There is no doubt one Spirit in both, but its consciousness does not compass both together, and religion appears as a part of existence, of activity, of striving, whose other part is life in Spirit's actual world. As we now know that Spirit in its own world and Spirit conscious of itself as Spirit, i.e., Spirit in the sphere of Religion, are the same, the perfection of Religion consists in the two forms becoming identical with one another."[23] Just as religious falsehood is the incongruity of religious ideas and social reality, so religious truth is the actual identity of religious and secular Spirit. Hegel's interpretation of his historical present, therefore, is that it is through the enlightened Christian church that the community of tolerance is beginning to become the universal community of man. The fundamental identity of the Christian church with the community of tolerance is seen in the fact that the collective self-consciousness of both is presented as the divine self-intuition. The need for religious and secular Spirit to become one explains why the new-born world in which Science is finally possible is to be found not at Bethlehem but in the aftermath of the French Revolution.

7B. Spirit as the Subject of Religious Knowledge

Religion is the knowledge which Spirit has of itself as Spirit. The subject as well as the object is Spirit. Just as religion as such is "the self-consciousness of the absolute Being," so in Christianity as absolute Religion, "the divine Being [*das Wesen*] is known as Spirit. This religion is the divine Being's consciousness concerning itself that it is Spirit."[24] But Spirit is a We, a universal or collective and not merely individual self-consciousness. That is why Religion has come before us as "the utterance of the congregation regarding its own Spirit," "the universal self-consciousness of the congregation," and "the certainty the congregation has of its own Spirit."[25] On the subject side religion is a mode of knowing quite removed from the individual in his Whiteheadean solitude, from Kierkegaard's Abraham alone before God.

But the social or collective subject of religious knowledge is not immediately aware of its identity with its object. "The object is revealed to the congregation from an alien source, and in this thought of Spirit it does not recognize its own self, does not recognize the nature of pure self-consciousness."[26] So far as this is the case the congregation "is not yet perfected in this its self-consciousness . . . It is not consciously aware what it is."[27] Why this is so and how it leads us beyond Religion are matters for the final part of this chapter. At present it is sufficient to note the fundamentally deceptive character of religious knowledge as a self-knowledge which does not know itself to be that.

Here it is useful to call upon the aid of a psychological model for understanding Hegel's view of Religion, the concept of projection. In its strict Freudian sense projection is a means of avoiding aspects of one's own self which are unacceptable, usually to the super-ego, by transplanting them onto some other person, object, or abstract concept such as fate. The individual sees his own hatred, jealousy, or lust, for example, in another person, but does not recognize it as his own.

With two modifications this concept nicely illustrates Hegel's view of Religion. The first is a loosening of the concept from its individualistic limitations. Just as Jung speaks of a collective unconscious, we can speak of a collective projection. The other modification expands the range of features which may be projected so as to include those acceptable to the subject. This expansion has already taken place in psychological theory in so far as such devices as the Rorschach Test and the Thematic Apperception Test are referred to as projective techniques. "Thus common practice has extended the Freudian concept so that it now includes . . . constituents that are acceptable or even admirable to the subject."[28] Both of these changes have been made in Erich Fromm's humanistic interpretation of religion as collective projection, making it an instructive commentary on Hegel.[29]

One is not to infer from the projective nature of Religion that it is an illusion. It is true that God's *esse* is *concipi*. "God is attainable only in pure speculative knowledge, and he is only in that knowledge, and he is simply that knowledge itself, for he is Spirit."[30] This means not only that the representation in which Spirit uncomprehendingly becomes conscious of itself is produced by the subject of religious knowledge, the congregation, but also that the object itself is constituted by that knowing. Actual Spirit in separation from religious Spirit is but an abstract and incomplete reality. Spirit is only truly Spirit as it knows itself in its gods.[31]

In other words Hegel wishes to speak of God as the product of human activity and thought without implying that God is but a figment of the imagination. In fact it is just in the context of emphasizing this character of God as produced by man that he sharply chides Enlightenment for taking Faith's God to be mere illusion.[32] There is, of course, an important element of falsehood in Religion as such on this interpretation, but as in every other sort of projection, there is also important truth, however distorted and disguised. Hegel finds religion to be neither a hoax perpetrated by priests and despots nor a wildly imaginative and primitive pseudo-science of nature. It is rather an essential element of the social experience which is its foundation; so essential, in fact, that Hegel reverses the order and finds it to be the ground of all human experience. You can tell a people by the gods they keep.[33]

There is perhaps no clearer exposition of this view of Religion than Emile Durkheim's *The Elementary Forms of the Religious Life.* Durkheim is full of "Hegelian" ideas. In this context the most important is his view that religious concepts are collective representations of collective sentiments growing out of social experience, and that the quasi-religious two-world philosophies of Plato and Kant are expressions of the tension between individual and society.

The fundamental question of his book—What is the origin of religion?—Durkheim interprets as asking what the ubiquitous features of human experience are which lead to dividing the world into profane and sacred, the world of the ordinary and the sharply separated world of ultimate significance and worth. Working on the methodological assumption that the most primitive religion will exhibit the essence of religion unencumbered by irrelevant accretions, he argues that totemism is the truly primitive religion. In doing so he not only rejects animism and naturism as candidates for the title of most primitive religion, but more importantly the implication normally associated with the presentation of both, that religion is a prescientific attempt to explain certain natural phenomena. From the outset he agrees with Hegel that Religion is not to be understood as a mode of knowing nature.

Seeking clues from totemism about the origin or essence of religion, Durkheim notes 1) that the separation between sacred and profane in totemism does not demarcate man as profane from certain religious objects as sacred, and 2) that sacred objects are not such in virtue of their own inherent qualities, but in virtue of participation in a power that survives the particulars. For example, the sacred emblems used in totemic ritual are frequently good for only one use and are destroyed after the ceremony is completed. Yet as symbolic of the totemic power, they are sacred. Similarly the human members of a totemic clan and the animal (or vegetable) members of the species from which it derives its name are transient, yet as participating in the impersonal power or life usually known by its Melanesian name, mana, they are sacred.[34]

Mana has a curious twofold significance. It is superior to the individual as that to which he owes veneration and respect. It has what Durkheim calls "moral authority." Yet it is at the same time the source of the individual's strength and vitality. The idea of a power or life which is at once sustainer and lord, sharply set off from the ordinary, immediate appearance of things does not come, Durkheim argues, from observing nature. It is grounded in the experience of social life. "Religion ceases to be an inexplicable hallucination and takes a foothold in reality. In fact, we can say that the believer is not deceived when he believes in the existence of a moral power upon which he depends and from which he receives all that is best in him: this power exists, it is society. . . It is true that he is wrong in thinking that this increase of vitality is the work of a power in the form of some animal or plant. But this error is merely in regard to the letter of the symbol by which this being is represented . . . and not in regard to the fact of its existence. Behind these figures and metaphors, be they gross or refined, there is a concrete and living reality. Thus religion . . . is a system of ideas with which the individuals represent to themselves the society of which they are members, and the obscure but intimate relations which they have with it."[35]

It is not difficult to account for ideas of God in these terms. "But whenever the tribe acquired a livelier sentiment of itself, this sentiment naturally incarnated itself in some personage, who became its symbol."[36] This personage is thus the culmination of a complicated rationalizing of the concept of mana with the help of imagination.

Durkheim's analysis of totemic sacrifice serves well to illustrate a paradox which the sociological theory purports to resolve. On the one hand sacrifice seems to involve the idea of communion and participation in which man finds the strength and confidence which come from divine favor. On the other hand he offers an oblation to his god, as if to say that his god could not get along without him. Who sustains whom?

Durkheim accepts the apparent circle. "It comes from the fact that the sacred beings, though superior to men, can live

only in the human consciousness."[37] When it is remembered
that the divine beings are symbols of society, the paradox is resolved. Man does create his gods and is yet sustained by them,
for he makes his own society, on which he is in turn dependent.
The purpose of the rite, be it sacrifice or any other, is "to re-
vivify the most essential elements of the collective consciousness. Through it, the group periodically renews the sentiment
which it has of itself and of its unity; at the same time, individuals are strengthened in their social natures."[38]

This digression on Durkheim has been introduced, not because it is free from theoretical difficulties of its own, but because it represents so clearly in non-Hegelian language Hegel's
fundamental idea about the relation of religion to society. It
shows that there is an interpretation of religion according to
which the dialectical transition from Chapter Six to Chapter
Seven of the *Phenomenology* is both more natural and necessary
than Hegel himself is able to make it seem. For many this transition is the central stumbling block of the entire *Phenomenology*.
It is often described more or less as Royce describes it. At the
level of Spirit we are involved with "the social order to which I
belong . . . a humanity in whose life I take part." But then we
leave this to discover a "super-social or religious realm."[39] This
may be considered a strength, since it seems to offer Hegel a
defense against the charges of statism or historicism; or it may
be considered a weakness, since it seems to represent a Stoic
sort of retreat from the real world and its problems to the inner
world where everything is reinterpreted but unchanged.

In either case this reading leads to a fundamental methodological problem which Hyppolite expresses as the question
whether at this point phenomenology turns into noumenology,
whether human experience and its description are suddenly
abandoned in favor of dogmatic pronouncements about
super-human realities.[40] If one assumes that when Hegel
speaks of absolute Spirit he is speaking of a super-human
Spirit, related but not relative to man, transcending the world
of human experience like the God of classical theism or the
Platonic Ideas, then references to absolute Spirit can only be an
embarrassment to his phenomenological approach and the
transition from Chapter Six to Chapter Seven a paradoxical *non
sequitur*. Whether or not one finds such a concept of absolute

Spirit intrinsically meaningful, and whether or not one finds its employment an advantage or a disadvantage from the political point of view, one will have to admit that the descriptive project described in the Introduction has broken down and been abandoned.

This is the wrong way to ask the right question. The question of Hegel's faithfulness to his own methodological requirements is nowhere more legitimate than at this point. But the way in which it is usually asked, a la Royce and Hyppolite, suffers from the double disadvantage of ignoring Hegel's own careful development of the concept of Spirit as a distinctly human We while at the same time making nonsense of the transition from Spirit to Religion. When Hegel's analysis of Spirit up to the section on Conscience is taken as the clue for interpreting the emergence of absolute Spirit there, the transition to Chapter Seven is a coherent and natural one, free of any sudden leaps to a super-human realm.

It is puzzling why this latter procedure has not been universally adopted. There appear to be two reasons why it has not. First, Hegel begins to speak of Spirit as absolute, and it is difficult to see how any human social reality could be described in this way, however aware of itself it might be. But when it is remembered that Hegel believed the emerging post-revolutionary world to be in its essence a society whose enlightened Christianity enabled it to be a universal community of reciprocal recognition or love, the difficulty is largely overcome. For if such an event had actually taken place it is not so clear that we would be reluctant to call it absolute Spirit. In any case, Hegel would have the right so to describe it, for it would embody a form of human consciousness whose truth was adequate to its certainty, whose reality was equal to its aspiration. There would be a human community completely free from domination or alienating otherness, whether between man and man or between man and God, and this society would know itself to be what it is. Its collective self-consciousness, having no need to go beyond itself, would be Absolute Knowledge. It would be human consciousness fully and genuinely satisfied, sheer blessedness.

Events have not been kind to Hegel's expectations, and it is appropriate to note that "were he alive today, so realistic a philosopher as Hegel would not be a Hegelian."[41] In other words, the right way to ask about Hegel's faithfulness to his descriptive method is not to suggest that this concept of absolute Spirit betrays that method from the outset; it is rather to ask whether the thoroughly describable event he believed to be taking place during his lifetime was actually taking place. From the perspective of our present the answer to this proper way of asking the question has to be negative. With this negative answer comes the judgment that Hegel was not able to be faithful to his descriptive method to the end. He thought the Kingdom of God had begun to dawn in a new and decisive form and he set about to describe it. But he was mistaken and it was not there.

This is perhaps the most serious criticism that can be made of the *Phenomenology*, especially since it derives from Hegel's own criterion and has such a direct and negative bearing on the possibility of transcending critical finitism and knowing the Absolute. But while these considerations are important for evaluating Hegel's project, they cannot govern its interpretation. That must be guided by the text and not subsequent events. This is all the more important since neither the meaningfulness nor the contemporary philosophical interest of Hegel's project depends on the accuracy of his historical projections. The inseparability of the question of Absolute Knowledge from that of the Kingdom of God is a philosophical thesis worthy of more attention than it usually gets in an atmosphere which is more likely to treat both questions as meaningless a priori. Similarly, to suggest that philosophy *per se*, not just political philosophy, is the expression of an essentially utopian striving is to throw interesting light on the history of the West, including the present moment, when philosophy in this sense has all but died out. Hegel's value to us is not tied to the possibility of our being Hegelians. He does not need to be infallible for us all to learn from him, whether we be Marxists or Christians, positivists or existentialists, language analysts or phenomenologists.

This brings us back to the task of interpreting Hegel and to the only partially answered question why absolute Spirit is so frequently interpreted as a super-human reality in spite of the good reasons against doing so. Beyond the fact that Hegel speaks of Spirit as absolute, he seems to emphasize rather than downplay the notion of transcendence, and this, too, is thought to require something on a theistic or Platonic model, or perhaps the Aristotelian νόησις νοήσεως νόησις which somehow manages to find its way onto the title page of Baillie's translation. But there are two ways in which the more nearly Feuerbachian-Durkheimian interpretation which the text calls for includes all the transcendence Hegel needs. The relation of the individual to God (society's collective self-consciousness) is still analogous to the transcendence of traditional philosophical theology. Durkheim makes this particularly clear. Further, the primacy given to the historical development of Spirit towards its absoluteness gives a horizontal transcendence in time which supplements the vertical transcendence of society to the individual. While this latter transcendence disappears with the dawning of the new world, the latter remains.

In summary, there is no need to treat Religion as the realm of the super-social. To do so is to abandon Hegel's careful development of the concept of Spirit just where he finds in it the solution he is looking for. The result is to render incoherent the transition to Chapter Seven by failing to see how Spirit is simultaneously subject and object of religious knowledge, thereby misconstruing the Hegelian sense in which Spirit can be absolute, transcendent, and divine.

7C. Vorstellung as the Form of Religious Knowledge

It was noted above that even though Hegel finds Christianity to be absolute Religion, he says its congregation "is not yet perfected in this its self-consciousness. . . It is not consciously aware what it is." The reason for this is that "its content, in general, is put before it in the *Form des Vorstellens.*"[42] Whereas Kant uses the term *Vorstellung* and the related verb to speak of representation in the inclusive sense of having some content present to consciousness, Hegel uses them as a technical term in contrast to *Begriff* or concept, often translated as notion. It connotes an essential bond with sense experience, and for this reason it is often translated as "pictorial thinking," "imaginative presentation," or "figurative thought." For Hegel as for earlier philosophical theology there is no way that sense bound categories can adequately express the divine. But for Hegel it is not the pictorial element which is the primary difficulty; it is rather that sense perception itself is the presupposed model for knowing. This means that the object of knowledge is viewed as external to the knowing subject. *Vorstellungen* thus express an externality of spatial and temporal relation which absolute Spirit purports to transcend. The unity and interdependence of Spirit are overpowered by multiplicity and independence in any *vorgestellt* subject matter. Religion, whose form of knowing is always *Vorstellung,* is therefore always consciousness and never self-consciousness.

This is a startling discovery, for Hegel has also been stressing the self-conscious nature of religious knowledge, the identity of subject and object, in direct conflict with what he now says about its form. But that is just the point. The apparent contradiction is avoided only by remembering the structure of projection. What is in fact an awareness of oneself may be taken to be an awareness of something other than oneself. Though the content may be that of self-consciousness, the form remains that of consciousness. Hegel finds this to be true of Religion as such. It is always self-consciousness, since the object apprehended is always identical with the collective religious subject. But from its own point of view Religion is always consciousness, since it takes the object to be an independent other, even if the object of religious awareness is not as wholly other as other objects.[43]

Christianity is no exception to this rule, either in Chapter Seven or in its two earlier appearances. At stake is the meaning of the incarnation.

Unhappy Consciousness views the divine as the unchangeable. In the incarnation the unchangeable seems to be brought down from its splendid isolation and united with man. "In point of fact through the unchangeable assuming a definite form the beyond as a moment has not only remained but is really more securely established. For if on the one hand the unchangeable seems indeed brought closer to the individual consciousness by taking the form of an actual individual, on the other hand it stands henceforth over against him as an opaque sensible particular with all the hard resistance of what is actual.

The hope of becoming one with him must remain a hope without present fulfillment." But religious consciousness requires more than this. "The external relation which at first obtains to the unchangeable in human form as to an alien entity must be raised to an absolute fusion [*Einswerden*]."[44] The presence which becomes absence by the contingency of human death is not the divine presence for which Unhappy Consciousness hopes. But hope is a certainty whose truth is still outstanding, and Absolute Knowledge is not to be found in any religion whose "faith is the assurance of things hoped for, the conviction of things not seen."[45]

Faith is also alienated consciousness, sharply in contrast to the self-consciousness, however insubstantial, of Enlightened Insight. Whereas the latter has only the pure self for its object, Faith is "the consciousness of what is given [*des Positiven*], the form of objectivity [*Gegenständlichkeit*] or of *Vorstellen*." It takes the divine to be "an objective being that lies beyond consciousness of self." For Faith "the divine falls out of thought into *Vorstellung*, and becomes a supersensible world which is supposed to be essentially other to self-consciousness." Like Unhappy Consciousness Faith seeks a sense of unity through its doctrine of kenosis. It thereby makes the divine an "unintelligible sensible actuality... The beyond has thus only been more specifically determined as remoteness in space and time."[46] Faith, too, remains mere consciousness.

Absolute Religion as described in Chapter Seven is still not free from the form of *Vorstellung*. For this reason "spiritual life is still burdened with an unreconciled division between a here and a beyond. The content is the true content. But all its moments, when placed in the element of *Vorstellen* have the character of not being understood [*begriffen*]. They rather appear to be completely independent elements, externally related to each other. In order that the true content may also receive its true form for consciousness, it is necessary for consciousness to rise to a higher plane of mental development, to elevate its intuition of the absolute Substance to the level of the concept [*Begriff*], and to bring its consciousness to the level of its self-consciousness for itself, just as this has already happened for us or in itself."[47] In other words, Religion has not yet caught up with "our" insight into what it is really all about.

The whole of Chapter Seven hinges on this distinction between *Vorstellung* and *Begriff*. Four pairs of contrasts summarize its meaning. As the preceding passage indicates, *Vorstellung* is bound to the dualism between the here and the beyond so that the divine is never fully present for the believer's experience. While he is beyond the desolation of "My God! My God! Why hast thou forsaken me?"—there remains as an essential aspect of faith the Psalmist's cry, "As a hart longs for flowing streams, so longs my soul for thee, O God."[48] This is why *Vorstellung* is associated with consciousness in opposition to the self-consciousness of *Begriff* in which, subject and object being identical, no such rift or absence is possible. In addition to these contrasts between *absence* and *presence, consciousness* and *self-consciousness, Vorstellung* means viewing the incarnation as an event, a *contingent* happening, while *Begriff* means viewing it as the expression of a *necessity*. What this distinction between event and necessity means is indicated by the final contrast, that of *individual* and *universal self-consciousness*. The incarnation means that God is present as observable human self-consciousness. But seen in the form of *Vorstellung* this refers uniquely to the historical event and the historical individual known as Jesus of Nazareth. To see the unity of the human and divine as a necessity, and thus in the form of *Begriff*, is to see the human self-consciousness in which God is present and united with man as the universal self-consciousness of the congregation which, in principle at least, incorporates all of humanity.[49]

Once again the question whether Hegel has kept to his descriptive methodology becomes unavoidable. Where God has become society's projected self-image and the incarnation means that mankind universally is divine, how can one speak any longer of Christianity? Is Hegel not telling us what he thinks Christianity ought to be rather than describing what it is when, as Hyppolite puts it, "the Christo-centric point of view of the Bible tends to disappear to make room for the universal Christ who is the community"?[50] Does not Kierkegaard have the right to be deeply offended, not so much at Hegel's view of the world but at the claim that it represents the final truth of the Christian faith?

We must proceed carefully here, for Hegel is careful not to suggest that he is a Christian theologian in the sense of someone like Anselm, who sought to give a conceptual exposition of the very faith taught in the scriptures and proclaimed by the church. He is most explicit in underscoring the difference between the truth of Christianity as *Begriff* and the way it was originally understood.[51] It is clear from his discussions of Unhappy Consciousness and Faith that Hegel sees the subsequent historical manifestations as more nearly the original understanding than the new understanding he presents. In fact he insists that as long as Christianity remains Religion it will see the incarnation as a unique event occurring once and for all in Jesus of Nazareth. Hegel is not for a moment pretending that his *Begriff* is telling us what the Bible and the church have been telling us for centuries.

But Hegel's descriptive method allows him to describe whatever he finds. If he finds a form of consciousness which calls itself Christian but understands the Christian message in the radically new way which Hegel designates as *Begriff* in contrast to *Vorstellung,* he is entitled to describe that too. That such a consciousness was prevalent in Hegel's time cannot be denied. One needs only to mention the writings of Kant, Fichte, and Schleiermacher during the last decade of the eighteenth century.[52]

Hegel does not hesitate to draw the consequences of this perspective, to which he is obviously sympathetic. At the beginning of Chapter Seven he suggests that Religion, which had previously appeared only in the form of consciousness, will now come forward as the self-consciousness of Spirit. So he describes the movement of Chapter Seven from Nature Religion to the Religion of Art to Absolute or Revealed Religion as a movement not simply to more and more adequate conceptions of the divine but primarily as the movement from consciousness to self-consciousness, that is, as a movement beyond the very form of religious consciousness to a new form of consciousness.[53] From its name, *Begriff,* and from its evident link with Absolute Knowledge, there is nothing surprising in the discovery that this new form of consciousness is the philosophical. The Christian congregation can become the bearer of this new mode of experience (which cannot strictly be called a form of consciousness) and of the Absolute Knowledge it makes possible only by radically transcending itself and ceasing to be what it has historically been. It must become a philosophical community instead of a religious community in the strictest sense. One is reminded of the relation of the Platonic republic to the Pythagorean communities. Neither the Platonic nor the Hegelian communities are to be composed simply of philosophers; yet philosophy is to permeate them as their Form or Idea. In Hegel's case this means that the collective self-consciousness of the community attains philosophic form, throws off the elements of unconsciousness involved in the structures of projection, and recognizes itself to be the truth of prior projections.

It would seem fair to say, then, in defense of Hegel, that his descriptive methodology has remained in tact in so far as 1) he is not purporting to describe traditional Christian faith but something clearly different from it in its essential form, and 2) he is describing something actual in the world, a point of view the essentials of which he did not invent. There remains, however, the claim that while the form is different, the content is the same. This amounts to saying that while the Christian religion is radically transcending itself in the movement from *Vorstellung* to *Begriff* it thereby finds its own true fulfillment. At this point Hegel does seem to have gone beyond the limits of pure description. It is tempting to read this claim as a prescriptive one, telling us how we ought to interpret the basic ideas of the Christian faith. But it is probably more accurate to see it as predictive, as the expectation that mankind's longing for the Kingdom of God and the lasting experience of the divine presence would find their fulfillment in the radical self-transcendence of Christianity.

From Hegel's time to our own there have been countless variations on this theme of salvation through a post-Christian Christianity. Since this gospel continues to be proclaimed even in our own time, it would perhaps be rash to say that history has decisively falsified it. But history's verdict on Hegel's hope has been extremely harsh.

Seen in this light Hegel's view of Christianity in the *Phenomenology*[54] is strikingly similar to Nietzsche's in the *Genealogy of Morals*. There Nietzsche applies to Christianity the principle that "all great things bring about their own destruction through an act of self-overcoming."[55] His argument there is that it was the Christian morality of truthfulness which really conquered the Christian God and that this same morality must end by turning against itself and discovering the deceitfulness of its passion for truth. In this way Christianity transcends itself both as dogma and as morality. Similarly, Hegel's Chapter Seven must be read as the application to Christianity of a major thesis of his about Spirit: "not the life that shrinks from death and keeps itself undefiled by devastation, but the life that endures, and preserves itself through death is the life of Spirit."[56]

Kierkegaard remains offended. And not without reason. For the implication of views like Hegel's and Nietzsche's is that Christianity is wholly an historical phenomenon like feudalism or capitalism. Since it has always claimed to be more than that its fulfillment could only be in the confirmation and not in the falsification of that claim.

NOTES

1. See Ch. 6, n. 87.
2. PhG, 639/482/698.
3. PhG, 644/485/703.
4. PhG, 651/490/709.
5. *Hegel's Phenomenology: Dialogues on the Life of Mind*, La Salle, 1965, p. 333.
6. PhG, 676/506/731.
7. PhG, 691/516/743. See E. R. Dodds, *The Greeks and the Irrational*, Berkeley, 1971, pp. 7, 14, and 30 f.
8. Jean Hyppolite, *Genèse et Structure de la Phénoménologie de l'Esprit de Hegel*, Paris, 1946, p. 533.
9. PhG, 699-702/521-23/750-53. This is in contrast to the religion of nature, which knows substance without subjectivity.
10. *Sacred and Profane Beauty: the Holy in Art*, trans. David Green, New York, 1963, p. 132.
11. SC, HTJ, 302-09/253-61. cf Hegel's speculation on life in Ch. 5 above.
12. *Ibid.*, 312-13/265-67.
13. *Ibid.*, 316/271.
14. *Ibid.*, 321-22/278, my italics.
15. *Ibid.*, 335-36/292-95.
16. PhG, 498/391/568-69. cf. 515/403/583.
17. PhG, 532/413/598.
18. PhG, 709-11/528-29/758-60. cf. *Realphilosophie*, II, 266, "The divine nature is not an other than the human."
19. PhG, 735/545/780.
20. PhG, 715/531/763, not "the complete whole of the individual spirit," as Baillie has it at the end of this passage. The influence of Lessing's *The Education of the Human Race* is to be seen here. On his threefold schema of man's religious history Judaism as the religion of the Father and Christianity as the religion of the Son belong to the childhood of the human race and are to be surpassed by an "eternal gospel" based on reason rather than revelation and as different from traditional Christianity as the latter is from Judaism. His contrast in *On the Proof of the Spirit and of Power* between the accidental truths of history and the necessary truths of reason closely parallels Hegel's distinction between *Vorstellung* and *Begriff*. See section 7C. below.
21. PhG, 718/534/766.

22. See note 14 above.

23. PhG, 628-29/475/688. Hegel had concluded *The Spirit of Christianity* by saying of the Christian church that "it is its fate that church and state, worship and life, piety and virtue, spiritual and worldly action, can never dissolve into one." HTJ, 342/301. Persuaded that Christianity is overcoming this fate, Hegel is not simply hostile toward it in the *Phenomenology*.

24. PhG, 434/350/513 and 709/528/758.

25. See notes 20 and 21 above and Ch. 6, n. 87.

26. PhG, 720/535/768.

27. PhG, 738-39/547/783.

28. Henry A. Murray, in a foreword to *An Introduction to Projective Techniques*, ed. Anderson and Anderson, Englewood Cliffs, 1951.

29. *Psychoanalysis and Religion*, New Haven, 1950, especially pages 49-52. It is not so clear that Feuerbach was as anti-Hegelian as he wanted to be in *The Essence of Christianity*.

30. PhG, 712/530/761.

31. See the citation from Schelling in Ch. 5., n. 27.

32. See note 16 above.

33. PhG, 630-31/476-77/689-90.

34. This is an illuminating perspective to bring to the romantic philosophy of nature and to Hegel's own early use of 'life' as a category.

35. *The Elementary Forms of the Religious Life*, trans. Swain, New York, 1965, p. 257.

36. *Ibid.*, p. 331.

37. *Ibid.*, p. 388.

38. *Ibid.*, p. 420. Hegel's own analysis of totemism and sacrifice fits this account perfectly. See PhG, 643-44/485-86/702-03 and 666-67/500/722-23.

39. *Lectures on Modern Idealism*, New Haven, 1919, p. 177.

40. *op. cit.*, pp. 515 f.

41. Emil Fackenheim, *The Religious Dimension in Hegel's Thought*, Bloomington, 1967, p. 224.

42. PhG, 738-39/547/783.

43. PhG, 635/479/693. Since religion always affirms some sort of bond between man and the divine Hegel says that the *Gegenstand* does not sink to pure *Gegenständlichkeit*.

44. PhG, 145-46/161-62/255-56. Kierkegaard's concept of contemporaneity with Christ is also a recognition that the believer never relates to the incarnation simply as an historical fact. What is puzzling

about Hegel's account is that he should speak of faith as fusion rather than recognition.

45. Hebrews 11:1 (RSV).

46. PhG, 478-83/379-81/553-56. On kenosis see Ch. 6, n. 31. On *Gegenständlichkeit* and *Vorstellung* see Ch. 6, n. 46.

47. PhG, 715-16/532/763-64.

48. Psalm 42:1 (RSV).

49. See especially PhG, 713-21/530-35/761-68 and 729-33/540-43/775-78.

50. *op. cit.*, p. 547.

51. PhG, 716-17/532-33/764.

52. Note especially what is said about the church in Kant's *Religion,* Schleiermacher's *Reden,* and Fichte's *Grundlage des Naturrechts* and *System der Sittenlehre.*

53. PhG, 625/473/683 and 638/482/696-97.

54. Nothing is here implied about Hegel's later views.

55. Third Essay, Section 27, Kaufmann translation. Nietzsche uses both *Selbstaufhebung* and *Selbstüberwindung* in this context.

56. See Ch. 1, n. 45. There is something right, then, in Altizer's attempt to enlist both Hegel and Nietzsche as allies in *The Gospel of Christian Atheism.*

CHAPTER EIGHT: Absolute Knowledge

8A. The Withering Away of Religion and the Marxian Critique

Hegel's final chapter is brief, as it can afford to be in the light of the thorough preparation for it. Complaints about its tantalizing brevity (with the usual explanations about the conditions under which the manuscript was completed) may reflect more on the critic's attention to the text than on Hegel's ability to say what he meant. The opening paragraph reminds the reader that he could by now write the conclusion for himself. At the same time it reminds the non-reader that Hegel's view of Absolute Knowledge cannot be found simply by reading Chapter Eight.

"Spirit as Revealed Religion has not yet overcome its consciousness as such; or what is the same thing, its actual self-consciousness is not the object of its consciousness. Spirit itself in general and the moments which distinguish themselves within it fall within the sphere of *Vorstellen* and in the form of objectivity [*Gegenständlichkeit*]. The content of *Vorstellen* is absolute Spirit. All that remains to be done is to transcend [*Aufheben*] this mere form, or rather, because this form belongs to consciousness as such, its truth must have already come out in the forms of consciousness."[1]

So far as "we" are concerned, nothing remains to be done, for "we" are supposed to have seen throughout the preceding chapter that the truth of Religion lies in correcting its misleading form by recognizing the divine to be nothing beyond us but the social whole of which we are parts. This is the cash value of the move from *Vorstellung* to *Begriff*, from consciousness to self-consciousness.[2] "We" who have carefully followed the development of Chapter Seven do not even need a short Chapter Eight to tell us that. But the truth which must have already come out in the preceding forms of consciousness must become the truth for religious consciousness itself. Hegel's account of Absolute Knowledge can remain within the limits of his descriptive method only if the consciousness he is describing

211

comes to see for itself what "we" are to have seen in Hegel's description of it. In other words, the self-transcendence of religion must in some sense be an historical fact and not simply a philosophical requirement or expectation.

Since that which is to be abandoned, *Vorstellung*, consciousness, and *Gegenständlichkeit* are definitive of religious consciousness as such, one can speak here of the withering away of the religious point of view. For just as Marx sees the pre-revolutionary, bourgeois state to be incompatible with truly human society, thus requiring radical transformation in the transition to socialism, so Hegel sees in divine transcendence, traditionally conceived, the last and most strategic stronghold of the philosophy of finitude in human knowledge. Only a radical transformation of that point of view can make the world safe for Absolute Knowledge.

Perhaps without realizing it, Hegel makes at this point his most direct assault on the Kantian thing in itself. For this Kantian doctrine not only entails the absolute, i.e., unsurpassable finitude of all human knowing; it is explicitly tied to the religious point of view which Hegel here seeks to transcend. The thing in itself is the thing as known by an infinite Creator, in contrast to which all creaturely knowledge can only be derivative and imperfect.[3]

Hegel calls this withering away of the religious point of view the "overcoming of the object of consciousness." Since he is dealing here with religious consciousness this object is God. His overcoming involves three elements: first, that the object shows itself as such to consciousness as a vanishing factor, that is, as something that does not remain incorrigibly other; second, that it becomes clear in this way that it is the alienation [*Entäusserung*] of self-consciousness which grounds objectivity [*die Dingheit setzt*], that is, that man makes the world he lives in; and third, that this alienation comes to have a positive significance for self-consciousness, namely in the discovery that man's world is not a brute fact but somehow his own creation. This knowledge is grounded in the pulsating movement of Spirit first outward, then inward. It arises "on the one hand through the fact that self-consciousness alienates itself. For in this alienation it establishes itself as object, or it establishes the object as itself, for the sake of the indivisible unity of being for itself. On the other hand, there is this other moment involved at the same time, that self-consciousness has just as much transcended [*aufgehoben*] this alienation and objectivity [*Gegenständlichkeit*] and has taken them back into itself. Thus it is at home [*bei sich*] in its otherness as such."[4]

Actually this summarizes four different processes which Hegel has presented. The *Gegenständlichkeit* of nature is overcome through knowing and labor, the theoretical and practical modes in which self-consciousness *die Dingheit setzt.*[5] As the argument of the first four chapters makes clear, this overcoming is not an obliteration; it rather presupposes a continuing otherness of the object, though not a brute otherness. The knowing and laboring self is "at home in its otherness as such."

Though knowing and labor may well be said to have a history, it is not man's encounter with nature which Hegel finds to be the heart of the historical process. This is rather found in the *Gegenständlichkeit* of the other self and its overcoming, not through knowing and labor but through love. The otherness of finite selves is overcome in the community of tolerance whose foundation is reciprocal recognition. The otherness of the Infinite Self is overcome in the discovery that the divine is nothing but this "nation of men related to one another by love."[6] Here, too, otherness does not simply disappear. But it loses that strangeness which leaves man estranged rather than at home in the presence of the other.

Marx's 1844 critique of Hegel's chapter on Absolute Knowledge takes the passage we have been examining as its focal point. The primary charge is that Hegel has illegitimately identified *Entaüsserung* and *Gegenständlichkeit*. In developing this critique Lukács suggests that it rests upon an ambiguity which Hegel builds into his use of the former term. On the one hand it has a strong sense akin to Marx's notion of fetishism, in which the meaning is that man's own creations win mastery over him. In this sense *Entaüsserung* has the sense of *Entfremdung;* it is alienation in the sense of estrangement and not simply of objectification. On the other hand there is a "broad philosophical universalizing of this concept: *Entaüsserung* then means the same as *Dingheit* or *Gegenständlichkeit.*" In other words it refers to the object of knowledge as such.[7]

For Marx these meanings are entirely discrete. It is to be

expected that man, as a natural being, will have the object of his knowledge and desire outside himself, just as he is the object of the knowing and desire of others. Objectivity is not a problem for him. His concern is solely with that inhuman self-objectification which he here calls estrangement and later calls fetishism.[8] By contrast he finds Hegel to have defined man solely in terms of thought and to be offended by objectivity as such, finding in it the "scandal of estrangement." Consequently his dialectic is exclusively that of thought and being. Having falsely identified *Entfremdung* and *Gegenständlichkeit* in the ambiguous concept of *Entäusserung,* he then offers an epistemological idealism as the solution to the real problems of life. As a comment on this part of Marx's argument Lukács quotes Engels' verdict "that finally the Hegelian system only represents a materialism whose method and content have been idealistically stood on their head."[9]

Marx has overlooked two important aspects of Hegel's argument. First, in the passage under consideration the primary reference is to God and not nature, as Marx constantly assumes. Since Marx is surely to be counted among those for whom in this instance any kind of *Gegenständlichkeit* would of necessity be *Entfremdung,* it is strange that it fails to see Hegel as a potential ally.

Second, and equally important, we have just seen that the "overcoming of the object of consciousness" properly refers beyond the primary reference of the immediate context and applies to nature as well. And we have been reminded that Hegel, too, in the earlier analysis of Self-Consciousness takes man to be a natural being with the object of his knowledge and desire outside himself. Why does Marx take the discussion of Absolute Knowledge to be a retraction of that position? It is because he has overlooked the significance of Hegel's language. It is true that Hegel's use of *Gegenständlichkeit* in Chapters Seven and Eight tends to equate it with *Entfremdung* as Marx says, for it is an objectivity which keeps man from being at home in his otherness which must be overcome. But this means that it is not objectivity or otherness as such which is the obstacle to human fulfillment, either in the case of nature or in the case of God. To repeat Hegel's formula, the goal is to be at home in otherness as such, that is, as other. Hegel's "idealism" leaves man fully embodied and situated in a world of nature and other selves. What he purports to have discovered is not that the *esse* of that world is *percipi* but that history has reached a point where man can be at home in his world.

Nothing in Hegel's argument suggests that on his view nature somehow ceases to be "out there." It is true that at the end of Chapter Eight he speaks of nature as alienated Spirit, though the same sentence describes nature in as materialist a formula as Marx could want. It is "nothing but the eternal alienation of its own existence, and the movement which produces the subject."[10] Perhaps more important for understanding Hegel's meaning when he speaks of nature as alienated Spirit is the fact that he makes a sharp distinction between the way in which nature and history can be spoken of as alienated Spirit. Nature is Spirit's "living, immediate becoming," while history is its "knowing, self-mediated becoming."

Lukács notices this important distinction that Hegel makes, but fails to see in it any corrective to the Marxian critique. He makes it to blame for the fact that "where Hegel discusses actual history [Chapter Six] the problems of nature are as good as completely gone."[11] He is right in noting that Hegel does not find man's encounter with nature and thus the history of alienated labor to be the motor of the historical process. This is a genuine difference from Marx which needs to be carefully spelled out. But it does not follow from this, as both Marx and Lukács conclude, that Hegel reduces the historical process to the history of knowledge. He finds Spirit's basic problem to be Spirit itself. That is why the historical process is interpreted in terms of the quest for reciprocal recognition and why the object whose "overcoming" is crucial to the emergence of Absolute Knowledge is God. It is strange that when Feuerbach presents a projectionist view of God Marx praises its materialism, but when Hegel does the same he repudiates it as idealist.

Since it is this question of God's status which primarily concerns Hegel in the opening paragraphs of Chapter Eight, they serve to recapitulate the themes of the previous chapter on Religion. But he quickly refers us to Chapter Six as well, describing the recognition achieved in forgiveness and the individual self which is "immediately universal" in the community of tolerance as "the reconciliation of Spirit with its actual consciousness," and as "the reconciliation of consciousness and self-consciousness." We thus have two accounts of what Hegel sometimes calls the overcoming of consciousness by self-consciousness but here describes as their reconciliation. One is in the context of religious Spirit (Chapter Seven), the other in the context of "consciousness itself as such" (Chapter Six). Since this reconciliation has the form of being in itself [*Ansichsein*] in the former and the form of being for itself [*Fürsichsein*] in the latter, the two are at first opposed. The community of tolerance and the church have not yet discovered their common identity. "The unification of both sides is not yet shown. It is this unification which concludes this series of forms of Spirit. For therein Spirit comes to know itself not only as it is in itself, or according to its absolute content, nor only as it is for itself, according to its contentless form or in terms of self-consciousness, but as it is in and for itself."[12]

This confirms our reading of Chapter Six as a sacralizing of the secular and Chapter Seven as a complementary secularizing of the sacred. Only the unity of the two perspectives, each one-sided in itself, permits a further stage of Spirit's development. Both involve the concept of "the self-intuition of the divine." But this concept is actualized "partly as acting, self-certain Spirit [the conscientious self] and partly as Religion. In the latter it won the absolute content as content, or in the form of *Vorstellung*, of otherness to consciousness. On the other hand in the former the form is just the self, for it contains acting, self-certain Spirit. The self realizes the life of absolute Spirit."[13] In other words the community of tolerance which appears at the end of Chapter Six is the fulfillment of the concept toward which it is striving only in so far as it comes to recognize the unity of its own self-constituting activity with the content affirmed by Religion. Its self-positing as the autonomy of the general will must understand itself as the subjectivity which is also the absolute substance known in Religion as God. The emergence of Absolute Knowledge means taking in dead earnest the affirmation of Rousseau's *Discourse on Political Economy:* "the voice of the people is in fact the voice of God."

In a similar way the religious consciousness must incorporate the perspective of Conscience. It must learn that the content which it takes to be basic, the sacred, is the self's own act. In doing this it learns to identify the city of God with the city of man and to overcome the fate which at an earlier time Hegel thought was insurmountable.[14]

As the religious and secular points of view thus confess and forgive one another, as it were, Spirit comes to the end of its long journey. "This last form of Spirit—Spirit which at once gives to its complete and true content the form of self and thereby realizes its concept, while remaining within its concept in this realization—is Absolute Knowledge. It is Spirit knowing itself in the form of Spirit; in other words, it is conceptual knowing . . . Spirit appearing in this element to consciousness, or what is here the same thing, produced by it in this element, is Science."[15]

Although Hegel talks freely here of Absolute Knowledge he has not abandoned his original concept of Spirit as the I that is We and the We that is I. He calls Science the "pure being for itself of self-consciousness. It is the I that is this I and no other I, just as much as the immediately mediated or transcended, universal I."[16] This means that just as it is the self which realizes the life of absolute Spirit,[17] so the bearers of Absolute Knowledge are individuals. But it is not as sheer individuals that they are the locus of Absolute Knowledge. Only as their personal self-consciousness can be said to be a particular expression of the collective self-consciousness which Hegel has been describing as absolute Spirit do they express Absolute Knowledge.

The story of Spirit's developing self-consciousness as presented in Chapters Six through Eight can be summarized in these terms: society is the reality which religion adores, and philosophy is the public discovery that this is so. Spirit's journey comes to its end and Science is born when, in Kojève's words, we learn "to say of man everything that the Christian says of his God . . ."[18] Like Lessing before him and Tillich after him Hegel allows his thought to come to rest only where Enlightenment's demand for absolute human autonomy is satisfied, but in such a way as to preserve some sort of "eternal gospel" or "dimension of depth."

It is understandable that Nietzsche, writing for his contemporaries, should have attacked the form of this compromise most popular in his day. But for us it is unfortunate that the target of his first Untimely Meditation should have been the epigone, David Friedrich Strauss, rather than his master, Hegel. There were thinkers of comparable stature, however, who challenged Hegel's attempted synthesis of Enlightenment and Christianity from the outset, Marx on the secular side, Kierkegaard on the religious. The story is beautifully told in Löwith's *From Hegel to Nietzsche*. Since there is so often an attempt to avoid discussion of these criticisms of Hegel by distinguishing the "existential" Hegel of the *Phenomenology* from the later System, it is well to note that the essential features of the synthesis against which Marx and Kierkegaard revolted are at the very heart of the *Phenomenology*. That Marx's own critique of Absolute Knowledge is seriously flawed in no way detracts from his judgment that "it is necessary to begin with the *Phenomenology*, because it is there that Hegel's philosophy was born and that its secret is to be found."[19]

8B. Science and Eternity

Before concluding his text with a preview of the system introduced by the *Phenomenology*, Hegel makes two crucial remarks about the relation of Absolute Knowledge to time.

First, Science is not ubiquitous with respect to time. It comes onto a stage from which it has been absent, not because it has been patiently waiting in the wings, but simply because it was not. "As to the existence of this concept, however, Science does not appear in time and actuality until Spirit has arrived at this consciousness of itself. As Spirit which knows what it is, it does not exist earlier."[20]

Since Science not only did not but also could not exist earlier than the events Hegel believes to be occurring in his own time, it is radically different from other modes of knowing. The knowledge of nature and the social and religious knowledge of Spirit are present wherever human experience occurs. Science does not have this generic character. It is a specific type of experience which occurs only when its temporal conditions have been met. This does not imply that philosophy is not to be found earlier in human history. The implication is rather that philosophy, so long as it has not achieved its professed goal of becoming Science, is only a highly reflective form of natural consciousness, the love of wisdom rather than its possession. As such it needs to be superseded just as much as the scientific and religious forms of natural consciousness. Philosophy is a task word, Science an achievement word.[21]

The second point about Absolute Knowledge and time is the problematic assertion that Science means an end to time. "Time is the concept itself so far as it is there and represents itself as empty intuition to consciousness. Therefore Spirit necessarily appears in time, and it appears in time so long as it does not grasp its pure concept, i.e., does not annul time [*nicht die Zeit tilgt*] . . . When this concept grasps itself, it supersedes its temporal form [*hebt er seine Zeitform auf*] . . . Time therefore appears as the fate and necessity of Spirit where Spirit is not yet complete within itself."[22]

Here the temptation is all but irresistible to think that whatever has gone on previously in the text, Hegel has finally and abruptly introduced a transtemporal, super-human Absolute, since such a being seems the only appropriate subject for this timeless knowledge. St. Thomas' God, whose eternity is "the simultaneously whole and perfect possession of interminable life," or Royce's Absolute, whose life is "present as a whole, *totum simul*," seem the only possible models.[23] It was only by finding an alternative to the theistic-Platonic model of transcendence that Absolute Knowledge as the synthesis of Conscience and Revealed Religion was possible. Now it is just that view of transcendence which seems to be the inescapable meaning attributed to that synthesis. A radical and inexplicable hiatus appears between the goal and the pathway to it. Worse yet, this conclusion would confirm the finitist view of human knowledge. The presence of a super-temporal absolute knower forms a standard of comparison by which any human knowledge, individual or collective, must be judged finite and imperfect. St. Thomas and Royce agree with Kant in making just this point.

These awkward results can be avoided only if the statements about time's annulment are taken in conjunction with the assertion that Science is an emergent reality. An emergent eternity is an odd bird, to be sure, and merely so to describe it, as we must, is to separate it irrevocably from the two models just mentioned. On the classically theistic model, eternity is thought of as "greater than" time, while on the Roycean type view it is

coextensive with time. Neither view permits an emergent eternity, one with temporal prerequisites. When Hyppolite asks—
"How is an Absolute Knowledge, in itself atemporal, able to
have temporal conditions in the existence and becoming of
humanity?"—he unwittingly calls pointed attention to the fact
that we are not here dealing with atemporal knowledge in any
usual sense.[24]

What then is the meaning of time's annulment which is
congruent with the parallel doctrine of eternity's emergence?
The answer requires our taking note of the fact that Hegel's
chief concern with time is not with either duration or succession
as such but with the externality of temporal relations. This is
particularly clear and close at hand in the critique of *Vorstel-*
lungen in religious knowledge. In this form the unity of human
and divine is conceived as a temporal event. In this sense reconciliation is viewed as a past or future event, in either case remote from all except the few contemporaries. Nostalgia and
hope thus play a primary and, on Hegel's analysis, a det-
rimental role in religious consciousness.

Now if the primary significance of time is separation and
externality, its abolition would be identical with the reconciliation with which Hegel's narrative culminates. That the divine is
fully present to human experience and not a past memory or
future hope does not entail anything negative about the durative and successive aspects of time in other respects. Breakfast
still comes before lunch. To speak of time's abolition is simply
to refer to the socio-religious event in which man is freed from
a world in which his ultimate values and joys are always beyond
his reach, whether in some past paradise or in some future
utopia, and enters the heavenly world (worldly heaven) in
which he is fully at home and fully satisfied. Heaven and eternity maintain their intimate connection on this view, but their
significance has little or nothing to do with the durative and
successive aspects of ordinary experience, and nothing at all to
do with the super-mundane. As in the New Testament they
serve as metaphors on the boundary between this age and the
age to come.[25]

The obvious advantage of this interpretation is that it gives
us a harmonious Chapter Eight and a harmonious
Phenomenology. It gives the former by taking Hegel's two state-

ments about the relation of Absolute Knowledge to time with equal seriousness. It gives the latter by retaining the humanistic interpretation of Spirit which the text has required up to this point.

While these harmonies are good reasons for accepting such an interpretation, there is a further important consideration. The use of language attributed to Hegel by this interpretation of his comments about time and (by implication) eternity is consistent with his regular demythologizing of other Christian categories.[26] The *Phenomenology* provides ample evidence for Kaufmann's judgment that "when Hegel avails himself of Christian categories, he never implies acceptance of Christian faith in the supernatural, in miracles, or in the incarnation and resurrection; he merely finds the Christian myths more suggestive and more appropriate anticipations of his philosophy than the myths of other religions."[27] Hegel may not be quite that cynical, but he surely is a master at the techniques of persuasive (re)definition. Nowhere is this clearer than in the *Phenomenology,* where the Holy Spirit turns out to be the church and the incarnation means that man generically is divine.

Perhaps it would be fair to compare Hegel's talk about the annulment of time and the emergence of eternity with the Marxian distinction between pre-history and history. In both cases the distinction is between an epoch of human history in which man's existence falls fundamentally short of its ideal and an epoch in which that ideal is concretely realized. At the point of transition Marx says history begins, while Hegel says it ends. Since this difference is purely semantic it is again ironical that Marx should have directed one of his sharpest attacks on Hegel against just this final chapter of the *Phenomenology.*[28]

He praises Hegel's critical analysis of religion, the state, and civil society, but finds the potentially negative dialectic swallowed up in an uncritical positivism at the end. The "philosophical dissolution" is followed by "the restoration of the existing empirical world." This is because Hegel overlooks the concrete human subject, the natural, embodied, sentient, living, drive-oriented, suffering self, and concerns himself only with the abstract subject, defined as self-consciousness. We get a sense of Hegel's perspective when we suppose a being which neither is an object nor has one. In spite of the fact that Hegel

introduces Self-Consciousness into the *Phenomenology* in terms
of animal desire and human intersubjectivity, Marx identifies
self-consciousness with man as thinker, as exclusively knowing
subject. So he finds Hegel to end up as a Stoic after all, retreat-
ing from the real world and its real problems to the inner world
of thought and its more easily soluble problems. Man's true
political existence and the true existence of the state turn out to
be the philosophy of the state, just as his true religious existence
and the true existence of religion turn out to be the philosophy
of religion. Philosophy as such is the overcoming of alienation.
Following Marx on this point Hyppolite describes philosophy as
the "prescription" which Hegel offers to alienated, unhappy
consciousness.[29]

What Marx has failed to notice is the emergent character of
Hegel's eternity. Hegel's clear position is that Science enters the
world only when certain historical conditions have been met,
conditions which are not events in the history of philosophy but
concrete social and religious transformations. Marx insists that
the true overcoming of alienation is only to be found in the
theoretical and practical humanism which he sets forth as
atheism and communism. He fails to notice that what Hegel sets
forth in Chapters Seven and Six respectively as the precondi-
tions for Science could easily be described as atheism and communism. For Absolute Knowledge is only the self-conscious ar-
ticulation of those historical events which involve the death of
God as traditionally conceived and the overcoming of the state.
Hegel's "atheism" is a rejection of theism which does not entail
that nothing should be thought of as divine, and his "communism" involves the abolition of the state and social classes,
but not that of private property. In both cases there are
genuine differences from Marx, but it is not these to which
Marx's critique directs our attention.[30]

One reason Marx does not see the emergent character of
Hegel's eternity, which could also be called the ideological
character of Absolute Knowledge,[31] is that he fails to notice
Hegel's consistent and careful preparation for his conclusion.
He says that Hegel does not see the alienation of self-
consciousness as "the expression, reflected in knowledge and
thought, of the real alienation of human life." In saying this he
overlooks Hegel's explicit treatment of Stoicism, Scepticism,

and Unhappy Consciousness as ideologies in just this sense, expressions in thought of the predominance of master-slave relations in daily life. He similarly overlooks the equally explicit treatment of both Faith and Enlightened Insight as similar expressions of the political and economic alienation of Culture. Consistent with this perspective Hegel could not hope to find Absolute Knowledge elsewhere than as the "ideology" of that human society which has concretely overcome the alienations which previously motivated the historical process, whether it be called the Kingdom of God or the classless society. We have seen, as Marx did not, that this is just what he does. The Stoicism which Marx attributes to Absolute Knowledge is a figment of his own careless reading. It is hard to agree with Hyppolite that "Marx is one of the best commentators upon Hegel."[32]

8C. The Phenomenology and the System

While Hegel does not offer his treatise to the world as a cure for its ills, he does present it as Science.[33] It was originally published with a title page that read, in part: "*System der Wissenschaft . . . Erster Theil, die Phänomenologie des Geistes.*" Towards the end of the Introduction he explains how the pathway to Science is itself Science. In so far as we see the necessity of the transformations which natural consciousness undergoes and which Hegel calls experience, the *Phenomenology* can be called the Science of the Experience of Consciousness. Presumably what is to follow will be Science in some other sense. Now, with the Science of the Experience of Consciousness concluded, Hegel is able to say something more about what it is we have been introduced to in the process. His account of Absolute Knowledge therefore not only seeks to synthesize the developments of Chapters Six and Seven; it also looks ahead to the System. Briefly put, the *Phenomenology* is a discovery; the System its development. Whereas the Phenomenology is our Virgil to lead us to the Kingdom of Truth, the System is our Beatrice to show us the splendors of that kingdom.

What has emerged in Absolute Knowledge is not just a new theory of knowledge but a whole new view of reality, a new ontology. This cannot be without its ramifications in every field of knowledge. It is the task of Science to develop these by reinterpreting first the forms of thought and then the contents of experience in the light of the new ontology.

The first of these tasks is what Hegel understands by Logic. He writes, "In [Absolute] Knowledge then, Spirit has concluded the development of its forms, so far as they are burdened with the now overcome distinction [of subject and object] involved in consciousness. Spirit has won the pure element of its existence, the concept . . . In that Spirit has thus won the concept, it develops both existence and process in this ether of its life and is Science. The moments of its movement no longer present themselves in it as determinate forms of consciousness, but . . . as determinate concepts, and as the organic, self-grounded movements of these concepts. While in the *Phenomenology of Spirit* each moment involves the distinction between knowledge and truth . . . Science does not contain this distinction and its supercession. Rather, since each moment has the form of concept, it unites the objective form of truth and the form of the knowing self in immediate unity."[34]

Such a Logic will be a theory of categories rather than a theory of inference. But unlike the Kantian doctrine of the categories it will not be premissed on the inadequacy of knowledge to its object. Quite the contrary. Hegel's ontologically grounded Logic will presuppose the unity of thought and being developed in the *Phenomenology*. The only question will be the adequacy of thought to its own demands. In this sense the Logic requires the *Phenomenology*, not for the detailed development of its categories, but for a proper understanding of their status.

Hegel's use of the term 'Absolute Knowledge' for both enterprises is not due to ambivalence, as if there were two separate projects with the same name. The two are parts of a whole which is Science. Neither by itself is Science as such, but both, as organic parts, are properly called Absolute Knowledge or Science. Since the ontological discovery and its conceptual development are strictly interdependent, both participate in the character of the whole.

But even the two together do not exhaust the nature of Science. For the new ontological standpoint must be brought to bear not only on the forms of thought but also on the contents of experience. Hegel no sooner refers to the future Logic than he remarks that its subject matter is abstract and is only fully grasped in relation to its limit. So as not to suggest an external relation between abstract form and concrete content as its limit, Hegel uses the language of alienation. The content of nature and Spirit as they reveal themselves to our experience is simply the external and outward form of the same inner truth comprehended as Logic. Put a slightly different way, thought is the inner life of Spirit, nature and history its outer life. Now that Spirit is fully manifest there is no longer a gulf between the two. So Hegel writes, "Science contains within itself this necessity to alienate itself from the form of the pure concept . . . Knowledge knows not only itself but also the negative of itself, its limit. To know its limit means to know how to sacrifice itself. This sacrifice is the alienation, in which Spirit presents its process of becoming Spirit in the form of free, contingent, happenings, intuiting its pure self as time outside itself and similarly its being as space." To speak of Spirit's being as space is to speak of nature, "Spirit's living, immediate becoming," while to speak of Spirit's self as time is to speak of history, its "knowing, self-mediating becoming."[35] According to this account one would expect the third part of the *Encyclopedia* to be a philosophy of history rather than the synchronic philosophy of Spirit it is, but the basic threefold structure of the System is plainly present.

These remarks about history and alienation lead Hegel to his final comment on the Scientific character of the *Phenomenology* itself. History has come to be seen as the self-alienation or externalization of Spirit in which it presents the whole wealth of its substance to public view. It reveals itself, but only in so far as Spirit learns to recognize itself in its outward manifestations. "Since Spirit's perfection consists in perfectly knowing what it is, its substance, this knowing is its turning inward [*Insichgehen*], in which it leaves its existence behind and gives its embodiment over to recollection."[36] The whole theory of Absolute Knowledge as Spirit's self-consciousness is summed up in this process of alienation [*Ent-äusserung*] and recollection [*Er-innerung*].

One may wish to call this Platonism, but it is evidently a very new kind of Platonism, for Absolute Knowledge consists in recollecting not the timeless but above all the historical.[37] "The path to the goal of Absolute Knowledge, or Spirit knowing itself

as Spirit, is the recollection of the Spirits . . . Their preservation, as free existence appearing in the form of contingency, is
history; but as comprehended [*begriffen*] organization it is the
Science of phenomenal knowledge. Both together, history
comprehended, form the recollection and the Golgotha of absolute Spirit, the actuality, truth, and certainty of its throne,
without which it would be something lifeless and lonely; only

> from the cup of this realm of spirits
> foams to him his infinity."[38]

To all of which Marcuse responds, "History, however, when
comprehended, shatters the idealistic framework."[39] History's
unkind treatment of Hegel's hopes has been stressed in the earlier sections of this chapter, and there is no need to rub salt into
the wound by further accounts of how his did not turn out to be
the definitive and ultimate epoch of human history. But it is not
so clear that the problem is properly diagnosed as idealism.
Over against the "materialist" view that history is primarily to
be understood in terms of economics and alienated labor,
Hegel's "idealistic" view sees master-slave domination in the
economic domain less as the basic reality than as the expression
of a deeper non-economic urge to dominate rooted in the need
for recognition. Hence the priority of love over labor in his historical dialectic. While it takes little comprehension of history to
see that the problematic of recognition or love was not resolved
even in principle by the revolutionary developments of Hegel's
time, it is harder to say that history has given a clear verdict between the "idealist" and "materialist" diagnoses of the problem.

Would it be fair to say, then, that the only major demonstra-
ble defect of Hegel's argument is its imperfect midwifery, its
radical overvaluing of the new births his age brought forth? I
believe not. It is not only that the actuality of reciprocal recognition is missing from Hegel's world; its possibility is missing from
his argument. As we have seen earlier, the original demand for
recognition is unmet because each individual is too concerned
with winning recognition to be able to give it. There is no love,
only the demand to be loved. Hegel does not present this as an
accidental situation of a few egocentric individuals but as the
universal and primordial relation of man to his fellow men.
Like Plato before him and Sartre after him he portrays human
existence as erotic. It is an emptiness needing to draw from a

fullness outside itself the resources it needs to be itself. Until it receives recognition it is too poor to give it.

Against the background of this analysis in Chapter Four the announcement in Chapter Six that reciprocal recognition has been achieved is sudden indeed. No account of how the vicious circle created by the demand to be loved may be escaped is given. No source of overflowing fullness which breaks into the circle is designated. Suddenly, like magic, individuals who have given themselves up to domination (if they are strong) or submission (if they are weak) and who have objectified these patterns in the form of social institutions cease to be what they have been. They become loving, accepting, tolerant, forgiving individuals, the founders of an entirely different type of human society.

If it had actually happened we might have been too happy to ask for an explanation. But since it didn't, the theoretical inadequacy of Hegel's analysis can scarcely be overlooked.[40] He has given us an Augustinian interpretation of history, joined to a Pelagian theory of its culmination. The latter is an unbelievable *Deus ex machina* just to the degree that the former is taken seriously. That is why the "idealism" of the *Phenomenology* has tended to become one or the other of two conflicting modes of existentialism. Sartrean existentialism takes the erotic structure of human intersubjectivity to be unsurpassable. It says of man, whose love is the demand to be loved and whose deepest project is to become his own foundation, no longer needing to be loved, that he is a useless passion. Kierkegaardian existentialism finds in the very God whom both Marxian materialism and Hegelian idealism took to be a major obstacle to human fulfillment that source of overflowing fulness which overcomes man's erotic emptiness and makes it possible for him to love.

Neither alternative would have much appeal for Hegel. He wanted to avoid this sort of either/or. But history seems to have disappointed his hopes in this respect as well.

NOTES

1. PhG, 742/549/789. cf. Ch. 7, n. 43 and n. 46.

2. Again in Chapter Eight the contrast between *Vorstellung* and *Begriff* is regularly assimilated to that between consciousness and self-consciousness.

3. This view is particularly strong in the second edition. cf. Ch. 1, n. 25.

4. PhG, 742-43/549/789-90.

5. This follows Hegel's 1805-06 analysis of language and labor as essential moments in Spirit's transcendence of animal nature. See *Realphilosophie*, II, 179-99.

6. See Ch. 7, n. 14.

7. *Der junge Hegel*, Zürich, 1948, pp. 684-86.

8. Marx's critique is found in *Die Frühschriften*, ed. Landshut, Stuttgart, 1968, pp. 270 f. English translation in *Karl Marx: Early Writings*, trans. Bottomore, New York, 1964, pp. 195-219. The critique of Absolute Knowledge is somewhat scattered in the Landshut volume, since he follows the original order of the manuscripts as given by Marx's own pagination.

9. *op. cit.*, p. 686.

10. PhG, 763-64/563/807.

11. *op. cit.*, p. 687.

12. PhG, 747-48/552-53/793-94.

13. PhG, 749-50/554/795.

14. See Ch. 7, n. 23.

15. PhG, 753/556/797-98. It is interesting to compare this passage with the one cited in note 13 above. Here he speaks of Spirit realizing its concept, there of the concept realizing itself. These seem to be interchangeable ways of describing the same process.

16. PhG, 753-54/556/798. cf. note 12 above where Hegel speaks of the "immediately universal" self.

17. See note 13 above.

18. *Introduction a la Lecture de Hegel*, Paris, 1947, p. 267. This passage is included in the English translation of selected portions, *Introduction to the Reading of Hegel*, ed. Bloom, trans. Nichols, New York, 1969, p. 73.

19. *Die Frühschriften*, p. 252. Bottomore, pp. 198-99.

20. PhG, 754/557/798-99.

21. See the Preface, PhG, VI-VII/12/70-71. For the distinction between task and achievement words see Gilbert Ryle, *The Concept of Mind*.

22. PhG, 756/558/800.

23. St. Thomas Aquinas, *Summa Theologiae*, I, Q. 10, Art. 1. Josiah Royce, *The World and the Individual*, New York, 1959, I. 341.

24. *Genèse et Structure de la Phénoménologie de l'Esprit de Hegel*, Paris, 1946, p. 575.

25. Oscar Cullmann has called attention to this characteristic of the New Testament in *Christ and Time*.

26. The implied comparison with Bultmann is fitting. He recognizes that the thrust of his work is to transform theology into anthropology, for "I am interpreting theological affirmations as assertions about human life." *Kerygma and Myth*, trans. and ed. Bartsch, New York, 1961, pp. 107-08. In this context Bultmann draws the parallel between Feuerbach and himself.

27. *Hegel: Reinterpretation, Texts, and Commentary*, Garden City, 1965, p. 274.

28. Here and in the following paragraphs reference is again made to the Marxian critique as designated in note 8 above.

29. *Studies on Marx and Hegel*, trans. O'Neill, New York, 1969, pp. 82 and 84.

30. When Marx says of communism that "it is the solution of the riddle of history and knows itself to be this solution," the Hegelian structure of his idea is manifest. *Die Frühschriften*, p. 235. Bottomore, p. 155.

31. Absolute Knowledge can be called ideological in the sense of being derivative, but not in the sense of being false consciousness.

32. *op. cit.*, p. 70.

33. Hegel's fullest discussion of what he means by Science comes in the Preface, which should be read in conjunction with Chapter Eight.

34. PhG, 761-62/561-62/804-05.

35. PhG, 763-64/563/806-07.

36. PhG, 764/563/807. cf. XXXIII-XXXIX/26-30/89-94.

37. At the end of Chapter Seven above Hegel's Kingdom is compared with Plato's Republic. Though there are no philosopher kings in the former, both societies are rooted in philosophical recollection.

38. PhG 765/564/808. On phenomenal knowledge see the paragraph in Chapter One following note 28.

39. *Reason and Revolution: Hegel and the Rise of Social Theory*, Boston, 1960, p. 16.

40. Here as earlier the disappointment of Hegel's expectations has no direct bearing on the *interpretation* of his text. But in this case it helps us to notice a difficulty which might otherwise have been overlooked.

INDEX

MEROLD WESTPHAL is Distinguished Professor of Philosophy at Fordham University. He is author of *Hegel, Freedom, and Modernity*; *Kierkegaard's Critique of Reason and Society*; *Becoming a Self: A Reading of Kierkegaard's* Concluding Unscientific Postscript; *God, Guilt, and Death: An Existential Phenomenology of Religion*; and *Suspicion and Faith: The Religious Uses of Modern Atheism*. He is co-editor (with Martin Matuštík) of *Kierkegaard in Post/Modernism*.